SEX, CLASS, and CULTURE

Lillian S. Robinson

D0709367

INDIANA UNIVERSITY PRESS
Bloomington and London

Manufactured in the United States of America

Library of Congress Cataloging in Publication Data

Robinson, Lillian S.
  Sex, class, and culture.

  Includes index.
  1. Women—United States—Addresses, essays,
lectures. I. Title.
HQ1426.R72   301.41′2′0973   77-15762
ISBN 0-253-35186-3   1 2 3 4 5 82 81 80 79 78

For my son, Isak Ethan,
born just in time to have
this book dedicated to him.

CONTENTS

ACKNOWLEDGMENTS

Permission to reprint the six articles listed below was granted by their original publishers:

"Dwelling in Decencies: Radical Criticism and the Feminist Perspective," *College English*, 32 (1971);

"The Critical Task," published as "Cultural Criticism and the *Horror Vacui*," *College English*, 33 (1972);

"Criticism—and Self-Criticism," *College English*, 36 (1974); all reprinted by permission of the National Council of Teachers of English.

"Modernism and History," *New Literary History*, 3 (1971), reprinted by permission of *New Literary History*.

"Criticism: Who Needs It?" from *The Uses of Criticism*, ed. A. P. Foulkes (Bern and Frankfurt: Lang, 1976), reprinted by permission of Verlag Lang.

"Who's Afraid of A Room of One's Own?" from *The Politics of Literature*, ed. Louis Kampf and Paul Lauter (New York: Pantheon–Random House, 1972), reprinted by permission of Pantheon Books.

Poems cited in the essay "The Keen Eye . . . Watching" are quoted by permission, as follows:

Alta, "Bitter Herbs," "First Pregnancy," "Pretty," "euch, are you having your period?" and "penus envy, they call it," Shameless Hussy Press.

Anita Barrows, "The Mutant," *Aphra*.

Madeline Tiger Bass, "To My Former Student, On the Occasion of Birth," from *We Become New* (Bantam, © 1975).

Summer Brenner, "Mother, they say you looked Irish," from *From the Heart to the Center* (The Figures: Berkeley, 1977).

Broadside/Crummell Press for excerpts from "Black Mother Woman" and "Who Said It Was Simple" by Audre Lorde, from *From a Land Where Other People Live*, © 1973 by Audre Lorde Rollins.

Rita Mae Brown, "Hymn to the 10,000 Who Die Each Year on the Abortionist's Table in Amerika," and "Sappho's Reply," NYU Press.

Olga Cabral, "Life and Death Among the Xerox People," from *We Become New* (Bantam, © 1975).

Jan Clausen, "A Christmas Letter," from *After Touch* (Out and Out Books: New York, 1975).

Doubleday and Company, Inc., excerpt from "In the Men's Room(s)" from *To Be of Use* by Marge Piercy, © 1972 by Aphra, Inc.

Farrar, Straus & Giroux, Inc., excerpt from "Women" from *The Blue Estuaries* by Louise Bogan, © 1952, 1954, 1957, 1958, 1962, 1963, 1964, 1965, 1966, 1967, 1968 by Louise Bogan.

Marjorie Fine, untitled poem.
Susan Griffin, "I Like to Think of Harriet Tubman," from *Like the Iris of An Eye* (Harper & Row, 1976).
Harper & Row, Publishers, Inc., excerpts from "the mother" from *The World of Gwendolyn Brooks*, © 1945, 1971 by Gwendolyn Brooks Blakely; "Daddy," by Sylvia Plath, from *Ariel* by Sylvia Plath, © 1963 by Ted Hughes; "With Child" and "Everyday Alchemy" from *Collected Poems 1918–1938* by Genevieve Taggard.
Houghton Mifflin Company, excerpts from the following poems by Anne Sexton: "In Celebration of My Uterus," *Love Poems*; "Christmas Eve," *Live or Die*; "Rapunzel" and "Little Girl, My String Bean. . . ," *Transformations*; "The Abortion," *All My Pretty Ones*.
Inkworks Press, excerpts from the anonymous poems "Riding the Subways" and "For L" which appeared in *Sing a Battle Song* (Oakland, Calif.: 1975).
Lucille Iverson, "Outrage" and "The Abortion," from *We Become New* (Bantam, © 1975).
Kayak Books, excerpts from "Poem in Which My Legs Are Accepted," "Poems for the New," and "Poem Wondering If I'm Pregnant," by Kathleen Fraser.
Judith Kerman, "That dream, at last" and "Exmatriate" from *The Jakoba Poems* (White Pine Press) and "Driving for Yellow Cab," © 1978 by Judith Kerman.
Jacqueline Lapidus, "Coming Out."
Audre Lorde, "To My Daughter the Junkie On A Train" from *New York Head Shop & Museum* (Broadside Press, 1974).
Jane Mayhall, "Tracing Back," from *We Become New* (Bantam, © 1975).
Honor Moore, "My Mother's Moustache," from *American Review* #19, and "Conversation in the Eighth Street Bookstore."
William Morrow & Co., Inc., excerpt from "Dear Oedipus" from *St. Ann's Gut* by Ann Darr.
Moving Out, excerpt from "My People" by Margery Himel.
New Directions Publishing Corp., excerpts from "About Marriage" from *O Taste and See*, © 1963 by Denise Levertov Goodman, and "The Mutes" from *The Sorrow Dance*, © 1966 by Denise Levertov.
W. W. Norton, excerpts from "A Woman Mourned by Daughters" and "The Fourth Month of the Landscape Architect" by Adrienne Rich from *Poems, Selected and New, 1950–1974*, © 1975, 1973, 1971, 1969, 1966 by W. W. Norton & Company, Inc.; © 1967, 1963, 1962, 1961, 1960, 1959, 1958, 1957, 1956, 1955, 1954, 1953, 1952, 1951 by Adrienne Rich.

Rochelle Owens, "All Owners of Meat. . . ," *I Am the Babe of Joseph Stalin's Daughter* (Kulchur Press, 1972).

Linda Pastan, "Notes from the Delivery Room," The Swallow Press.

Random House, Inc., excerpts from "The Lost Baby Poem" from *Good News About the Earth* by Lucille Clifton and "Matrilineal Descent" and "Lesbian Poem" from *Monster: Poems by Robin Morgan*.

Kathryn Ruby, "Portrait of a Woman," from *We Become New* (Bantam, © 1975).

Muriel Rukeyser, "The Question" and "Ann Burlak," Monica McCall/International Creative Management.

Susan Fromberg Schaeffer, "Housewife."

Elizabeth Lynn Schneider, "Elegy," *Earth's Daughters* #5/6.

Karen Swenson, "The Evening Gown."

Wallace and Sheil Agency, Inc., excerpt from "The Bumpity Road to Mutual Devotion" from *Living in the Open* by Marge Piercy (Alfred A. Knopf, 1976).

Yvonne (Chism-Peace), "Rachel at 13" and "Rachel and the Truth" from *We Become New* (Bantam, © 1975).

Laurie Zoloth. "Women's Work: Nursing, the Cheery Aspect" and "Labor."

I am grateful to the professional staff of the Buffalo and Erie County Public Library, where much of this book was written. A grant from the Julian Park Fund, administered by the Faculty of Arts and Letters at SUNY/Buffalo, paid for the making of the index. Those parts of the manuscript that I did not type myself were done by Ruth Geller and Linda Phillips-Palo, both of whom applied their editorial sense as well as their mechanical skill to what I was trying to say.

Each of these essays, finally, owes something to an editor who invited its submission and smoothed its infelicities, a panel chairperson who asked me to participate in a conference, or a friend who commented on early versions of the text. This generous group includes, most notably, Ralph Cohen, Rebecca Dobkin, Josephine Donovan, Ellen DuBois, Theresa Epstein, Thomas R. Edwards, Jr., Martha Fleischer, Peter Foulkes, Ira Gerstein, Katya Gilden, Louis Kampf, Charles Keil, Paul Lauter, Susan McAllester, Dora Odarenko, Richard Ohmann, and Norman Rudich. Lise Vogel's contribution to what I think and write is by no means restricted to her collaboration on one of the essays in this volume; her relentless critical intelligence has been and remains a formative element in my own development for which I am deeply grateful.

Introduction

SEX. CLASS. CULTURE. They're big words—or, even more problematically, they're large concepts expressed in deceptively short and definitive words. This collection makes no claims to all of the unity or the comprehensiveness its title may connote. Had my editor permitted me the ponderous conventions of academe there would have been a subtitle, the words to the right of the colon specifying that my book offers Essays in Marxism, Feminism, and Criticism, or perhaps, though with less ideological precision, Theoretical and Practical Essays. In either version the central term would be "essays" and that is quite literally what this volume presents—a dozen essays, attempts, forays into critical territory where social reality and cultural production share a common unguarded border.

There is nothing tentative about these efforts. Indeed, when I reread the older pieces I am struck by their tone of assurance and conviction; however little confidence I may have had in my own abilities, I was always certain that the issues themselves were of genuine importance. Nor is my description of the contents as twelve discrete attempts intended as an apology for some absence of cohesion in the book. I believe that the collection does come together as an integral whole, with a certain consistency of approach that overrides the process of elaboration and correction through which the individual essays evolve.

In an amusing book called *Radicals in the University*, Edward

E. Ericson, Jr., produced a New Critical reading of contemporary radical critics.* Ericson's discussion of my first literary publication, the short article called "Dwelling in Decencies," castigates it for failing to come up with a unifying strategy for the liberation of women. I would hate to think that my expectations for myself are lower than those of my right-wing critics. But I do believe that the development of a revolutionary theory of culture that could explain our present condition and point out future directions is a more complex process than those who are satisfied with the received wisdom can apprehend. Not only is it slow and painstaking, but, by its nature, it is a collective endeavor. Such a theory depends at every stage of its elaboration on the touchstone of practice, and not critical practice alone, but the realities of social history and social movements. I am, moreover, less certain than Mr. Ericson—or than I once was myself—of the necessary and immediate connection between literature and women's liberation. In fact, this is one of the themes that is explored from different perspectives and to different conclusions in a number of the essays. It is not precisely that I feel *unequal* to the challenge to enunciate—or, rather, to have enunciated in ten pages back in 1970—a comprehensive analysis of culture and revolution in their special relation to the female sex, but rather that, as someone for whom each term in the statement possesses a personal urgency, I must constantly question the value, as well as the form, of the enterprise.

The painful emergence of my own assumptions about the relations that do or that might exist between cultural criticism and the world of social action is one reason why I believe it may be helpful to explain the genesis of each essay and, where appropriate, the changes that I have made or have refrained from making for the present edition. Such a discussion should serve to make the particular essays more accessible. It should also clarify the

---

*Edward E. Ericson, Jr., *Radicals in the University*, Hoover Institution Publications 144 (Stanford, California: Hoover Institution Press, 1975).

design of the work as a self-contained, though hardly self-sufficient, whole.

In early 1968 I was a graduate student at Columbia University, teaching freshman English and suffering from an advanced case of dissertation block. I had passed my orals two years before, and now, having produced very little prose and nothing of value, I seemed to have been overcome by premature senility. What no one had told me was that the topic I'd chosen was not a thesis, but a life's work. What no one there *could* have told me and what I lacked the conceptual apparatus to work out for myself was that it was somebody else's life work: the contradictions between the literary theory I was trying to elaborate and the history in which I lived were too strong to ignore and too painful to confront. I think I assumed I would go on like that forever.

It was during the Tet Offensive and I couldn't sleep at night. I'd been politically involved since my undergraduate years, in the civil rights and ban-the-bomb struggles, then the movement against the war in Vietnam. But in those years before the new feminism, the pressures of graduate school and the personal life of a woman in her twenties had combined to make me increasingly less of an activist and more of a sympathizer. From my two-room apartment full of cats and craziness, I sympathized with the Vietnamese. Now, during Tet, it became more than that, as I began to understand that those people were not just helpless victims of the U.S. war machine, that they were able to fight back militarily, as well as morally, and that they could *win* militarily. Those barefoot peasant guerrillas were actually going to win against the armies of the richest and most powerful nation in the world! It was inspiring—in both an historical and a more intimate sense—and, at the same time, deeply troubling for someone with my pacifist history. One day, in an elevator at Columbia, I overheard someone from the French Department speak of an NLF victory as a certainty: *Mais ils se battent pour leur patrie, ces gens-là*. I realized that I had come to agree with the pronouncement and the conviction behind it. Of course they would win, and of course it was right that they should.

At night I listened to the radio for whatever WBAI could tell me about what was happening in Vietnam and, between bulletins, I read. One night I stayed up until dawn reading Virginia Woolf's *A Room of One's Own*. Its feminism impressed and moved me, but I felt that both the sexual and the political climate had changed sufficiently in the intervening forty years to call for a contemporary response. I knew that what I was listening for on the radio had something to do with it, although I was unsure about how to make the connections. I wanted to write something, even that night, but I knew I *shouldn't* write anything except my impossible dissertation. Instead, I went in to my freshman class on Literary Forms, where I was supposed to be introducing Fiction that day, and delivered an extempore rap about the origins of the English novel, the evolution of the female audience and female authorship, and the relation of these factors to the oppression of women. I talked out my essay and went home to listen to the war news.

Shortly afterward, Columbia University went out on strike. As I became active in the events of those weeks, it seemed as though my insomniac obsession with events in Southeast Asia was sweeping through the academic calm of my daylight haven, revealing the connections that had always subsisted between the two. The incidental effect on how I talked and taught about literature was enormous, but I was not yet able to see what it might have to do with the writing of "professional" scholarship and criticism. I got arrested twice during the strike period and, as a result, was thrown out of graduate school, an experience that taught me a great deal more about the world I lived in than all my doctoral seminars had managed to do. My political activity continued, but eventually I was reinstated as a student and hence as an apprentice teacher through something called Executive Clemency. In those pre-Watergate years the phrase was an unfamiliar one to us, the process itself mostly ironic.

As the Fall term advanced, and with a much stronger sense of how things fit together, I began applying for my first full-time university job. At MIT, the place that interested me most, the appointments committee wanted a sample of my written work. I had met the head of their Literature department a few weeks earlier, and it didn't seem nice to lay a chapter of my moribund thesis on him, but I had nothing else to send. Then, remembering the Virginia Woolf essay that had had neither motive nor audience, I decided to write it so as not to bore Louis Kampf with my dissertation. It took me ten days. I had never read any feminist criticism except what is in *A Room of One's Own* itself or in Mary Ellmann's *Thinking About Women,* which had just been published; I'd never been to a women's meeting. One evening while the essay was in progress I had a drink with an old boyfriend. He asked what writing he'd interrupted, and I immodestly explained that I was updating Virginia Woolf on Women and Fiction. Competitive wit had always been the mode between us, so I added: "You could call it, 'Who's Afraid of A Room of One's Own?' " I did.

By the time the essay was published, it already had a dated quality.* For the present collection I was tempted either to eliminate it from the contents or to revise it by excising all the embarrassing passages and bringing the rest into conformity with my present political and literary positions. I have done neither, because my most recent reading of the piece made it clear to me that it had some validity as an historical document. Not only does it mark a clear stage in my personal development, but it reflects the thinking of that period in the contemporary women's movement.

In preparation for the planned revisions, for instance, I read Juliet Mitchell's *Psychoanalysis and Feminism* and reread a

---

*Although Kampf and Lauter had accepted it early in 1969 for the anthology that was to become *The Politics of Literature,* and I made my final revisions early in 1970, the book was not published until mid-1972. Historical reasons for this delay are explained in the compilers' introduction to that collection. The result, I believe, was that the book as a whole, and my contribution as part of it, missed their proper time and audience.

number of other neo-Freudians, particularly those who attempt to "reconcile" Marxist and psychoanalytic theory. The assumption behind this endeavor was that the attack on Freud in "Who's Afraid of A Room of One's Own?" was misdirected—though not, I believe, mistaken—and that it was essential to take seriously the reasoning of those Freudians who share some part of my world view before I could take them on. Both hypotheses may well be true, but I am convinced that it is not correct to bring a nine-year-old article into that debate by making its half-dozen pages on Freud respond to arguments that had not been advanced at the time I was initially trying to think through these questions. The very fact that my piece anticipates—and thus, at some years' distance, appears to reiterate—similar discussions in a number of early women's liberation documents, notably the work of Weisstein, Millett, Figes, and Firestone, makes it imperative to recognize and respect the position as an authentic and significant one. For this reason, whereas I felt able to make additions, sometimes in the form of footnotes, to other parts of the essay where developments since 1968 have altered or confirmed some judgment of mine, this section, which is far more important in the general scheme of my argument, could not be changed without doing violence to my sense of history and my sense of intellectual honesty.

Now, in rereading the essay, I am impressed by some other features that seem to characterize my own process of development and that of the emerging feminist movement of which I was a part. One is the open concern with sexuality, specifically with the politics and the liberatory potential of heterosexuality, that is one of the article's organizing principles. Although I state unequivocally in the essay that the Sexual Revolution then at its apogee was neither sexual nor a revolution, there is a sense in which that nonrevolution nonetheless established the premises of my thinking and the terms in which it occurred. The very primacy of the issue and the insistence on its political nature were consequences of the assumptions and the unfulfilled promises of prevalent late-'60s sexual ideology.

This preoccupation with sexual questions is noticeable on a rereading precisely because the movement—and more particularly its left wing—has since concentrated its analytic and social energies on other facets of women's lives. Although I have one colleague who blames it all on overreaction to Germaine Greer, I believe that the reasons for this turn are historically complex and have to do with altered conditions faced by the left as a whole. What is clear is that by the time Midge Decter and Norman Mailer published their antifeminist tracts, there was a sense that the entire sexual framework from which they were arguing was very much beside the point; both books therefore end up seeming conservative in a double sense. In any event, the ways in which "Who's Afraid of A Room of One's Own?" reflects and recapitulates the sexual concerns of its time do not represent "errors" that my present judgment would correct, but rather serve as a reminder of a direction we did not take—for better or for worse—and actually, I suspect, for better *and* for worse.

This earliest essay stands at one extreme on the question of the relationship between cultural criticism and feminist theory. Because *A Room of One's Own* provided the initial impetus for my own piece, and because all of Virginia Woolf's social theorizing starts from the cultural situation of women, "Who's Afraid of A Room of One's Own?" is unself-consciously literary in its approach. Like Virginia Woolf, I write as if cultural analysis and criticism were universally accepted as literary modes in themselves, so that there is no question that what I am doing counts as *writing*. On a somewhat less innocent level, Woolf's literary feminism contributed to the fluidity—and the occasionally dangerous facility—with which the essay moves back and forth between literary and historical events, between fiction, criticism, social theory, and personal experience. Similarly, my approach is literary in the sense that it treats ideas and schools of ideas as if they were capable of acting in history as they do in literature, rather than having historical forces behind them. Once more, however, I believe the particular phase in the life of the women's liberation movement has as much to do with this direction as the influence of *A Room of One's Own;* at any rate, the same conflation of social systems and ideas may be found in the founding literature of contemporary feminism, even in the works of those of us who sought at least some of our ideas and methods in the Marxist tradition.

The five articles grouped together in the "Theory" section constitute a sequence, although the process by which they develop from, build upon, and contradict one another was not clear to me until I had been engaged in it for some time. Written between December 1970 and February 1975, they reflect the evolution of my attempt to understand how cultural criticism might be brought into closer relation with daily life itself and with movements to change the conditions under which we experience it. Which is to say that not even the earliest essay repeats the unexamined assumption about the naturalness of the relation that characterized my Virginia Woolf essay and its literary model. I think that my own political evolution in what in retrospect seems like the short period between the composition of "Who's Afraid of A Room of One's Own?" and the next piece would have called my naïve literary feminism into question anyway, but the circumstances that impelled me to write the first of the theoretical pieces in this collection made the self-scrutiny inevitable.

Between 1968 and 1970 I was mostly an activist, but the demands that practice made on me entailed the study of theory, so that I was learning from books as well as from my immediate experience. First of all, I joined the women's liberation movement in New York and later in Boston, identifying with groups that understood the oppression of women in the context of world capitalism. At the same time, I never abandoned work in community organizations or in the antiwar/antiimperialist movement on campus, participating as well, and with greatly varying degrees of success, in the struggle to force those groups to take the woman question seriously and to change their own sexist practice.

A lot of important things happened to me in those two years. I learned to talk with other women and know such talk for a social process, not a pseudotherapy or a futile sob-session. With that support, I learned to take part in large meetings and to give public speeches with some confidence. I visited Cuba. Through the "power-structure research" that was the New Left's great intellectual contribution, I came to understand that there was an international ruling class. Eventually, and by means of a rougher process, I also recognized that there was a working class, apprehending the significance of this first of all in terms of my own family background and identity, then as an attribute of other individuals and communities, then as a force that operates on a world-historic scale. For the first time in what had only superficially seemed a busy academic and political life, I had a sense that my well-being and my self-definition didn't depend on what man I was sleeping with. I was arrested a couple more times.

During that period I wrote leaflets, political journalism, and feminist pamphlets that were about women's lives, not about books about women's lives; I also learned how to write collectively. The closest I got to criticism was to provide translations and commentary for a group of Cuban poems. Also, after perhaps fifteen years of silence, I began writing poetry again, mostly for my own notebooks, but sometimes for publication. My academic work was concentrated in teaching, as I began to design and offer courses in what was eventually to be called women's studies. When I thought about it, I assumed I still had dissertation block; but now at least I understood that there was something wrong with the subject itself, and I also realized that I still had no notion of how to translate social insights into critical practice, for I had no access to critical theory.

There was no way, particularly at the height of the war in Southeast Asia, to be a woman at MIT and to be struggling only for "women's rights." The place was like a men's locker-room, but it was all too apparent that the same system that socialized most women to fear and fail at scientific subjects was also responsible for the grotesque uses to which that male-dominated skill was being put. To teach about sexual politics in such an environment was, necessarily, to teach about the world in which my students, male and female, were expected to function as technological cadres. I knew, of course, that there were women's groups that did not share my perspective, but it literally never occurred to me that the influence of that sort of feminism could survive in a literary context; the books my students and I were reading had such a different lesson to teach. So I went to the MLA and lost my innocence.

Nineteen seventy was the first year that the Association's Commission on the Status of Women offered forums and workshops reflecting a feminist approach to the discipline. These discussions of content paralleled and complemented the Commission's other activities, which chiefly concerned women's getting and holding jobs in a profession where sex discrimination was rampant and only sometimes overt. I felt rather alienated from the nonliterary issues that were central to the women at MLA. Some of my response undoubtedly had to do with the peculiarities of my position at MIT. At that time I was fighting to keep my job. After a sit-in in the office of the president, and especially after most of us had been let off with probation by the criminal courts, MIT wanted to do *something* to the students and teachers involved and found it had no procedures by which to discipline faculty. In the months preceding the MLA convention, therefore, a faculty committee had been holding hearings in order to design a judicial code by which we could be prosecuted after the fact. I knew that a number of my student friends had been suspended and it seemed unlikely that I would have a job for the following year. My problem wasn't exactly a model case in sex discrimination, although there was plenty of that at issue, and the MLA women seemed to have no room for political complexities.

Similarly, I had a hard time understanding their attitude toward affirmative action. Women's groups nationally were just beginning to use the universities' status as federal contractors to insist on application and enforcement of the nondiscrimination stipulated in those contracts. And the strategy was working. Research contracts and granted funds come from various branches of the government, of course, and entail many different kinds of work. In 1970, however, the greatest number of contracts—and by far the largest dollar amounts—were awarded by the Department of Defense and its military components. Not only was MIT the largest defense contractor among U.S. universities, it was the nation's fifth largest defense contractor overall! The movement with which I worked at MIT took action to protest the Institute's involvement in directly war-related research—work, for instance, on the MIRV (Multiple Intermediate-Range Re-entry Vehicle), the "stabilization" of military helicopters, and a device with the Orwellian name of "moving target indicator"—and in counter-insurgency research, both international and domestic, in the social sciences. We wanted those contracts not to exist on any terms; and I felt it was grotesque to imagine that it would benefit women in general to win some jobs or promotions at MIT through blackmail based on the contracts' affirmative action clauses.

The feminist criticism to which I was exposed at the MLA convention shared the limitations of the other feminist activities: neither involved a thoroughgoing critique of academic institutions and academic work. Just as the legalistic approach to sex discrimination and affirmative action entailed no sense of the actual social functions that higher education serves, so too, the criticism on display reflected an unexamined acceptance of the methods and values of traditional criticism—except for their sexism, of course. Careers were to be built on the successful accommodation of feminism to conventional methodology, but I am convinced that most of the feminist criticism whose narrowness distressed me was not conceived or executed for opportunist reasons. (Indeed, it has often proved professionally unhealthy for a woman to concern herself with research and teaching in the field of women's studies. Many departments tend to regard pursuit of this new discipline as abandonment of literary scholarship and criticism. Their persistence indicates that large numbers of women nonetheless feel impelled to continue work they believe to be·important. I may consider their efforts shortsighted, but they are hardly as myopic as the departments that refuse to shelter them.)

As a participant in the early surge of the movement for women's liberation, I had felt myself to be part of the mainstream. I had seen my literary work as being one part of my contribution to this growing social force. At MLA my particular concerns represented a minority position among the feminists, and even the customary vocabulary—words like "movement" and "consciousness" and "action"—was applied to unfamiliar phenomena. I felt that the possible directions feminist *criticism* might take reflected different perceptions of feminism itself, and in the commentary I gave at my own session I tried to point this out. For the first time in a group of women, I had an experience we talked a good deal about in those days, the sense of being tolerantly ignored. As Jean Tepperman's poem, "Witch," expressed it,

> They waited for me to finish
> then continued the conversation.

In my own life, I'd always identified Tepperman's "they" as men, especially avuncular professors and participants at New Left meetings. Now I had a new place in which to feel impotent and invisible.

When I returned to Boston, I learned that *College English* would devote a forthcoming issue to convention activities centering on women in the profession. I rapidly turned my notes into the article called "Dwelling in Decencies," which became the first of the pieces collected here to be published. The article strikes me today as funny, angry, and remarkably prescient, although the polemic it contains might have been more deliberately and more accurately focused. It establishes the connections between feminist criticism and the whole of feminist theory, thereby asserting, if not satisfactorily demonstrating, that thinking about women and literature ought to take place in the context of the women's movement as a whole; at the same time, I tried to make it clear that the best goals of that movement were diametrically opposed to those of the defining institutions of class society. My fear that feminist studies, in an attempt to justify its acceptance as a respectable part of academe, would become indistinguishable from that which it was designed to criticize has been realized in far too many cases, but in my post-MLA despondency I totally underestimated the potential vigor and breadth of the genuinely feminist scholarship made available in the past five or six years. Most of the changes I have permitted myself are editorial and move in the direction of clarifying points I believed I'd already made. The one conscious anachronism that I have introduced occurs in the labeling of tendencies within the women's liberation movement, where I employ the present designations, "radical feminist" and "socialist feminist," to replace the then-current but inexact polarity of "feminists" and "politicos."

Once my article was completed and in the mail, I found myself discussing the issues it raised with friends from the movement whose work was in other branches of women's studies. Out of these discussions came (eventually abortive) plans for a radical conference on feminist scholarship and the article entitled "Modernism and History." In the summer of 1971, Lise Vogel, one of the women with whom I had worked in political organizations and study groups, asked me to collaborate with her on an article for a journal's symposium on "modernism." This time instead of simply declaring, as I had in my earlier paper, that feminist criticism had to understand sex within a context also defined by class and race oppression, Vogel and I examined each of the three social categories in its impact on both culture and criticism. Since Vo-

gel's background was in art history, a field in which I had also
done some graduate work, our arguments make reference to
visual as well as literary examples, and the flexibility with which
we move from one to the other makes for a more comprehensive
theoretical approach than a focus on one medium would.

In the six years that have passed since we wrote the article,
both Vogel and I have continued to develop our views on the
issues it addresses. The changes I have made here, with my
coauthor's approval, reflect only a small part of that development.* Although we analyze the cultural implications of sex,
class, and race, recognizing that they are overlapping categories
presenting discrete sets of problems, we place too much emphasis
on individual identity. That is, we concentrate on race, sex, and
class as personal attributes of artist, critic, and audience, an approach that enables us to distinguish the work of art from its
purely formal history and return it to the world of human realities,
but that fails to place it in that larger human history in which
class, race, and sex function as *social* forces. The chief result of
this focus is that the paper cannot fully integrate its Marxism—
which necessarily centers on broad historical forces—with its
criticism—which focuses on private identity and the responses it
evinces. Our understanding of Marxist theory was, in any event,
at a rather primitive level, and the editor of *New Literary History*
wisely proposed relegating most of the direct citations from Marx
and Engels to a single long footnote. For the present version I
have eliminated that note completely, since I find that certain of
the historical and materialist assumptions from which we worked
are in fact reflected in the critical passages, and that the others are
more adequately and effectively applied in the later essays.

Elsewhere in the article, we have attempted to strengthen some

*The later essays in this volume suggest my own intellectual trajectory. Lise
Vogel, who is better known for her theoretical and historical writings on women's
work and the family, has also written about women and art. For a more sophisti-
cated treatment of the questions posed in "Modernism and History," I recommend her piece, "Fine Arts and Feminism: The Awakening Consciousness,"
Feminist Studies, 3 (1974).

of the original critical points, particularly in the discussion of Monet's water lily paintings; but both of us have restrained the impulse either to bring every judgment into harmony with what we now think or to reopen those areas on which we disagreed when we wrote the article and whose old resolution may represent an unsatisfactory compromise. In one place, though, I have added a sentence directly addressing the concerns of those who have attacked the article for "confusing" modernism (which is Good) with formalism (understood as Bad).

While "Modernism and History" was still in press, *College English* began to send me comments they'd received on my earlier article, "Dwelling in Decencies." One of them offered some praise of my article by way of introduction to a lengthy plug for a left sectarian literary review with which I had long since lost patience. In a brief response, I attempted to lay out what I thought a radical critic was supposed to do, what I'd been trying to do myself, and how the journal that was being publicized at my expense fell short of what was needed. Because I was discussing what purported to be a Marxist journal, I was moved for the first time in print to consider the issue of the working-class audience, the culture addressed to it, and the possible role of criticism with respect to it. For this reason I wanted to reprint the article in the present collection while eliminating all references to the particular occasion of its composition. The result is the piece called "The Critical Task," which recasts the arguments I advanced in "Cultural Criticism and the *Horror Vacui*" as a discursive note, instead of a reply to something else. Unfortunately, by removing my essay from the polemical context in which it was conceived I have also removed most of its wit, since the journal had been too large and obvious a target to resist. I think, however, that even this somewhat denatured version of my remarks suggests the directions in which my two later theoretical pieces were to move.

This essay also constitutes a kind of chronological bridge, for in 1972 I made two decisions that considerably slowed down any production in the area of cultural theory: I began work on an

entirely new dissertation topic, and I accepted an appointment at
SUNY/Buffalo. My old job at MIT seemed secure, but I had
realized by now that MIT was hardly the ideal environment in
which to pursue teaching and scholarship about women and that if
I were really serious about feminist studies I needed to be working in a program committed to that field. Politically, moreover, I
was increasingly impatient with what I saw as the demographic
unrealities of Boston–Cambridge, and felt that my work might
make more sense if I carried it on in a more "normal" American
industrial city. The move to Buffalo and the doctoral work
influenced the content, as well as the pace, of my subsequent
ventures into cultural analysis.

When choosing a new subject for my dissertation, I was determined to find one within my original period of specialization,
the European Renaissance, and also to explore the new terrain of
women's studies. As I began work, it was rapidly borne in on me
that I had learned about the "Renaissance" as a designation of
style, and that what history I had assimilated was presented as the
"background" to cultural events. From a perspective informed
by the theoretical approach I had been developing in my essays, I
recognized that my critical subject required a grounding in social
and economic history; and as I began laying the basis for a new
understanding of the period I was already supposed to know, this
outlook had an impact on what I wrote about critical theory.

Thus, in September 1973, when I was asked to give a paper at
the English Institute as a part of a series on "The Literature of
Politics," I took the opportunity to reexamine the cultural significance of race, class, and sex from a more historical point of
view than I had been capable of earlier. In this piece,
"Criticism—and Self Criticism," I drew a distinction between the
personal and the social history that are shaped by sex, class, and
race, and attempted to demonstrate that art belongs to the public
dimension of experience. At the same time, I used Marx's
analysis of commodity fetishism to describe the way traditional

criticism misapprehends and alienates the work of art, and I tried to connect the making of art to other forms of production under capitalism.

I did not revise this article for publication until the middle of 1974, after I defended my Ph.D. dissertation. Since I had already accepted the invitation to write another article, "Criticism: Who Needs It?" which I began later that year and completed in early 1975, I was able to conceive of the two as complementary and thus produce an essay that was more an elaboration than a correction of earlier efforts. In "Criticism: Who Needs It?" I return to the question of class and culture from a perspective shaped by life in Buffalo. This leads to consideration of the mass media forms directed at the working class. I attempt to understand what they have to do with culture and criticism as I had previously understood them and—far more important—as they needed to be understood by the working-class movement. My assumptions about the role of culture in the life of a movement are no less global here than they were when I was imitating Virginia Woolf, but they no longer take it for granted that culture and revolution are the same thing. The process of reevaluating what I think I know and integrating what I learn is a constant one, assuring that "Criticism: Who Needs It?" is far from definitive. Nonetheless, I have kept editorial changes in both pieces to a cosmetic minimum, reserving to myself the sense that further approaches to cultural theory will have to depend on further practice of criticism and politics.

In the spring of 1975, I completed arrangments with Indiana University Press to compile this collection of my essays. The five theoretical pieces were already written, as was "Who's Afraid of A Room of One's Own?" which is not so readily classifiable as either cultural theory or practical criticism. What remained was to try my theories out in practice with a series of pieces addressed to the same audience for which I had written the earlier articles.

The half-dozen essays included in the last section of this book make no claims to "cover" the possible ranges of subjects to which Marxist and feminist methods can or should be applied. Rather, they reflect the eccentricities of my tastes and information, as well as some accidental events in my intellectual life.

"Woman under Capitalism" summarizes my doctoral work but, since it was written more than a year after my defense, it begins to compensate for the onesidedness of that manuscript's thesis, recognizing sexuality and statecraft as parallel themes in Renaissance heroic epic rather than insisting that the former invariably pointed to the latter. My interest in television is at another pole of my professional concerns. "What's My Line?" brings together some of the themes of my lectures and conference papers at the same time that it adumbrates the longer study of television and daily life in which I am now engaged.* While these essays grew out of intellectual preoccupations with which I had been, as it were, "officially" concerned, others originated in what were supposed to be hobbies, areas in which I was not a specialist. For instance, "Why Marry Mr. Collins?" is a direct result of discussions with Martha Fleischer and her students about Jane Austen.

Often the essays have served more as ways of figuring out what I think and why than of simply setting down what I already know. Thus, writing about the poetry of the feminist movement helped me to come to terms with a school or tendency within contemporary American literature with which I identify as both poet and critic, but with whose political limitations I remain uneasy. "On Reading Trash" tries to explain—to myself, first of all—why I am an avid reader of the historical romances sold in drugstores. And "Working/Women/Writing" grows out of my disagreement with a publisher about a selection from the scrapbook *I Am a Woman Worker* that I wished to include in a proposed anthology. The publisher rejected the selection: it was "not moving." I found it

---

*The book is scheduled for publication by Indiana University Press.

very moving. This was the origin of my concern with defining a usable feminist aesthetic. My 1976 MLA paper dealt with this topic. Writing down my ideas helped to clarify them, and the ensuing discussion from the floor—lively, controversial, and varied as it was—helped even more. The present, much-expanded paper thus reflects what I took away from that session as much as what I brought to it.

A preoccupation that runs through all but one of these essays concerns work, particularly the work that women do, in its relation to cultural expression. Perhaps such an interest is inevitable on the part of someone who understands the centrality of labor to our present social system but whose own "work" involves explaining aspects of life that belong to the territory defined as "leisure." I believe, however, that interest in this theme is more than a personal idiosyncrasy, and that its presence in five of these essays serves not only to unify my efforts in practical criticism but also to underscore some issues that are of the highest importance in our common understanding of cultural experience.

Generally speaking, however, the twelve essays that make up this collection come together more like a dozen segments of some larger but still unfinished design than like the pieces of a satisfactorily completed puzzle. This effect is intentional; the major tasks in the field of culture, as in history itself, still lie before us, and only some of their outlines are as yet perceptible. The articles in this volume are meant to provoke—or perhaps "stimulate" is a more diplomatic word—critical interest and further work on the issues I bring up. Although I like to win arguments as much as the next person, I cannot pretend that these studies of sex, class, and culture are anything more than the beginning of a debate. They are not the last word.

Sex, Class, and Culture

PART ONE

Critical Theory

Dwelling in Decencies: Radical Criticism and the Feminist Perspective

I reached the point of thinking you were right, and that your culture was the true one. . . . By a hair, I missed becoming one of you.
    —The Schoolboys of Barbiana, Letter to a Teacher

I

FEMINIST CRITICISM, as its name implies, is criticism with a Cause, engaged criticism. But the critical model presented to us so far is merely engaged to be married. It is about to contract what can only be a *mésalliance* with bourgeois modes of thought and the critical categories they inform. To be effective, feminist criticism cannot become simply bourgeois criticism in drag. It must be ideological and moral criticism; it must be revolutionary.

Having begun thus bluntly, I feel tempted to retreat somewhat, to equivocate and speak optimistically of "steps in the right direction." Literary theory has existed so long without a self-conscious female component that I hesitate to find fault when one is forthcoming. Nonetheless, I am convinced that established criticism cannot provide the intellectual means to advance in what will prove to be right directions.

Even criticism that calls itself radical frequently falls into masculine habits of expression: the human antecedent takes the pronoun "he" and the human generalization is sexually par-

3

ticularized as "Man" or "mankind." The existence of these terms may be a lexical accident, their survival an anachronism. But their continued use by professed radicals reflects a grave failure of consciousness. Those who recognize the class and racial bias of traditional literary study have paid, at best, only perfunctory notice to its sex bias. If radical critics are sexist, however, that does not mean feminists can ignore what they tell us about literature and criticism. Rather, we must construct a method that applies radical insights about culture and politics, but does so in the context of a coherent feminist analysis.

To some extent, the terms of this discussion recapitulate debates within the American women's movement. The questions I pose about our discipline reflect a larger question about ourselves: can women be liberated in our present political economy, or is more fundamental change required? For those of us who choose a radical response to this question, there is a more strategic problem. I am referring to the tension between radical feminists, defined as those who believe that the basic social conflict is between the sexes and socialist feminists, who believe that the fundamental conflict is between classes and that sexism is a part of that struggle. This is not merely a sectarian quarrel, and I bring it up in a literary discussion because much of my present argument depends on the definition of "feminism." In this paper, I characterize as feminist women's consciousness of being "the other" in a male-dominated system. Within the limits of literature, at least, women's exclusion is clearly shared by all nonwhite and working-class men. High culture is a male domain, but not all men may participate in it. Recognition of these facts does not make my approach less feminist. It does suggest the critical direction I think we should pursue.

II

My earlier unsupported allusion to bourgeois ideology probably had two immediate effects: it made me a marked woman and it alienated part of my audience. I hope this response is not irrevocable, for my use of the term is quite precise and is meant as neither random invective nor (red) flag-waving. None of us is to blame for our exposure to certain training, including a conditioned revulsion to the rhetoric of class warfare. We are at fault only if we insist—in the face of all evidence—that the realm of the mind is above that struggle, that it is some abstract Agora where ideas duel gracefully among themselves, all unconscious of whose interests they serve.

What happens then is that we perceive history—literary history above all—as the consecutive predominance of certain ideas, schools and values, independent of the conditions or the people that produced them. Marx and Engels observed that it had not occurred to the philosophers who were their contemporaries "to inquire into the connections of German philosophy with German reality, the relation of their criticism to their own material surroundings."[1] Similarly, the literary profession has *chosen* to ignore the class nature of the categories and standards it employs. This is something that women, in particular, cannot afford to do.

I have called certain categories of thought "bourgeois," choosing a term that entails class rather than gender connotations. As I have said, I think that cultural criticism helps us to clarify what "class analysis" has to do with feminism. When I characterize an idea as bourgeois, I am doing so in the traditional Marxist sense:

> The ideas of the ruling class are in every epoch the ruling ideas: i.e. the class which is the ruling material force of society is at the same time its ruling intellectual force. The class which has the means of material production at its disposal has control at the same time over the means of mental production, so that thereby, generally speaking, the ideas of those who lack the means of mental production are subject to it. The ruling ideas are nothing more than the ideal expression of the dominant material relationships, the dominant material relationships grasped as ideas.[2]

Italian adolescents have expressed the same view somewhat more colorfully: "How could a young gentleman argue with his own shadow, spit on himself and on his own distorted culture while using the very words of that culture?"[3] Both of these arguments involve observations about the nature of the dominant ideology and the difficulty of formulating a critique from within its sphere of influence.

Feminist theory may avoid the class question, but it is quite explicit as to women's sense of being culturally disinherited. It may seem that I needlessly polarize the issue by insisting on the relations between material and ideological power. Aren't there many bourgeois women, after all? Well, no. The wives and daughters of the ruling class do not somehow mystically partake in *someone else's* relation to the means of production.

> The category [woman] seems to cut across all classes; one speaks of working-class women, middle-class women, etc. The status of women is clearly inferior to that of men, but analysis of this condition usually falls into discussing socialization, psychology, interpersonal relations, or the role of marriage as a social institution. Are these, however, the primary factors? In arguing that the roots of the secondary status of women are in fact economic it can be shown that women as a group do indeed have a definite relation to the means of production and that this is different from that of men. The personal and psychological factors then follow from this special relation to production, and a change in the latter will be a necessary (but not sufficient) condition for changing the former.[4]

Women are not the in-laws of class society. The uniquely female relation to social production is embodied in women's traditional tasks in the home, housework, child-rearing, even supervision of housework and serving as hostess. We are used to borrowing sociological vocabulary and speaking of women's "rôle," but it is useful, first, to comprehend it materially. And it is vital to do so if we are to understand that vast body of literature in which female characters acquire, question, accept, or modify their "rôles," the social definition of woman.

Just above, I used a Marxist source because I think it very cogently summarizes one side of a vexed economic question. But

I first encountered a proposal to "capitalize" household duties in a less doctrinaire setting, the writings of Virginia Woolf. Addressing a man of the ruling class, Virginia Woolf says, "you should provide a wage to be paid by the State to those whose profession is marriage and motherhood."[5] In suggesting this, with a sense of futility but not of irony, Virginia Woolf recognizes the psychological effects of economic conditions; payment of a regular salary to unpaid women workers is, she states, "the most effective way in which we can ensure that the large and very honourable class of married women shall have a mind and a will of their own." She also translates into material terms the feeling of "otherness" typical even of women who are "of" the bourgeoisie. For instance, she explains her repetition of the phrase "educated man's daughter" to designate such a woman:

> Our ideology is still so inveterately anthropocentric that it has been necessary to coin this clumsy term . . . to describe the class whose fathers have been educated at public schools and universities. Obviously, if the term 'bourgeois' fits her brother, it is grossly incorrect to use it of one who differs so profoundly in the two prime characteristics of the bourgeoisie—capital and environment.[6]

So when I speak of the bourgeoisie and the intellectual productions that support it, I feel I am doing so as a feminist, referring to a group from which women are by and large excluded and in whose interest that exclusion is justified.

III

Annis Pratt has outlined how "feminist" critics can make use of bibliographical, textual, contextual, and archetypal modes. My response has been to say that feminism is necessarily alienated from those modes—at least as we have come to understand them. It remains for me to suggest something to put in their place.

As women, we should be aware of how idealization serves oppression. Throughout much of our literature, fanciful constructs of the ideal female, her character and psychology, have obscured the limitations suffered by actual women. Worse, they have encouraged expectations and behavior that only strengthen the real oppression. Feminist critics are not likely to ape male poets in sentimentalizing the female spirit. But there is a kind of idealism to which we become susceptible when we explore the question of feminine consciousness. For we, too, have a tendency to ignore its material basis.

Granted, this is a kind of play on words, but it is not intended to blur the distinction between "idealization" and "idealism." In literature, to idealize means to ignore, perhaps to "transcend," reality. The philosophical tendency called "idealism" means to ignore material conditions, treating ideas as if they were causes or motivations in themselves, the "unmoved movers" of history. Whereas the former is more or less the opposite of realism, the latter is the opposite of materialism. I see no point in reopening all the books that give us a view of "feminine consciousness" unless we have a firm grasp of what *anybody's* consciousness is. From a Marxist perspective, "the production . . . of consciousness is at first directly interwoven with the material activity and the material intercourse of men, the language of real life. . . . Life is not determined by consciousness, but consciousness by life."[7] Perhaps this sounds more like an assertion that works through repetition of key phrases than an argument. In another place, Marx reiterates the idea and fills in some of what may appear to be rhetorical gaps:

In the social production of their life, men enter into definite relations that are indispensable and independent of their will, relations of production which correspond to a definite stage of development of their material productive forces. The sum total of these relations of production constitutes the economic structure of society, the real foundation, on which rises a legal and political superstructure and to which correspond definite forms of social consciousness. The mode of production of material life conditions the social, polit-

ical and intellectual life process in general. It is not the consciousness of men that determines their being, but, on the contrary, their
social being that determines their consciousness.[8]

How would feminist criticism based on this view of consciousness differ from what Annis Pratt calls "contextual" criticism?
For one thing, she speaks of contextual analysis as considering
"the relevance of a group of works, even if artistically flawed, as
a reflection of the situation of women. . . . [The critic] should be
'feminist' in going beyond formalism to consider literature as it
reveals men and women in relationship to each other within a
socio-economic *context,* that web of role expectations in which
women are enmeshed." I think I understand what "context"
might mean when freed of sociological terminology, but I cannot
deduce what kind of literary criticism it might inspire. The only
examples which Pratt provides us have to do with the exigencies
of the literary marketplace, not the full material situation of
author or characters. Beyond this, we are apparently being asked
to regard the book as an historical artifact revealing its "context"
and at the same time the product of a context that we should
somehow "take into account" as we read.

Perhaps writers themselves give us a better idea of how to
proceed. Novelists and playwrights, even when they mystify
womanhood, usually consider it almost a matter of course to
relate their characters' psychological circumstances to their
material situation. And even when the "resolution" is a highly
suspect one, we are frequently made to see how it is materially
conditioned. Many books about women concentrate on the moral
and social "choices" they make; their authors almost always
show us how little material scope for choosing they really have.
This is clearly more than just telling us how much money someone has or can get—although writers, when speaking of women,
are astonishingly explicit about these facts. It is a matter of relating the economic and cultural experience of class to someone's

sense of herself and to what happens in her life. It also means understanding the extent to which sexual identity itself is a material fact.

To be specific, what is it that Becky Sharp wants and how does she come to want it? What really *happens* to Eugénie Grandet? What if either of them were a man in the same circumstances? Those are obvious examples, perhaps, but I need not rely only on them. I could give you instead Isabel Archer, Anne Eliot, Lily Bart, Cranford's Miss Matty Jenkyns, or Constance Chatterley. None of these is a feminist heroine or a "simple" case of economic determinism. None of their creators was—to understate the case—a Marxist. But all of them give us information about the intersection of class and gender that we have not as yet learned to interpret.

IV

I have not taken up Annis Pratt's four categories in their original order, because the mode she calls "contextual" is the only one that can be considered feminist at all. The others are much more firmly entrenched in standard lit-crit assumptions and it is harder to see how they can be useful to us. I hasten to repeat that it is not something "old-fashioned" or stuffy about traditional criticism that I object to, but rather its use in the service of ruling-class interests. It should be clear, for instance, that sexual stereotypes serve *somebody's* interest; they are not the result of what some writer "happens" to believe because of a particularly noble (or vicious) mother or because of myths about Motherhood. Similarly, a prevailing ideology about sexual love—something that literature certainly promotes—has a great deal to do with basic social relationships and institutions. It is no accident that certain groups benefit from their existence and that others are oppressed by them. I have mentioned two central aspects of Western literature. They exist whatever critical posture we choose to adopt. But criticism does determine the way they function for us. These two are also specifically sexual ideas; current critical fashions devote great attention to more general themes like "Man's" isolation, alienation, and individualism. It has clearly been convenient for the operation of our society for us to believe in and teach these themes as "universals"—to say nothing of the greatest bourgeois theme of all, the myth of pluralism, with its consequent rejection of ideological commitment as "too simple" to embrace the (necessarily complex) truth.

These last observations are an oblique introduction to my remarks on archetypal criticism. As I understand it, archetypal criticism is the application to literature of Jungian psychology. Nothing could be more harmful to a coherent and fruitful reading of "the literature of women" than Jungianism, with its liturgical pronouncements about The Masculine and The Feminine—not to mention The Universal and The Innate. That such criticism has very real and very negative social effects seems to me undeniable. But its implications for women are particularly sinister. If we find that heroines "manifest interestingly parallel characteristics during their psychic development," this does not mean that we should perpetrate generalizations about the female psyche as specious as those that define the male psyche. Of course it is infuriating that the male psyche has been treated "as if it, itself, defined the human soul." But it is also infuriating that the human soul has been defined so oppressively, and we should not correct only the lesser injustice. There are, indeed, parallel characteristics in the lives of fictional women. We should not make a fetish of these, but consider why they exist. To what extent do they coincide with the social reality of women's lives? Where they do not, to what end did their authors impose this development? What are the social effects of literary conventions dealing with women? These are important questions, but they are far from the realm of psychic archetypes.

The bibliographical question, too, has been incorrectly posed, for it assumes what it attempts to prove: that our principal focus should be neglected works that can in some way or other be classified as "feminist." This is only one of the tasks of a feminist critic, particularly when she is also a critic of culture and society. I agree that feminist writings and the "literature of women" as a whole must be reexamined. But to limit ourselves to that area is to imply that feminists have nothing to add to analyses of the male literature that makes up the great body of "our" literary tradition. We have a significant contribution to make to the radical criticism of that tradition—a contribution that is not encompassed merely by saying "ugh!" and turning away.

It is true that the literary mistreatment of women has been compounded by the critical mistreatment of women's literature. Mary Ellmann points out some of the ramifications of this in *Thinking About Women:* assumptions about "feminine style," sexual analogy, treating women's books as if they *were* women. Carol Ohmann's essay, "Emily Brontë in the Hands of Male Critics," is a history of one such case. It incisively documents the critical habits of more than a century with regard to *Wuthering Heights,* a novel whose "sex" was unknown for the first years of its life. Women authors generally and those, in particular, who are "only" concerned with female psychology, are treated with a most destructive combination of condescension and neglect.

Sometimes it is worse than that. I have recently read through Fred Pattee's *The Feminine Fifties,* a book that is listed in one of Annis Pratt's footnotes and that she apparently considers a step in the right direction.[9] It is a general history of American literature in the decade before the Civil War and the adjective is supposed to describe the decade itself. Alluding to the fashion of alliterative designations for periods, the author says:

> There are at least ten "f" words that describe phases of the decade: *fervid, fevered, furious, fatuous, fertile, feeling, florid, furbelowed, fighting, funny.* . . . To find a single adjective that would combine them all—can it be done? Would not such a word be a veritable world in itself? Unquestionably. That I have found this word, however, my title reveals."[10]

Pattee concludes the first chapter with an even more vicious observation. He says it was "a feminine period undoubtedly. Thomas Cholmondely, of London, to whom Thoreau in 1857 sent a copy of the second edition of *Leaves of Grass,* could sum up the poems and the poet with this startling verdict: 'I find reality and beauty, mixed with not a little violence and coarseness—both of which are to me effeminate.' Not only did this characterize the early Whitman and his work, but the decade as well. . . ."[11] This history devotes considerably more space than most to women writers and the feminist movement. But the results are what you might expect from someone who accepts and appears to delight in sexual stereotypes, who puts women's rights between inverted commas, and who cannot usefully distinguish between what is female, feminine, feminist, and effeminate. Had it merely neglected women, Pattee's book would have been just a rambling and inoffensive piece of writing. Its emphasis on the "feminine," however, makes it dangerous.

A book that Annis Pratt castigates for its "old feminist" stereotyping is Josephine Lurie Jessup's *The Faith of Our Feminists.*[12] I think this "study" of Edith Wharton, Ellen Glasgow, and Willa Cather is worse than stereotyped. It is both antifeminist and thoroughly reactionary. Jessup's thesis is based on the identification of feminism with any form of female independence; her bias is implicit in her opening remark that "straightaway woman discovered her limitation she set about denying it."[13] Pursuing a theological metaphor throughout, she regards feminism as the cult of Athena and thus can describe it triumphantly as "a faith which waned during the lifetime of its most distinguished adherents."[14] Her own theology is less clear. She stresses but fails to analyze the relations of each of the three writers to the Episcopal Church and remarks almost inconsequentially at the end of her book that the trouble with present-day American literature is that "we lack Dante's inscription [*sic*] 'In His will is our peace."[15]

Her politics are clearer and they are the reason why I give any attention at all to this eccentric volume. For Jessup's views are a vulgarization of bourgeois values of a sort not normally acknowledged in books of criticism. She believes in "spiritual triumphs" and in an author's "paying tribute" to the opposite sex. She makes many novels feminist victories by showing how someone's death or destruction was a "moral" defeat for the (often unidentified) enemy. Yet she appears to resent these imagined triumphs. At the same time, she thinks that male writers have done better by the female sex because they have idealized it. Similarly (and I suppose paradoxically), she claims that women writers have given male characters dignity: "Even at its bitterest, feminist fiction never describes the human male as the end-product of slum situations, or a creature peculiarly given to incest and inversion, or yet merely a fighting-and-lusting animal."[16] It is as if she thinks *writers who describe it* are responsible for the depravity that results from social conditions; treating people with dignity would thus consist in imagining more privileged moral types. Jessup generally has trouble with "social conditions." She believes Dreiser "the realist" is saying the same thing as Wolfe "the romantic," which is that "man, good as an individual, somehow [sic] absorbs and spreads contamination through group living."[17] Ironically, she seems to have chosen her subject because, for these three novelists, "life defines itself less often as a conflict between the individual and society than as a struggle between the sexes."[18] Besides, male writers are distressing because their social comment is so diffuse. "The feminist, for her part, has just one complaint. She disapproves of sexuality."[19] Perhaps I am over-emphasizing these two stupid books. But they are what you find when you go looking for studies of the literature of women. They may be the nadir, but they certainly provide reason enough for feminists to turn to our own literature.

Most literature, however, is not our own, and that is why I do not think there is a bibliographical problem. Much of what we have to do involves instead the rethinking of familiar material. "Is one to extol or to expose? This is a question of attitude. What attitude is wanted? I would say, both."[20] My citation is ironic in some measure; we shouldn't need Chairman Mao to tell us that feminist politics can expose something essential about the literature of and by men. "Exposure" does not mean simply repeated revelation of sexism. Even self-proclaimed feminists speak as if Kate Millett's *Sexual Politics* were definitive and exhaustive. Millett has made a beginning by discussing political implications of the language and themes of literature. Her method is suggestive, not prescriptive, and there are other ways to unmask sexist bias and place it in historical perspective.

There are questions, moreover, that will occur to us and not to other critics. I think, for instance, of *Ulysses,* which makes Annis Pratt flinch as a feminist while, as a critic, she acknowledges its literary worth. For the moment, let us set aside the question of "literary worth" in works that are ideologically repellent. Instead, let us think of how to approach the novel not as a feminist one moment and as a critic the next, but as a feminist critic. Annis Pratt says she responds to Molly Bloom on the chamber pot as a black militant must to stereotypes of Negro servants.[21] The solution is not to ignore it and go on to something else. On the contrary, I believe only a feminist knows what Molly Bloom is really about and can ask the questions that will demonstrate the real functioning of sexual myth in Joyce's novel.

A simpler example is the Nausicaa episode, which proceeds through representation of the thoughts of Gerty MacDowell and Leopold Bloom. As Tindall describes it, "For Gerty's part . . . [Joyce] wickedly chose the style of a cheap Victorian 'novelette'—what he called 'a namby-pamby jammy marmalady drawersy . . . style with effects of incense, mariolatry, masturbation, stewed cockles.' The ultimate indecency of the chapter is not Bloom's action but this style, which, embodying and presenting Gerty, is Gerty."[22] We should recall that in this chapter

whose symbol is "Virgin" and in which Bloom reflects on the
"womanly woman," Gerty-Nausicaa is also Milly, Mary, and
Molly. What is the function of Joyce's stylistic parody—and the
venom behind it? (And what are the politics of Joyce's relationship to the kind of prose he imitates? To the women who read and
wrote it? It is interesting that Hawthorne made specific reference
to Maria Cummins's *The Lamplighter,* one of Joyce's sources for
the Nausicaa style, when he inveighed against the "d——d mob
of scribbling women." Was Joyce, too, just pissed off at the
competition? Or is there an idea—even an ideology—in the background?)

What is the significance of the literary equipment with which
Joyce provides Gerty and Molly, on the one hand, Bloom and
Stephen on the other? What does Tindall intend when he says that
Joyce employs the parodic style "wickedly" and that it is an
"indecency"? What does it mean for women in general, and
those of the lower classes in particular, to realize fiction as Gerty
does? Why is this "trash" the literature they are fed? Is there a
way of reading and identifying with books that women typically
adopt in our society? How come? If her style "is" Gerty, how has
that come about? What is the significance of her lapses from it?
Why are her fantasies more contemptible than anyone else's?
These are not rhetorical questions, and there are many more we
might profitably ask. The answers to some of them would lead to
a better understanding of this section of *Ulysses* and of the novel
as a whole. Others will turn us away from the book to issues
concerning the sociology of literature. What has criticism to say
about the real Gerty MacDowells? What are the effects on them
and on society of escapist fiction and its characteristic style? And,
always, *cui bono*—who profits?

V

The question of style is the hardest, though hardly the most
important issue, because it is the place where literary and social

norms seem at first to be least compatible. It is also the one where the bourgeois critic feels most secure about the importance of the endeavor and the correctness of his judgments. Throughout Annis Pratt's essay there is an emphasis on textual criteria that are somehow independent of ideology. Thus, she can speak of some feminist works as being historically useful, although "artistically flawed"; and of the critic who considers context "without for a moment suspending her textual judgment"; and of works "which are resonant and craftsmanlike, if [male] chauvinistic examples of the fictional art." I shall spare all of us the ritual invective against the New Criticism. But I do not believe we have hitherto had objective standards by which to judge literary art, so the application of a feminist perspective will not mean adding ideology to a value-free discipline. *Thinking About Women* shows one aspect of "textual analysis," the phallic approach to writings by and about women. I do not suggest that we elevate anachronism into criticism, demanding that the writers of the past meet present-day expectations of political awareness, but rather that we consider what relation form has to moral and ideological content.

Along with spurious objectivity, I wish to discard the notion of critical "disinterestedness" that is one of Matthew Arnold's legacies to our profession. It is clear that to Arnold a disinterested approach does not mean a dispassionate one, but one that treats ideas in their "proper" intellectual sphere and does not attempt to involve them in the realm of practical political action. As I said before, I do not believe there is a separate domain of ideas and I think that it is dangerous to behave as if there were. But Arnold hardly intended a separation of the critical faculty from standards of moral judgment. Nor did he think that "style" is independent of ideology, otherwise what does it mean to deflate jingoist pretensions by repeating "Wragg is in custody"? Criticism has progressed so far into formalism that we have forgotten not so much that art has content but that *content* has content.

I have been using the word "morality" as if it still meant some-

thing in intellectual circles. In reality, it is one of those platitudi-
nous babies that are always being thrown out with the bath water.
For, when we recognized that there was no moral permanence,
we apparently decided that there was no basis for moral judgments. We failed to acknowledge that morality is social and that it
has material causes. Moral certainty itself began to look a bit
naïve, whatever its nature. When I read *Heroines of Fiction*, I
was appropriately amused by its approach to moral questions. In
the introductory chapter, Howells describes the hallmarks of
nineteenth-century literature as "voluntary naturalness, in-
structed singularity." Defoe is an earlier writer who has these
qualities, but does not share Howells's modern morality. "He
was, frankly, of the day before we began to dwell in decencies,
before women began to read novels so much that the novel had to
change its subject, or so limit its discussion that it came to the
same thing. . . . Because of his matter, and not because of his
manner or motive, his heroines must remain under lock and key
and cannot be so much as raised in mixed companies."[23] Of
course, Howells is an easy target for those claiming more sophis-
ticated sexual standards. Poor deluded soul, he thought he knew
what "goodness" was, in writing and in behavior, and he thought
that they were the same thing. The decencies in which I should
like to dwell are quite different from Howells's unexamined
categories, and draw rather different conclusions from the fact
that women read fiction. But maybe there was something worth
rescuing from his tub-load of assumptions—before they all went
down the drain.

Sartre once asked whether it would be possible to write a
"good" anti-Semitic novel in the wake of Nazi genocide. Someone replied that Céline has done precisely that. I imagine we
would all counter by asking, "What do you mean 'good'?" A
radical kind of textual criticism might well be able to answer that
question. It could usefully study the way the texture of sentences,
choice of metaphors, patterns of exposition and narrative relate

to ideology. I call such an approach radical and insist that feminism is intrinsic to it because up to now we have been very narrow in defining what we mean by the "content" that "form" is supposed to convey. In my education, for instance, much attention was devoted to such concepts as Metaphysical Wit, but our attention was never directed to the social conditions that informed the making of those conceits. I never inquired how they functioned *off* the page. Radical criticism of texts would obviously be more meaningful than a standard that simply said, "This is acceptable, that is not" without showing how this and that worked. It would thus actively demonstrate that ideology need not be dogma, that it can provide critical tools to broaden our present vision.

Proletarian critics of the '30s are frequently sneered at for praising authors of whom "no one today has heard," while attacking those whose reputations have grown since then. Their detractors act as if the voice of the people had spoken and rejected the Communist position, when what happened was the enthronement of an opposing critical fashion. Radical criticism should be able to do more than point out a "correct line" on sex or class. Applying our analysis to texts will determine, as dogma would not, what it *means* to keep saying, "That is a sexist book—but it's great literature."

*   *   *

I began by referring to a *mésalliance* between "feminism" and established critical modes. It might be amusing to extend the conceit to speak of oppressive relationships, bourgeois mindfuck, and foredoomed offspring. A more exact simile, however, would be the shotgun wedding. Some people are trying to make an honest woman out of the feminist critic, to claim that every "worthwhile" department should stock one. I am not terribly interested in whether feminism becomes a respectable part of academic criticism; I am very much concerned that feminist critics become a useful part of the women's movement. Old feminism concentrated on legal and human rights within essentially unaltered institutions. New feminism is about fundamentally transforming institutions. In our struggle for liberation, Marx's note about philosophers may apply to cultural critics as well: that up to now they have only interpreted the world and the real point is to change it.

NOTES

1. Karl Marx and Frederick Engels, *The German Ideology,* 1845-46 (New York: New World-International, 1967) , p. 6.
2. Ibid., p. 39.
3. The Schoolboys of Barbiana, *Letter to a Teacher* (New York: Random House, 1970), p. 90.
4. Margaret Benston, "The Political Economy of Women's Liberation," reprinted from *Monthly Review,* September 1969 (Boston: New England Free Press, 1969), p. 13.
5. Virginia Woolf, *Three Guineas,* 1938 (New York: Harcourt, Brace and World, 1963), pp. 110-111.
6. Ibid., p. 146, note 2. In the first sentence, I take it she means "androcentric."
7. Marx and Engels, pp. 13, 14, 15.
8. Karl Marx, "Preface to *A Contribution to the Critique of Political Economy,*" 1859, in Karl Marx and Frederick Engels, *Selected Works in One Volume* (New York: International, 1968), p. 182.
9. Fred Lewis Pattee, *The Feminine Fifties* (New York: Appleton, Century, 1940).
10. Ibid., p. 4.
11. Ibid., p. 111.
12. Josephine Lurie Jessup, *Faith of Our Feminists* (New York: Richard Smith, 1950).
13. Ibid., p. 9.
14. Ibid., p. 117.
15. Ibid., p. 118.
16. Ibid., p. 88.
17. Ibid., p. 87.

18. Ibid., p. 18.

19. Ibid., p. 117.

20. Mao Tse-tung, *Talks at the Yenan Forum on Literature and Art* (San Francisco: China Books, 1965).

21. Actually, the stereotype she uses is Jack Benny's Rochester, who is far from obsequious and seems to me to follow, rather, the old dramatic convention of the clever servant. But we might well ask what the uses of that convention have been to class societies.

22. William York Tindall, *A Reader's Guide to James Joyce* (New York: Farrar, Straus and Cudahy, 1959), p. 193.

23. William Dean Howells, *Heroines of Fiction,* Volume I (New York and London: Harper and Brothers, 1901), pp. 2-3.

Modernism and History

(with Lise Vogel)

I

THE exponents and the detractors of modernism are in surprising accord about what makes a work of art or criticism "modernist." For Clement Greenberg, to whom the term is a measure of quality, "the essence of modernism lies . . . in the use of the characteristic methods of a discipline to criticize the discipline itself, not in order to subvert it, but in order to entrench it more firmly in its area of competence."[1] Both aspects of this definition—the centripetal nature of modernism and its almost complete identification of criticism with art—are recognized in Louis Kampf's less respectful analysis: "One of the principal reasons for the dominance of criticism . . . is the disintegration of any firm notion of artistic form. . . . The act of esthetic perception has turned into criticism, but a criticism almost entirely concerned with defining the object and our perception of it: in short, epistemology."[2]

Whether it is invoked evangelically or pejoratively, "modernism" suggests an overriding emphasis on the autonomy of the work of art and its formal characteristics, on the permanence of modal change, and on the independence of critical judgment. The peculiar term "modernism" embodies in itself some of the problems presented by this constellation of ideas. It is a period designation whose suffix connotes at once a style and a creed. "Modern" would describe any work produced in the last hundred years or so; addition of the suffix "ism," however, implies a school or tendency, to which only certain of those works belong. The effect of this—both conceptually and semantically—is to detach culture from history, so that modernism becomes a critical stance for works of art from all periods. The work of art is isolated not only from tradition but from those considerations of content, patronage, and audience that brought it into being. Moreover, because of the integration of criticism into modernist culture, the critic is presumed to possess a consciousness equally free of the demands and limitations of history.* To the modernist critic, "formalism" is a negative term, connoting a narrow and absolute position that lacks the philosophical inclusiveness of "modernism." If we seem to use the two terms interchangeably in our arguments, it is because we believe the distinction to be illusory and even intellectually dishonest.

In recent years, there have been a number of attempts to re-situate the work of art in its history. These efforts have been based on assumptions about the relevance of subject matter to form and of social or psychological environment to cultural prod-uction. They have pleaded with critics to add "contextual" considerations to their formal analyses and apply "flexible approaches" when investigating the art of the past. In reality, they have all been extensions of the maxim that circumstances alter cases; nonetheless, they have implicitly accepted *certain* social and material circumstances as the norm, others as exceptions.

---

*"To impute a position or a line to a critic is to want, in effect, to limit his freedom. For a precious freedom lies in the very involuntariness of esthetic judging: the freedom to be surprised, taken aback, have your expectations confounded, the freedom to be inconsistent and to like anything in art so long as it is good—the freedom, in short, to let art stay open." Clement Greenberg, "Complaints of an Art Critic," *Artforum,* VI, 2 (October 1967), 38.

Despite its greater attention to the "history of ideas," such criticism still denies certain concrete properties to the work of art or its point of view. Its underlying assumptions are that *if* art has a race, it is white; *if* it has a sex, it is male; *if* it has a class, it is the ruling one. But these matters are almost never part of the "social context" we are urged to examine. When we consider the critic, the situation is clearer, for here is someone to whom we may safely attribute a race, a sex, a class. The problem is whether and to what extent these various memberships inform consciousness.

*   *   *

For this [Swiss] village, even were it incomparably more remote and incredibly more primitive, is the West, the West onto which I have been so strangely grafted. These people cannot be, from the point of view of power, strangers anywhere in the world; they have made the modern world, in effect, even if they do not know it. The most illiterate among them is related, in a way that I am not, to Dante, Shakespeare, Michelangelo, Aeschylus, Da Vinci, Rembrandt, and Racine; the cathedral at Chartres says something to them which it cannot say to me, as indeed would New York's Empire State Building, should anyone here ever see it. Out of their hymns and dances come Beethoven and Bach. Go back a few centuries and they are in their full glory—but I am in Africa, watching the conquerors arrive.

James Baldwin

"It is obvious that good art has no sex." So *Art News* tells me. So I have learned to agree. But reading the categorical statement takes me back to my old, "naive" responses. I already had my Master's in art history when my husband and I spent a summer in Europe. One afternoon, at the Alte Pinakothek in Munich, we stopped in front of Boucher's *Reclining Girl*. She is lying on her belly, naked, her elbows supporting the upper part of her rosy body and her legs spread wide apart. My husband looked for a moment and observed with mock pedantry, "Ah yes, a nude of the turn-her-over-and-fuck-her school." But *I* didn't want to turn her over and fuck her. Nor did I want to compete with her candid

sexuality. What I felt was her exposure and vulnerability—and I
felt that I shared them. We were both supposed to believe that this
portrait of a teenaged mistress of Louis XV "is a triumph of simple
and memorable design, and shows Boucher's delight in the sheer
painting of flesh." As I progressed through graduate school, even
such contradictory judgments as this began to come naturally to
me too.

Anonymous

I reached the point of thinking you were right, and that your
culture was the true one. Perhaps we . . . were still dreaming with
a simplicity you had left behind centuries ago. Perhaps our dream
of a language that everyone could read, made of plain words, was
nothing but a fantasy ahead of its time. By a hair I missed becoming one of you. Like those children of the poor who change their
race when they go up to the university.

Schoolboys of Barbiana

For a long time I have been obsessed with the emotional
possibilities of baroque architecture. I have traveled, gotten
grants, studied, looked and looked—and I have been deeply
moved. But at whose expense were my sensibilities deepened by
the experience of Rome? And why is the joy of a refined esthetic
emotionally available to me—a middle-class academic, an
intellectual—but not to others? When I last stood in the Piazza
Navona, watching my fellow tourists more than Bernini's foun-
tains, I hardly dared think of the crimes, the human suffering,
which made both the scene and my being there possible. I stood
surrounded by priceless objects—and I valued them. Yet I hate the
economic system which has invested finely chiseled stone with a
price. Our esthetics are rooted in surplus value.

Louis Kampf

The passages above reflect some of the ways that race, class,
and sex may be present in a work of art or the critical response to
it.[3] Far from representing "special cases" requiring "flexible approaches," these elements are the very basis of our experience,

seeking recognition in the work of art that is supposed to express
it and the criticism that is meant to interpret it.

II

To be conscious of race, class, or sex with respect to high culture
is to be conscious, first of all, of exclusion. The black, the
woman, the worker, and the peasant are all forced to acknowledge the existence of a mainstream, self-proclaimed as the whole
of "culture," in which they do not—or do not fully—participate.
But "exclusion" is not in itself a critical position; to be the Other
is, by definition, to be the element that is *not* the subject, defined
only in relation to it and only negatively. For each of the excluded
groups, the extent and the nature of its exclusion differ and dic-
tate a different criticism and different cultural alternatives.

Racial exclusion presents the clearest case. In terms of both
cultural heritage and social environment, the black person is excluded from white culture.* The black confronts a body of art that
does not acknowledge his or her existence and experience and
that appears richly (or smugly) self-sufficient. In the selection
cited, Baldwin sees himself as the outsider in white Western cul-

---

*Throughout this essay, we have had in mind the cultural situation of the black
person in the United States. The vast majority of the world is "non-white," and
the cultural problem is somewhat different for colonialized peoples. Frantz Fanon
has described the complexities of this consciousness; for example, he recommends "the following experiment. . . . Attend showings of a Tarzan film in the
Antilles and in Europe. In the Antilles, the young Negro identifies himself *de facto*
with Tarzan against the Negroes. This is much more difficult for him in a European theater, for the rest of the audience, which is white, automatically identifies
him with the savages on the screen. It is a conclusive experience. The Negro
learns that one is not black without problems. A documentary film on Africa
produces similar reactions when it is shown in a French city and in Fort-de-
France. I will go farther and say that Bushmen and Zulus arouse even more
laughter among the young Antilleans. It would be interesting to show how in this
instance the reactional exaggeration betrays a hint of recognition. In France a
Negro who sees this documentary is virtually petrified. There he has no more hope
of flight: He is at once Antillean, Bushman, and Zulu. . . . Quite literally I can say
without any risk of error that the Antillean who goes to France in order to convince himself that he is white will find his real face there." Frantz Fanon, *Black
Skin, White Masks*, 1952 (New York, 1967), pp. 152-53, nn. 15 and 16.

ture, unable, whatever his gifts and education, to "pass" and assimilate into it. Even the folk art of European peasants is part of the tradition that shuts him out, while the folk art of his own people is alien to it. Yet Baldwin accepts the claim of supremacy that Western culture makes for itself; he invokes the great names of European culture with despair at his own incapacity to realize their works completely.

Through this very exclusion, however, the black has another possibility: to reject the white man's culture and create one that reflects and speaks to the black condition. Where Baldwin mentions Africa only to recall the shame of the conquered, other blacks see African civilization as a source of tradition and pride for an autonomous black American culture. It must be understood, however, that it is not Africa Baldwin is ashamed of, but defeat and powerlessness. He does not deprecate tribal music and dance when he sees that Bach's music evolved from its European counterpart. But because the "glory" of past European centuries was expressed in imperial ventures as well as in great art, the most important thing Baldwin knows about his African forebears is that they were victims of European conquest. He does not seek to reconstruct their folk music because the fact of enslavement has made it irrelevant to him.

Baldwin's views in that early essay were not definitive, and they are not at issue here. However, his stress on the cultural significance of oppression raises questions about the extent to which a black American is ever free to say, "That culture is Whitey's thing; I've got my own." Albeit gently, Baldwin brings up the issue of power in the discussion of culture. The two issues are linked in Baldwin's contrast between his situation as the first black man to appear in a Swiss village and that of the first white in an African one:

> The white man takes the astonishment as tribute, for he arrives
> to conquer and to convert the natives, whose inferiority in relation
> to himself is not even to be questioned; whereas I, without a

thought of conquest, find myself among a people whose culture
controls me, has even, in a sense, created me, people who have
cost me more in anguish and rage than they will ever know, who
yet do not even know of my existence.[4]

The black who takes part in a separate black culture is still living
in the midst of a society dominated by whites. To ignore that fact
in black art would be to falsify the black experience in America.
An art that made this black experience its subject and built from
there would clearly be sacrificing autonomy in the modernist
sense of esthetic inviolability. But it could be a force for real
autonomy in that real world where experience takes place.

At least, nobody doubts the reality of racial exclusion. Those
whose exclusion from the cultural tradition is based on sex or
class have a more ambiguous problem of consciousness. Obviously, none of the three categories is discrete, and a single individual possesses all three characteristics. The white woman may
share all the tastes and concerns of the bourgeoisie if she is born
or marries into it. In this country particularly, such a woman is
eagerly welcomed into the cultural world in the role of
consumer—as collector, appreciator, patron, enthusiast, and
"preserver." Her experience is not wholly excluded from the
world of art, because she does participate in the experience of her
class and also because she has learned to interpret that experience the way the dominant culture does. Or to feel a proportion-
ate guilt and inadequacy should she fail to do so.

Nonetheless, most of us have some moment when we wonder
what *Beatrice* thought about Dante's sacred and profane loves, or
like the episode of the Boucher nude, when our vision is neither
hypocritically neuter nor second-hand male. At such moments, it
is impossible to deny that the critical mind, as formed in our
society, has a gender and that the truth, viewed from this perspective, is more nearly the reverse of what one has been taught.
The white woman's response to her exclusion as a woman may be
epitomized as, "That's not the way it is; my reality is the opposite."

Such moments are rare, however, and until a woman accepts a consistently feminist position, they are accompanied by discomfort and embarrassment. These feelings often result in her acceptance of critics' undervaluing art that does express her own reality. In any event, it is not so much a separate culture that can come out of this consciousness as a separate point of view, for both artist and critic.

It must appear almost superfluous to insist that high culture is a ruling class preoccupation. After all, historians of art and literature learn as a matter of course about court intrigues and patterns of patronage, royal favorites and discriminating prelates, when they study a given period or school. We take it for granted that the social milieu of art includes courts and counting houses, cathedrals and drawing rooms, but we do not acknowledge that these are rather exclusive environments.

Obviously, it is difficult to acknowledge that Western art and criticism exclude certain classes from participation without admitting that a class system exists. The past is less trouble: of course they had social classes back then, but our sophistication demands tolerance; oppressors and victims are equally dead, and anyway how could one study the cultural history of that vast majority who did not leave enduring monuments? In discussing the present, however, and especially in matters of culture, it is crude to mention exploiting and exploited classes. The cultural euphemism for the working class is the "less well-educated." The onus is thus placed on the individual rather than on social conditions, and the real causes and effects are implicitly reversed. Whereas, in reality, people have less education because they are working class, the euphemistic formulation implies that they are working class because they have less education. Lack of education explains, for instance, why some people do not go to museums even when admission is free. In short, certain people do not have access to culture because they are uncultured.

The Schoolboys of Barbiana are able to articulate a position that cuts through egalitarian pretenses and the mystique of "education." Their view may be formulated as: "That's *your* culture, Teacher; real life is over here." We shall be referring rather frequently to the *Letter to a Teacher* because it is a rare expression of working class exclusion from bourgeois culture and a self-conscious alternative to it. The Barbiana letters are unique in the totality with which they reject bourgeois culture. For those who lack the rigorous sense of class that informs their critique, some partial accommodation is possible. As long as one does not insist that real life—and hence artistic truth—is elsewhere, as long as one accepts the assumptions of high culture, one is welcome to partake of it. In fact, the elements of "our" cultural tradition are packaged in museums and anthologies for easy access on the part of those willing to receive it on its own terms. The semantics of this acculturation process are revealing: a working-class person acquiring "culture" is said to be concerned with "self-improvement" and is coming in contact with "the finer things," with "spiritual values."[5] Such a person is certainly not becoming bourgeois, but is assimilating part of bourgeois ideology instead of struggling against it on the grounds that unreality means untruth. That person is rejecting what the working class *knows* to be true and, in this sense, "changing race." At present, most working people do not have the confidence in the validity of their own experience from which cultural alternatives could develop. Nor are the irrelevancies of art attractive enough to co-opt them. So they remain outside of culture, unable even to define its function in the system that oppresses them.

III

The problem for cultural theory is to determine the significance of the exclusions based on class, race, and sex and the critique to which they give rise. For the modernist, this is not difficult, for he can take refuge in his formalist concerns, secure in his conviction that other matters are irrelevant. But those who concede that art has social and ideological content may try to find a place for considerations of race, class, and sex. They will probably be quick to distinguish two distinct cases: works in which those elements are acknowledged in the subject, and those where they are not. With its characteristic flexibility, contextual criticism occasionally expands its vocabulary of special cases to allow for a female point of view where sexuality is the subject, a black point of view where race is, a non-elite point of view where class is. It is useful to explore such instances before broaching the knottier question of whether they constitute critical "exceptions" or demand a whole new "rule."

Sexuality is a central issue in much of Western art and literature, and women have often been prominent among the consumers of culture; nevertheless, criticism has rarely recognized that their experience might make women interpret art differently from men. "We, men, women, and Ph.D.s, have always read . . . [literature] as men."[6] This is true because criticism has denied the existence of a gender point of view or, where it has acknowledged it, dismissed the female one as peculiar, marginal, and subjective.

The dominant tendency denies that men and women have separate ways of perceiving sexual content in art. In the case of the visual media, formal analysis often goes a step further and tries to ignore the *existence* of sexual content. It is probable, for example, that the patrons and purchasers of painted female nudes invested in them at least partially because they enjoyed looking at naked women. But today only a naïve or exceptionally candid man admits that facet of his appreciation of a Titian, a Rubens, or a Boucher. The masterpieces of Western painting are not, after all, supposed to serve the same function as the Playmate of the Month. We are expected to look at the nude as an exercise in form and design, much as Levey does for half of the description cited earlier of the Boucher nude. The sexual element is to be admitted only in cant phrases like "Boucher's delight in the sheer painting of flesh.'' Painters like Boucher and Rubens inspire an entire lexicon of euphemism in which words like ''sensuous'' and ''delight'' take on a curiously alienated, unfleshly quality.

In less overt instances of sensuous delight, one is supposed to ignore the sexual implications of female nudity. The study of life-drawing, for example, has become a traditional part of an art student's training, and no sexual construction is to be placed on this attention to the nude. Yet at precisely the time when an art ''curriculum'' was being formalized and the non-sexual aspect of the body touted, a double standard was at work. As Linda Nochlin documents, female art students were not normally allowed to draw from an undraped model, regardless of the model's sex or that of their classmates.[7] Nochlin's thesis has to do with the inequality of technical opportunity for men and women prevalent in art until quite recently. But she does not underline the bland hypocrisy that could uphold the sexual neutrality of the nude and at the same time bar women from learning to draw it on account of its sexual content.

Nowadays, we have progressed so far into formalism as to be shocked at such an attitude. Male and female art students may work side by side, drawing from the same nude model, because both are expected to look at her in the same asexual way. But what of the woman art student who rejects the alienation from her own body inherent in that way of seeing? Or the female critic who knows what a particular nude may symbolize or what heights of color and brushwork were involved in painting it—and who yet sees that she is looking at the nude from inside just another such symbol? And her counterpart in literature, who has learned to identify with the persistent masculine ''I'' that echoes through Western poetry, when she finds that she has allied herself with a convention that violates her own responses?

The obvious fact is that when sex is the subject we are not learning the whole truth if we hear only from the sex that has consistently dominated ''our'' culture and its ideology. The full significance of the Boucher nude eludes anyone who talks about tactile values or simple and meaningful design quite as much as it does someone who merely wishes to turn the original over and fuck her. Identifying the subject as one of Louis XV's mistresses, Levey, parenthetically flippant, adds "little as that particularizes her." At this point, we are presumably supposed to smile at the delightfully sensuous monarch who, in addition to a series of official mistresses, had his own whorehouse of adolescent girls— so many, indeed, that they are hard for history to enumerate or distinguish. The "unparticularized" girl is just one more object for sensual delectation, along with the smoky fragrance from the large censer, the velvet cushions and the silken draperies, as she lies there so suggestively that only the unimaginative would see the need to turn her over. To be reminded of Sade and Laclos is perhaps overly impressionistic. But to call that girl a victim is merely to state a fact. An empathetic response to that aspect of the picture may be subjective, but it is *no more so* than insistence on seeing her as part of a pleasing pattern or an obscene titillation, and it comes closer to what the picture really is.

When we use expressions like "the truth" and "what it really is," we are suggesting that the work of art inhabits a world where it not only reflects but influences values, ideas, and action. That it exists, in short, in the same world that we do and belongs, as we do, to history. It is evident, for example, that literature reflects and codifies prevailing ideologies about sexual love. And it is equally clear that it becomes part of that ideology and exerts influence upon society, on the way people conduct and interpret their lives. Reading a love poem, then, is not merely an excursion into the poet's subjectivity, but rather an exploration of the culture that reader and writer share. Now the lover in that lyric, the "I" who speaks to us, is almost always a man. He presents certain ideas—conventional or eccentric—about what he feels, how his lady treats him, what she and her sex are like. There is only one active element in the poem, one person whose thoughts and sentiments are realized for us. It is his point of view and not that of the passive partner that the reader perforce adopts. For any individual woman reader to do this means acceptance of a certain psychic distortion and alienation. More important, in her acceptance, such a reader is also acquiescing to the poem's entry into and continued effect upon the culture in which she is living her own life.

The factors of race and class present a generally similar situation: modernist criticism does its best to deny that they ever really are the subject of art, but once their critical vision is admitted, it transforms the entire experience. It used to be fashionable, for instance, to read black novelists as if their use of race were archetypal, a symbol of that isolation and alienation that is supposed to be universal to the human condition. But today, race is usually acknowledged as a subject of art made by blacks and whites.

Once again, as with women, the subject group's lack of objectivity is thought to invalidate its criticism of such art. If blacks complain that black people are almost totally absent from European and American painting except in subordinate roles, the counter-argument claims that depicting black pages or maidservants in Western painting only reflects the life of the court or the courtesan as it was; it is misplaced sensitivity, and anachronistic to boot, for blacks to be offended by it. Objections to the perpetual servant role assigned to blacks on the screen were long dismissed on the same grounds. With the introduction of films providing a wider range of black types, there should have come some recognition of how the old servant stereotype was not only realistic but implicitly normative. It thus had its effect on the society *outside* the film.

The "oversensitivity" of those who are slighted is a biased position, to be sure, but so is acceptance of their subordination. Both authors of this article were educated in a school system that had its own Index of reading matter offensive to one ethnic group or another. *Huckleberry Finn,* for instance, was excised from the curriculum not because of racism, about which an argument could be made, but because of a racist epithet. And many "classics" were forbidden because they reflected anti-Semitic attitudes. As Jewish adolescents who had enjoyed such prohibited works as *The Merchant of Venice* outside of school, we felt this merely demonstrated the folly of censorship. In later years, however, we have talked with people of an older generation who vividly remember the sense of injury aroused by some of those works. One mother of a friend spoke of having read *Ivanhoe* as a book-loving girl and being deeply hurt by the character and fate of Rebecca. Although far from supporting the censorship of such books, we have stopped shaking our heads at these readers' lack of historical tolerance and begun to consider what it means. Anti-Semitism was never a material force in our lives, so it was possible for us to accept the attitudes in Shakespeare and Scott as "the way they felt then" and proceed to the real point of the work. But as recently as a generation before our own, American Jews had undergone real anti-Semitic experiences as well as reading about them. Their response, therefore, had validity in their culture and at that point in history. Tolerance would have implied acquiescence in their own oppression as well as that in the book.

It is difficult to speak intelligibly about class in a society where a mechanical egalitarianism, driven by "education," is supposed to prevail. Although many people recognize and castigate the pop-sociological jargon about poverty, with its talk of cultural deprivation, underprivilege, and the like, the similar rhetoric of class equality seems to escape them. The realities of a class-stratified system (and the potential for struggle within it) are disguised by such phrases as "Middle American," "lower middle class," and "blue collar middle class."[8] Even to use the term "working class" is to label oneself and, in some circles, to discredit whatever else one says. All this makes it hard to identify and discuss class as the explicit subject of recent art or literature.

Its presence is generally acknowledged, however, in the study of past centuries, when it was the bourgeoisie that was the class struggling for recognition and power.

An instructive instance is the Renaissance *topos* about true nobility, a convention that harks back to the time of Dante and his contemporaries of the *dolce stil nuovo*. These highly educated young men of bourgeois origin were understandably preoccupied with the question of their own status. For themselves and their audience, they needed to justify and facilitate the "success" of those who won it through personal endeavor rather than aristocratic lineage. In highly abstract poems, they persistently explore the problem of whether aristocracy is a matter of birth or personal attributes; deciding, inevitably, on the latter, they proceed to consider what personal qualities and experiences make a natural gentleman (and "born lover"), someone possessed of "the gentle heart." Throughout the Renaissance, the issue was to be reopened in poetry, drama, and theoretical dialogues of all sorts, with advice and assistance being proffered from all sides to those attempting to make good without an aristocratic background. To be sure, there also was a "blood-will-tell" or "you-can't-keep-a-true-born-prince-under-a-bushel" tradition, but it merely stated the converse, that aristocrats did have true nobility, never that the quality was restricted to them. In the novel, which was to be the bourgeois literary form *par excellence,* the theme remained a central statement.

Ironically, though perhaps not surprisingly, the same assertions about class and the individual that expressed the aspirations of a bourgeoisie rising against the aristocracy now serve to consolidate and preserve its power against incursions by the proletariat. Although only one element in the system of bourgeois ideology, these ideas reinforce the claim to dominance of the ruling class. The notion that certain people, whatever their class origin, have the personal qualities necessary to success, and that such success is actually attainable, simultaneously justifies retention of a hierarchy and places blame on the individual for failing to rise in it. Once the bourgeoisie is in control, even the strongest antiaristocratic statements in bourgeois literature become an instrument of domination and a weapon of reaction in the class struggle.*

IV

Where the subject matter of art has explicit race, sex, or class content, this content must be understood and experienced to the full extent that it participates in meaning. But what about works of art whose subject matter seems only peripherally, if at all, involved with questions of race, class, or sex? Are those works not immune to the critical approaches we have been suggesting? We would answer that they are not.

Monet's water lily paintings provide an example of apparently neutral subject matter. With real insight, modernist critics point to "the apparent dissociation of colour and brushwork from object" in these canvases; they observe that "image and paint surface [seem] to exist on separate levels of perception"; and they suggest that "Nature, prodded by an eye obsessed with the most naïve kind of exactness, responded in the end with textures of color that could be managed on canvas only by involving the autonomous laws of the medium—which is to say that Nature became the springboard for an almost abstract art."[9] What possible class or race content could be integral to the experience of these paintings? The Schoolboys of Barbiana would tell us immediately: "Monet's water lily paintings are part of *your* culture, Teacher."

Monet's painting belongs to the Western tradition of high art in its capitalist phase. In the 1870s, the Impressionists sought to create a new vision of the world: a new modern form to correspond to a modern subject matter. But the bourgeois society for

---

*None of these observations is novel. But most commentators situate the class event parallel to the literary one, rather than relating them causally. The "rise of Puritanism," for instance, is *related* to the rise of the middle class and to individualism, but the causality is, if anything, normally reversed.

which they created the new style rejected them. In the dramatic words of Marx and Engels:

> The bourgeoisie . . . has left remaining no other nexus between man and man than naked self-interest, than callous "cash payment". . . . The bourgeoisie has stripped of its halo every occupation hitherto honoured and looked up to with reverent awe. It has converted the physician, the lawyer, the priest, the poet, the man of science, into its paid wage-labourers.[10]

Such a bourgeoisie could not but regard the paintings of the Impressionists as strange and useless artifacts, or even recognize the liberatory threat implicit in the new style.* The crisis in the Impressionist movement in the 1880s and the subsequent development of various new kinds of painting was in part a response to bourgeois society's rejection of early Impressionism. It was a time of intense labor struggles in Europe and America; the social crisis undoubtedly influenced the need artists felt for change, especially for generating new styles in the last decade of the century.

Monet, like many others, moved away from the recurrent nineteenth-century dream of a modern art for the modern public. His late painting style represents a withdrawal into lonely individualism, into a fragmented world of intensely felt sensations, into the minute analysis of private experience, and even, in the huge water lily friezes, into the attempted construction of an alternate environment as a means to reunite the self with the world. From here, as the critics cited above observe, it is but a short step to abstract art.

No matter how painful and how lonely an artist's existence might have been, the Schoolboys of Barbiana would understand what a luxury it is to be able to withdraw from the realities of

---

*The comparative acceptability of "avant-garde" art and artists to the bourgeoisie in the middle of the twentieth century corresponds to a more advanced stage of capitalism, one requiring for its survival a much stronger dose of ideological mystification throughout society.

bourgeois society. They know well that it could hardly be worse than the pressures created when "a worker stays by his stamping machine eight hours a day, in constant fear of losing his arm."[11] Many artists of the late nineteenth and twentieth centuries tried, at great personal cost, to withdraw, yet in the end they created an art for the bourgeoisie: a happy, decorative art, shimmering with light and color; or an anguished art, full of private pain; or a scientific, rigorous art, as "required" by modern times. Whether abstract or not, all such art has a definite class basis in that it is an art of leisure, decoration, and escape, available only to one small sector of society. To the extent that it is an "expression of spiritual values," "a portrayal of the inner landscape," etc., the values and landscapes were and remain basically those of that sector. Monet's water lily paintings speak to the alienation of the artist and his bourgeois audience. That we can at best place Monet's art in parallel with the contemporary social upheavals testifies to its successful isolation; those groups whose social identity excludes them from the world of high culture are excluded as well from the world of the water lilies.

Certain types of genre painting present additional examples of art that is supposedly free of potential race, class, or sexual reference. Representations of domestic interiors and "everyday" objects, painted with intense involvement in the material reality of the subject, appear sporadically in the course of the history of Western art. Their appearance tends to coincide with periods in which the patrons and buyers of art had a special involvement, themselves, with the material reality of objects. The vast trade network and the prosperous urban life of Roman antiquity must be seen as the social background not only for the *Satyricon* of Petronius, but also for still-life, landscape, seascape, and genre scenes in Roman art. Similarly, the development at the end of the Middle Ages of international trade and a large "middle" class of merchants, craftsmen, and entrepreneurs corresponds to the appearance, particularly in fifteenth-century Northern painting, of a meticulous interest in the tangibility of material objects. Not until the seventeenth century in Holland, however, does this interest achieve sufficient independent validity to be expressed in a vast production of paintings geared to it; the acceptability of still-life, genre, and similar modes as autonomous subject matter is established. This brief survey suggests the presence of a class content in such painting, content whose relevance is well established in historical discussions of art. What is less generally recognized is the existence of a gender point of view in still-life and domestic-interior paintings.

The vision of the Dutch genre painters who produced for the seventeenth century art market was, more than that of any painters before them, unobscured by "spiritual" illusion. When they took the domestic environment as subject, it became an explicitly material collection of tangible objects. Far from discovering that "there is great painting without an important subject-matter," the Dutch painters realized in their works the very deep significance of material objects for the daily experience of the rising mercantile class: objects had at last been established as simple commodities to be manufactured and sold by the bourgeoisie on the market.[12] The production of articles for direct use, rather than exchange on the market, was on the wane, and the future lay in the hands of the burghers. The artists sold them paintings that lovingly celebrated objects in their new essence as exchangeable commodities and as private property. The peculiarly insistent clarity, the urgent involvement with physical texture, and the ever-present intensity of the naturalism in these paintings force us again and again to confront the objects as material possessions. The buyers of the paintings identified themselves with the unseen burghers who owned the objects represented in them; both buyer and "owner" were of course men, normally with families. The objects burst gloriously forth from the canvas out at us, and we realize that they are to be felt as *our* possessions, *our* conquests of reality. Yet they are merely household objects and environments—the conquests we have made are those of the male burgher who heads the household. The "neutral" observer has not only a class but a sex—he is a man.

In the course of the seventeenth century, the nature of the burgher's family was changing. Women and children had traditionally been useful, if severely subordinated, contributors to the participation of the family in production and consumption; now, in the bourgeois sectors of society, they were more and more transformed into unsentimentalized private property. Women and children were becoming, *without illusion,* merely wives to be acquired, offspring to be produced, daughters to be exchanged—in short, they were becoming commodities. Their very existence as human beings could begin to be called into question. In this context, the nature of the placing of women and children in scenes of domestic interiors becomes clearer. Strangely immobilized, they often participate in the paintings not as modest caretakers of the household goods, but as passive objects, part of the inventory. At the extreme we have Vermeer, frequently and intelligently described as an artist who, "though we look in vain for a still life by his hand, was perhaps the greatest still-life painter of all time."[13] In other words, women, children, objects, and their domestic environments were clearly seen and depicted in their social reality as material possessions, the itemization of accumulated wealth that validated the experience of the burgher.

Two hundred years later, the reduction in art of people, especially women, to the status of objects was complete. Both in the drawing class and in finished works of art, the human body was, although sometimes ambiguously, denied its actual life and sexuality. The ballet dancers, hairdressers, and "keyhole" nudes in Degas' paintings are the distant cousins of the women in the seventeenth century Dutch interiors. By the nineteenth century, however, they had become even more dehumanized; no longer the private possessions of one bourgeois, they were manipulated like puppets and fragmented into their constituent parts. Degas wrote in his notebook:

> Of a dancer do either the arms or the legs or the back. Do the
> shoes—the hands—of the hairdresser—the badly cut coif-
> fure . . . bare feet in dance, action, etc., etc.
>   Do every kind of worn object placed, accompanied in such a way
> that they have the life of the man or the woman; corsets which
> have just been taken off, for example—and which keep the form of
> the body, etc., etc.[14]

The women have become objects, while the objects can only
grasp at life.

The seventeenth-century Dutch interiors and the nineteenth-
century Degas dancers, hairdressers, or nudes are unusually clear
examples of paintings in which the living existence and sexuality
of the women portrayed have been eroded. To the extent that we
reconstruct the original male-dominated context in which the
paintings were produced, we are justified in discussing the women
as more or less inanimate objects. Yet here, as with the Boucher
nude, the female observer's point of view produces a different
response. In these paintings, she identifies not with the invisible
possessor but with the objects possessed, not with the voyeur but
with the women seen through the keyhole. She recognizes her
own predecessors, women who, like her, tended to be more
things than *people* to the men who observed and lived with them.
The reality of her experience and of her response is part of what
these paintings mean.

In literature, not even modernist criticism has been able to
convince many readers that ideas are entirely irrelevant. Our
problem is less to demonstrate that literature does convey ideas
than to show that those ideas have a class origin and a class
function. What we mean when we say that an idea is bourgeois is
that it arises out of the circumstances of the present ruling class
and that it helps in some way to justify or perpetuate the
hegemony of that class.

It is not difficult, from our present point in history, to see how
certain ideas served to bolster past societies controlled by a

monarch or an aristocracy. In such a system, ideas about natural hierarchy, order, and divine sanction clearly shored up the dominant institutions. Literature that expressed and promulgated these ideas can be readily identified, its social function traced. The current ruling class, the bourgeoisie, derives its power from a different system of production and profit. The old myths of aristocracy did not meet the needs of the new ruling class, which could not claim legitimacy from a permanent hierarchy, a fixed social and moral order, or divine will. A new set of ideas, those evolved during the bourgeoisie's struggle for supremacy, had to be codified. It was and continues to be the function of bourgeois culture to express those ideas in new art, of criticism to "discover" them in existing monuments.

In our remarks about bourgeois definitions of "nobility," we chose an example that had to do specifically with the subject of class; most elements of the ideology we call bourgeois are not so direct. They have to do, rather, with fixed categories in "human nature" and "the human condition" that emphasize what is ideal, absolute, and private over what is material, fluid, and collective. According to bourgeois literature, the important events of history are the events of inner history. Suffering is portrayed as a personal struggle, experienced by the individual in isolation. Alienation becomes a heroic disease, for which there is no social remedy. Irony masks resignation to a situation one cannot alter or control. The human situation is seen as static, with certain external forms varying but the eternal anguish remaining. Every political system is perceived to set some small group into power, so that changing the identity of the group will not affect our "real" (that is, private) lives. If the work of literature does not make these notions sufficiently explicit, the critic helps to locate them in their context of "universals."

Thus simply expressed, the elements of bourgeois ideology have a clear role in maintaining the status quo. Arising out of a system that functions through corporate competition for profits,

the ideas of the bourgeoisie imply the ultimate powerlessness of
the individual, the futility of public action, and the necessity of
despair.

V

What we are aiming at is not just a better way to read poetry or
look at pictures, but a way to understand our own experience as
historical beings. In this we are going beyond the customary
frontiers of criticism—certainly of modernist criticism. We are
suggesting that the work of art exists in a real, rather than ideal,
world, and that the critic is not an ahistorical being—lacking gender, race, and class—any more than the artist, the patron, or the
public. Blindness to the race, sex, or class content in art brutally
reveals the extent to which consciousness is affected by circumstances.

    What are the consequences of asserting that the critic is a
human being who exists in history, and that consciousness comes
out of real life? It is a sad fact that anyone wishing to answer this
question and elaborate such a position is forced each time to
review the same fundamental concepts. Circumstances and real
life in the United States have produced a situation in which the
precise use of such categories as "capitalism," "bourgeois,"
"exploitation," or even the mere citation of Marx, too often produces in the reader a sudden inability to understand. What is even
more frustrating is the reader's stubborn innocence of the nature
and sources of that inability, and the constant refusal to evaluate
it. Still, times are changing, and obstinacy may eventually be
overcome by endurance—we begin at what we believe to be the
beginning.

    Criticism based on the view of consciousness developed in this
essay remains a rarity. It differs from "contextual" and "social
history" approaches in that it goes beyond the mere placing of the
work against the background in a sort of silhouette arrangement.
It refuses to isolate the work of art as something distinct from its

social environment; instead it recognizes that the work is itself a part of that environment and functions in it. Modernism, by contrast, seeks to intensify isolation. It forces the work of art, the artist, the critic, and the audience outside of history. Modernism denies us the possibility of understanding ourselves as *agents* in the material world, for all has been removed to an abstract world of ideas, where interactions can be minimized or emptied of meaning and real consequences. Less than ever are we able to interpret the world—much less change it.

As the twentieth century advances, culture increasingly participates in the maintenance of bourgeois ideology; its main vehicle, both in criticism and in art, is modernism. "Great" art and literature enter the curriculum of working class and black high schools and of two-year colleges. They appear in modernist guise, stripped of their full historical meaning and transported to the timeless realm of universals. By teaching art and literature in this way, the educational system tries to do to the students what it has done to the subjects: it implicitly denies them their own full historical identity and instead suggests that they too are isolated, unconnected, and powerless. Art has been forced to support and critics have up to now perpetuated this ideological mystification. The Schoolboys of Barbiana resist it; our task is to replace it.

NOTES

1. Clement Greenberg, "Modernist Painting," *Arts Yearbook*, 4 (1961), 103.
2. Louis Kampf, "The Permanence of Modernism," *On Modernism: The Prospects for Literature and Freedom* (Cambridge, Mass., 1967), pp. 6, 8.
3. The passages cited are: James Baldwin, "Stranger in the Village," *Notes of a Native Son* (Boston, 1955), p. 165; private communication from a female colleague, August 1971; The Schoolboys of Barbiana, *Letter to a Teacher* (New York, 1970), p. 128; Louis Kampf, "Notes Toward a Radical Culture," in *The New Left,* comp. Priscilla Long (Bos-

ton, 1969), p. 424. References in the paragraph about Boucher come, respectively, from *Art News,* 69 (1971), 60 and Michael Levey, *A Concise History of Painting from Giotto to Cezanne* (New York, 1962), p. 218.

4. Baldwin, p. 164.

5. Quoting Jan Myrdal, Louis Kampf remarks that spiritual values are the ideology of the ruling class ("Notes," p. 427).

6. Carolyn Heilbrun, "Millett's *Sexual Politics:* A Year Later," *Aphra,* 2 (1971), 39.

7. Linda Nochlin, "Why Are There No Great Women Artists?" *Art News,* 69 (1971), 23ff. See especially pp. 32-36.

8. This grotesquerie occurs in the Literary Guild account of K.B. Gilden's *Between the Hills and the Sea* (New York, 1971). Even in describing a novel about trade union struggles, it appears that blurb-writers are unable to acknowledge that its protagonists are members of the working class.

9. George Heard Hamilton, *Painting and Sculpture in Europe, 1880-1940* (Baltimore, 1967), p. 18; Clement Greenberg, *Art and Culture* (Boston, 1961), pp. 43, 42.

10. Karl Marx and Frederick Engels, *Manifesto of the Communist Party,* in their *Selected Works in One Volume* (New York, 1968), pp. 37-38.

11. The Schoolboys of Barbiana, p. 82. The Schoolboys are here comparing the pressures endured by teachers to those that industrial workers undergo: "We read . . . that your teaching hours are 'enough to drain the psychophysical capacities of any normal human being.' A worker stays by his stamping machine eight hours a day, in constant fear of losing his arm. You would not dare say this sort of thing in his presence."

12. E. H. Gombrich, *The Story of Art* (London, 1950), p. 323. We cite here an easily accessible popularization of the widespread, and characteristically modernist, notion that "the Dutch specialists . . . ended by proving that the subject-matter was of secondary importance."

13. A typical observation about Vermeer; the example cited here is Vitale Bloch, in *Burlington Magazine,* 94 (1952), 208. The "rehabilitation" of Vermeer as one of the masters of Western painting occurred, interestingly enough, only within the last hundred years, that is, under modernism.

14. Cited in Linda Nochlin, *Impressionism and Post-Impressionism, 1874-1904* (Englewood Cliffs, New Jersey, 1966), p. 63.

The Critical Task

AN IDEOLOGICAL critic has three fundamental tasks: to identify a
worthwhile subject, to determine what to say about it, and to
communicate her views. Reduced to such generalities, the points
hardly seem worth making at all, for the responsibility of the critic
concerned with social issues does not appear very different from
that of any other critic. Much depends on how those categories
are interpreted, and whether one accepts one's choice of topic,
one's literary argument, and one's mode of expression as political
acts, with political roots and political consequences. Unless it is
based on such awareness and shaped accordingly, ideological
criticism can be as sterile as academic criticism, or, even worse,
can become an unintentional parody of it.

High culture, the stuff on which journal articles feed, has received relatively little attention from the American movement.*

*At first, I wrote "The American left," but I think our self-descriptive term
"the movement" is more precise. To speak of a "left" implies the existence of a
full ideological spectrum, with a right and various kinds of centers, such as traditionally appears in Western Europe. Here, where the boundaries are less well
defined or understood, the word "movement" conveys more exactly the kind of
social force it is.

In some few cases, this neglect stems from a preoccupation with directly material conditions that preclude interest in superstructural phenomena like culture. For the most part, however, it is founded on the usually unexamined assumption that high culture is not where it's at, that it is no longer the principal—or even an important—means of transmitting bourgeois ideology. Thus, while the movement has demonstrated an almost obsessive interest in mass media and its alternatives, it has, *de facto*, assigned a low priority to traditional culture. We have not produced a theorist like Georg Lukacs, Ernst Fischer, or Christopher Caudwell—and we have not felt the lack.

The women's movement has been the only segment of the New Left to examine both high culture and popular media. In fact, all the major "women's liberation" books that have appeared in the past couple of years have been works of cultural criticism. (I am not referring to the women's press or pamphlets, which have, of course, been concerned with a wide range of issues, but rather to such book-length studies as Mary Ellmann's *Thinking About Women*, Kate Millett's *Sexual Politics*, Shulamith Firestone's *The Dialectic of Sex*, and Eva Figes' *Patriarchal Attitudes*, all of which are primarily involved with cultural criticism.) These efforts may betray the class origins of the movement that produced them, but at the same time they help to illuminate the source and the nature of certain received ideas and thus to situate our present cultural condition in its history.

In my essay "Dwelling in Decencies," I addressed myself to some of the pitfalls of feminist literary criticism. The principal danger I perceived was an unquestioning acceptance of the bases and methods of bourgeois scholarship in the work of women trained in academic modes who are belatedly discovering that their discipline has a gender. As academics, these women share with their colleagues certain assumptions about the primacy of high culture, and they lack the sociological perspective that underlies cultural criticism coming out of the movement.

It is not my intention to go to the other extreme and deny the political significance of culture. I would point out, rather, that one must not confuse culture with its particular modes of expression. The ruling class is materially sustained and reinforced by the circulation of certain ideas. But in admitting this cultural hegemony, one must consider the diffusion, the audience, and the influence of the forms and levels of culture. Since the bourgeoisie is the class in power, the dominant ideas are the ideas of that class. A corollary of this is that if one wishes to fight the ruling class, one must be able to fight its ideas. But if "cultural hegemony" is not merely a catchphrase, the ideas of the bourgeoisie are everywhere. So one must begin by combatting them in the areas where they are most pervasive, have the widest audience, and serve the most vicious purposes. These related propositions do not deny the presence of reactionary views in the works of, say, D. H. Lawrence. The question is whether it matters much that they are there.

Now, academics tend to believe that high culture is the central *locus* of ideas and forms. Radicalized academics, who identify the social origins and nature of those ideas, still see their occurrence in high culture as a key experience. Knowing that Lawrence remains a widely read and influential novelist, they do not investigate what this description means. Widely read by whom? Influential upon whom? If one recognizes the almost rhetorical character of these questions, one sees the difference between a novelist's being the darling of intellectuals and his being objectively influential. It should be possible to acknowledge that the choices that intellectuals make have a disproportionate weight in our culture, without swallowing the entire myth about their power and "responsibility."

An example of the kind of myth-making to which I refer is the current reexamination of the 1950s. Almost by definition, the Cold War assigned a high priority to the production and distribution of ideas. The paramilitary idiom accompanying the exchange of a theatrical company or a ballet troupe was one obvious symptom of the role of culture during that period. A more important one, of course, was the funding of cultural and propaganda enterprises by the CIA and other government agencies. Whether they support or deprecate it, few observers would, at this remove, deny the part literary critics played in the Cold War. But it is one thing to acknowledge that, and quite another to label the '50s the Age of Criticism, as many of its participants do.

Most people, after all, lived through the Truman–Eisenhower years without suspecting it *was* the Age of Criticism, because for them it was nothing of the sort. Yet they were all subjected to overtly anti-Communist propaganda, along with a constellation of other ideas that reinforced the social status quo. The mass media were the most important source of those views. It is true that to some extent the media were merely translating and popularizing themes that originated in high culture. But it is interesting to consider the *differences* between the attitudes expressed in the literature and criticism of the period and those embodied in movies, television dramas, and popular magazines. Where the latter preached a meliorative, integrative philosophy and what came to be called "conformism," the intellectuals were creating and being exposed to a precisely opposite image of the individual: isolated, alienated, eccentric, despairing. The problem is complicated by the fact that the mass culture was being produced by people who have to be defined as intellectuals and who had some familiarity, themselves, with the themes of high culture. And *criticism* of popular culture was being written almost exclusively by such people. It seems to me that this contrast—paradoxical or dialectical—is worth studying, as is the actual content of the cultural products beamed at the working class, the people who have least to gain from the continued hegemony of the bourgeoisie.

The analogy with our present situation should be clear. It may be important to examine high culture, but one should also consider its audience and what kind of investment that audience has in what sorts of changes. At the same time, it is necessary to give much more serious attention to mass culture if one believes, as I do, that *its* audience is going to have a lot more to say than the intellectuals about how we change power relations in this country. Again, contrasts between the "message" of media aimed at different classes prove especially revealing. The special problems of "youth culture" are another important facet, but they have to be understood as part of a more general analysis of the media, as does the packaging of the high cultural tradition for consumption by high school and college students from the mass culture audience.

In much of my work I discuss the limitations of a feminist criticism that does no more than expose sexism in one work of literature after another. At the same time, I have attempted to outline what feminist criticism should look like and to place it in the context of historical materialist interpretations of culture. My emphasis has not been simply on the absence of a "class analysis" from criticism that calls itself feminist, but on the futility of equating *exposure* with criticism. There is not much difference between Millett's unmasking Lawrence as a sexist and a more class-conscious critic's exposing that sexism in the context of his other reactionary views. Real criticism would mean providing an interpretation of the material under discussion on the basis of one's insights into it. Millett's feminist perspective at least enables her to *read* Lawrence rather than merely denouncing him.

If one accepts the view that real life determines consciousness, then it must also inform art, which is the expression of consciousness. Art is not neutral, but derives its specific content from a society conditioned by divisions of class, race, and sex. Even where these three categories are not explicitly the subject of a work, awareness of how they operate illuminates the social origins and social functions of that work. Race, class, and sex also constitute a vantage point for criticism, a way of looking at a work that locates it historically and helps us understand what it really is. Questions of gender are often inseparable from questions of class. In each case, it is essential to move from the ritual *assertion* that art has something to do with race, sex, and class to what one can learn by assuming from the beginning that it has a great deal to do with them.

Just how significant the critical process is depends, of course, on how it is communicated. For the academic, this is simply a matter of publishing in a journal read by those likely to be interested in one's subject. It is expected to provoke no action beyond, perhaps, that of a tenure committee or a reader aroused to pursue or demolish one's argument. The ideological critic, however, faces more difficult problems in finding the right audience, the right medium, and the right action.

For academic readers, it is appropriate simply to lay out some radical possibilities for criticism. But for an audience able to perceive the connection between what is said and their own conditions of life, one's ideas have to be part of a program of cultural and political alternatives. Ideological criticism must take place in the context of a political movement that can put it to work. The revolution is simply not going to be made by literary journals.

Criticism—and
Self-Criticism

"WHAT CENTURY ARE YOU IN?" When I was at Columbia, the first question one asked a fellow graduate student in English or Comparative Literature was always about the person's sub-field, the literary period in which she or he was specializing. The verbal formula was as unvarying as the ritual question itself and, even when it was my own habitual conversation-starter, I noticed its peculiar ontological implications. What did it signify to *be in* a certain century? It would have been considered inexcusably flippant to reply that, along with one's interlocutor, one's classmates, and one's teachers, and whether one liked it or not, one was "in" the twentieth century. Yet our education did little to shed light on what it might mean to be "in" any other period. This essay is an attempt to examine the meaning of that question, the correct answer to it, and the reasons why I think it is of such urgent importance for us, as humanists, to be aware of the historical situation of our work—to know what century we are in.

My initial method is anecdotal, but it develops into what I think is a more systematic attempt to connect the disparate pieces. The first anecdote concerns a rather mysterious experience I had in a museum some years ago. I was about to begin graduate study in the history of art, and took my work and myself very seriously. At the Byzantine Museum in Athens one afternoon, I stationed myself in front of a large triptych with a Madonna and Child in its central panel, and began taking notes to record my professional observations and responses. After a few minutes, a woman I took to be a museum attendant approached me, speaking in Greek and pointing from the icon to me and back again. My Greek is very poor, but her words, the repeated gesture, and the frenetic signs of the Cross she was tracing in the air between us eventually got through to me. She was asking whether the icon was an object of veneration to me— that is, if I were a Christian. I said—or, rather, indicated—that I was not. Growing more excited, the woman grabbed my arm and led me across the room to a smaller icon depicting what was presumably an Old Testament scene. There was Hebrew writing in the background of this picture, and my self-appointed guide and persecutor went through her rapid gesticulations again, somewhat more sternly: was *that* what I was? The anti-Semitism evoked both pride and defensiveness and I agreed that, like the picture and the funny lettering, I, too, was Jewish. With as little irony as I could manage, I thanked the woman for showing me the icon and returned to the triptych that had first attracted my notice. But the damned woman wouldn't let me alone. She kept on talking and gesturing, trying to pull me away from the Madonna and back to the painting I "belonged" in front of. Finally—and most meretriciously—she told me that it was against the rules to write in the Museum and that I would have to put my notebook away. At this point, exasperated, I gave up on the triptych and moved on to take notes about an enormous Byzantine angel several rooms away.

My response to this incident has passed through several distinct phases over the years. At the time, I was mostly annoyed at the interruption of My Work and at the racism that prompted it. But I was also faintly amused at the naïvete of this poor woman, who apparently thought that art had a meaning and a function, that those possessed social and ideological import, and that, if you couldn't relate to them on that level, you had no business in the place. As the incident receded in time and an elite graduate education—in art and later in literature—made further inroads into my good sense, the anger diminished and the amusement grew, for I was increasingly convinced that the critical approach implied by the old woman's actions was pathetically innocent. More recently, a vision of both art and criticism as political expressions has forced me to reevaluate the assumptions of the woman in the Byzantine Museum. Although I still believe I have the right to admire and analyze what I do not worship, I have begun to think that, on some level at least, the woman knew a lot more than I was ever taught about the function of culture and criticism.

Another aspect of the problem is reflected in the experience a friend of mine has been having with an article he published in 1970. By way of illustrating some effects of humanist training on one's historical perspective, he began the essay with a two-paragraph discussion of what it had been like for him to be a successful graduate student "in" the eighteenth century, identifying intellectually with the literary culture of Alexander Pope, while remaining "ignorant of the larger culture . . . [surrounding] the masterpieces" he studied. Most graduate students, he wrote, suffer similar limitations:

> . . . the Enlightenment is little more than a vague rumor to them, as is the industrial revolution and urbanization; the fact that there was a popular culture central to the lives of the vast majority of the population simply does not come within their field of professional concern. I began to feel uneasy about my work when it dawned on me that I really agreed with the objectives of the Enlightenment.[1]

The passage goes on to describe how the author came to understand that there was a disjunction between his imaginative life, rooted "in" the eighteenth century, and the constellation of political and cultural attitudes shaped by his own material and historical experience. The world his literary education had encouraged him to embrace was, of course, politely free of distinctions based on class, race, or ideology, so it took him some time to realize that neither Swift nor Pope would have received him socially. His mannered fantasy had been a grotesque anachronism: "the Jewish socialist from Washington Heights, sitting in his Chinese garden swapping epigrams with Dr. Arbuthnot!"

Reading these remarks in their original context—an article about the politically compromised nature of literary study—I considered them a wry and rather modest attempt to demystify and make sense of fragmented experience. My colleague was performing that act for which liberal education is supposed supremely to prepare us: he was attempting to know himself, he was asking that fundamental question, "What the fuck am I doing?" Some people read the passage very differently, however. For whatever motives, they see it as a pathologically subjective approach to "our" cultural tradition. Whenever a political attack is directed at the author from within the profession, these paragraphs are exhumed, paraphrased, and caricatured. He is widely believed to have projected some kind of private paranoia onto the great writers of the eighteenth century, decided on the basis of that paranoia that these distinguished men would have snubbed him, and developed an implacable grudge against them. Having refused the invitation to a timeless and gracious world he'd ceased to believe in, he found himself in the classic position of the child who not only points out the Emperor's embarrassing nudity, but proceeds to inform the rest of the crowd how far *they'd* sold out by praising the softness of the insubstantial velvet, the shine on the nonexistent cloth of gold. At my friend's own institution, a retired dean—an individual who had once managed to quote Montaigne in support of procedures leading to dismissal of my colleague and myself—wrote an appeal for gentlemanly values in humanities teaching. In this document, which was printed and distributed at university expense, he heaped scorn on an unnamed professor who, convinced that Pope and Swift would have disliked him personally, refused to teach their works in his own courses and prevented others from doing so in theirs!

I encountered the third bit of anecdotal evidence while reading the entertainment section of the Sunday *Times*. On the front page, the headline over an article by Walter Kerr posed the angry question: WILL WE EVER SEE THE BACCHAE AS EURIPIDES WROTE IT?[2] My immediate reaction was to answer, "Of course not, schmuck," and move on to livelier reading. When I returned to the article, however, I discovered that the argument was somewhat more subtle than anticipated. Kerr was inveighing against a current London production of *The Bacchae,* which a director from the Third World had interpreted as antiimperialist drama, with Dionysius representing the liberating energy that moves an oppressed people. Nor was this the only recent version of the play that distressed the reviewer, for he also dismissed *Dionysius in 69* as an "apologia for the counter-culture" and a "limp" one at that—surely a most un-Dionysian attribute.

Despite the headline, the critic was not calling on us to recreate the conditions under which *The Bacchae* was first produced. (What's the matter, Kerr, you want to go fight in the Peleponesus? You want *slaves?*) All he asked was a faithful rendering of the text—the *English* text, of course—with, perhaps, a discreet adoption of some few techniques characteristic of Attic theater: the chorus, maybe the masks, but no men playing Maenads, I bet, and for heaven's sake not all that sitting around on hard stone benches. Kerr was not suggesting that we reproduce—or even consider— the social forces within which *The Bacchae* functioned when Euripides wrote it, forces that may well be obscured by translating the play into the terms of our own modern history. Rather, he wanted a denatured *Bacchae* that did not document Athenian experience or Athenian theater, but that remained equally unsullied by twentieth-century tensions. In such a play, the references to gods, wives, kings, and servants, to wars, epidemics, and power politics, do not represent social experience, but are transfigured on a higher, asocial realm. They are seen as expressions of timeless, "universal" categories that are as stylized as wearing white robes or speaking in verse. The tragedy does not take place somewhere, but Everywhere; it is freed from having to be about something, in the interests of being about Everything. I think I understand the travesty Kerr wants to see in the theater because it is the same *Bacchae* I have encountered in the classroom, the one that was taught to me and that I was encouraged to present to my own students as the departmentally-sanctified Real Thing. (Fortunately, throughout Euripides' tragedy, Dionysius the Liberator wears a smiling mask.)

These three vignettes share a concern about our ability to recognize and respond to the distinction between subjective and objective categories of historical experience. In each of the *exempla,* some questions are raised about the proper relationship of individual experience to the apprehension of a work of art. Although Alienated Man—existentially isolated and despairing in a world of subjective forms—is the contemporary bourgeois hero, he is no one's idea of a good critic. Even the modernist critic, immersed in those same subjective forms, normally retains a certain responsibility to the social act of communicating insights and helping to render aesthetic experience intelligible. Given these assumptions, the only difficulty is to identify which are the subjective elements of consciousness, which the objective ones.

I would maintain that, as the products of social experience, the personal responses evinced by the people in my three anecdotes are by no means subjective. The consciousness informed by membership—especially what could be called active membership—in one's race, one's class, or one's sex is an objective phenomenon. The idea that "life is not determined by consciousness, but consciousness by life," is probably too familiar to require much elaboration. For my present purposes, however, it is worth looking at how Marx and Engels completed the paragraph in which they originally made that pronouncement: "In the first method of approach the starting-point is consciousness taken as the living individuals; in the second it is the real living individuals themselves, as they are in actual life, and consciousness is considered solely as *their* consciousness."[3] What the authors are trying to do here is to remove the clouds of abstraction that surround the notion of consciousness as long as it is understood as a force capable of either constituting or determining life. Although it adds a more rigorous note, the term "consciousness," thus idealized, has no more precision than the word "soul," and becomes its secular equivalent. This form of mystification can be avoided only if we remember that the vague polysyllable "consciousness" has to belong to real people, that it possesses no being or significance apart from people, and that its specific content must depend on the nature of real people's experience.

The historical materialism that *The German Ideology* begins to enunciate takes issue, then, with idealist theories—theological, philosophical, or psychological—that perceive consciousness as the determinant of experience. Yet, taken out of context, the initial statement of the position would still seem to leave room for the grossest and most self-indulgent solipsism, for if *your* consciousness is determined by *your* life and *my* consciousness is determined by *my* life and we all have our own idiosyncrasies and our own suffering, then in the expressions of consciousness—in the arts and their interpretation, for example—pretty much anything is legitimate. The continuation of that paragraph suggests, however, that it is not personal history that Marxists regard as central to consciousness, but social history. And that when we talk about individuals producing their lives and their lives, in turn, determining consciousness, we are talking about the *social* production of human life.

Of course, we all have individual histories and those histories constitute part of the psychic and intellectual baggage we bring with us to a new experience, including our first contact with a given work of art. If, say, a mysterious dark bird appeared one day and pecked out your Uncle Herbert's eyes, the incident is probably going to be relevant to your reading of certain poems by Edgar

Allan Poe and Wallace Stevens. Indeed, the event might be of such overriding importance in your mental makeup that you couldn't get much out of "The Raven" or "Thirteen Ways of Looking at a Blackbird," and that's too bad. If I can't get much out of, say, "Prufrock," these days, because I read it as a woman, that is also too bad. But I refuse to believe that the two kinds of damn shame are in any sense equivalent.

In "Modernism and History," Lise Vogel and I freely acknowledged that members of oppressed groups often respond subjectively to the content of art. We insisted, however, that such a response was no more subjective than that of the dominant culture—merely more overt. My own present position amounts to a reconsideration of even that qualified admission. It is founded on the view that, when there is a difference between personal and social experience, it is the latter, properly understood, that has the primary role in the understanding of art. Thus my friend's Jewishness, or the London director's African origins, like my femaleness, are qualitatively different, in their effect on consciousness, from the multitude of personal eccentricities and private details that also mark our lives and that have a more limited, though quite genuine, social basis. And the opinions we advance—my socialist friend's belated support for the Enlightenment, my youthful preference for aesthetic form over the Christian god as an object of worship, Walter Kerr's yearning for a "pure" production of Euripides—do not reflect the accidental operation of casual tastes, but are ideological products of the same categories of class, race, and sex, acting as historical forces. The *Times* does not "happen" to have a theater critic who wants to keep Dionysian energies in their place (Periclean Athens is about far enough, in space and time). And I am not a working-class misfit who was spontaneously convinced that art was made for art's sake.

I have asserted rather categorically that social experience is not only different from private experience but that, acknowledged or not, it is the dominant force in the making of art or criticism. This assertion remains to be supported and justified. It seems to me that bourgeois criticism inverts the categories of objective and subjective and thereby distorts the kind of relationship that subsists between art and audience. That is, it behaves as if the work of art, which it perceives as a product of the artist's subjectivity, has a certain objective life, an autonomous reality, of its own; we, the critics, are subjective beings, and, though our mission is to apprehend the work in its full (objective) reality, the process is to some extent mediated by our own subjectivity. From this perspective, the interchange between the work of art and its interpreter appears as a relationship between a subjective being and an objective thing. And the sensitive, informed work of critical interpretation, itself apparently an autonomous and objective thing, seems to enter into a relation with that other thing, the work of art. The only language we have to describe the process makes all this seem like a right and natural and inevitable condition. (Witness my own near-personification of "bourgeois criticism" in the course of this very discussion.)*

But in fact we are not simply ambulant subjectivities; we are the products of human history and of certain material developments within it. And the work of art is a *work,* the product of human labor, socially (though in our culture not often collectively) produced. It is made by a historical being using socially developed means to arrive at a social expression. Not only is the artist situated in history, but the art itself is. It is quite true, that is, that the artist's consciousness contains elements other than those determined by class, race, and sex or the operation of those forces in particular conditions. The artist has a biography, a subjective history, and also a craft, a relation to the formal elements of the art. And she or

---

*I realize that some readers will be less distressed by the personification than by my characterizing some—indeed, most—criticism as "bourgeois." There is no other term, however, that is comprehensive enough to describe newspaper reviewers, New Critics, self-proclaimed "structuralists," and the run of literary historians. I imagine each of them would be as quick to deny participation in the same "mainstream" as any of the others. If this is so, I prefer to use what I believe is the right term, and trust that my subsequent argument will demonstrate its appropriateness.

he may be convinced that those elements are the whole point of any work of art. But the formal components—as well as matters of "style"—are social facts. In the twentieth century, new styles in the arts have frequently been received with questions about whether this thing that the orchestra was playing was really music or whether this object hung for exhibit was really to be regarded as a painting. Under the hegemony of modernism, the answer is always, "Yes, it is art." But the persistence of the question means that, even if the barriers are flexible, there remains the assumption that, at any *particular* moment, there is some commonly agreed on view of what is and what is not a work of art. In a sense, the more flexible the boundaries of acceptable form, the greater our awareness that those boundaries exist.[4]

If the creator and the means of art have an historical, a social existence, then there is something exceptionally peculiar about the critical mode I described earlier, wherein the reified interpretation, the work of criticism as thing, engages the work of art as thing in some kind of relationship. Our present stage of material civilization has confused the situation so that the world of art comes to resemble that of religion: "In that world the productions of the human brain appear as independent beings endowed with life and entering into relations both with one another and the human race."[5] A human relation, initially established between people as historical beings, thus comes to assume "the fantastic form of a relation between things."[6]

The source of these observations is Marx's chapter on Commodity Fetishism in the first volume of *Capital*.[7] This may suggest that I think an analogy exists between the situation in art and that of material production. In fact, I would go further and say that I think it is more than an analogy, for the work of art is not only a product of the brain but of the hand—that is, of a labor process. And it is a literal, not a metaphorical product. One aspect of this fact is that, in order for the artist to survive and for the work to have an impact on the social world, it has to enter the capitalist market, to be actually or potentially bought and sold.

Does my use of Marx's term mean that the work of art is not only a thing but the specific kind of thing called a commodity? And does it matter for cultural theory whether it is a commodity or not? I think it does matter for an understanding of what critical fetishism means, and for that reason I wish the answer to my first question were simpler. Everything that can be placed on the market is not a commodity; as Marx points out, "in order to sell a thing, nothing more is required than its capacity to be monopolised and alienated."[8] He also makes it clear in a number of places that the kind of commodity he is discussing (and hence the kind that can be fetishized) may be reproduced in any quantity by the application of labor.[9]

I believe that the way modern art has responded to and made use of the technology of advanced capitalism shows the extent to which it is coming to fit this second definition, to share with conventional manufactured commodities the capacity of being reproduced by the application of labor. In the nineteenth century, works of art were not commodities in the strictly analytic sense of the term; in the twentieth, they are still not the same as other objects, but they are somewhat less special.* What is more important, however, is the way they are perceived, for our critical approach to them is increasingly conditioned by our participation in a culture where the autonomous life and mental processes of commodities are taken even more as a matter of course than when Marx first named the curious phenomenon.

If we are to be able to see the work of art for what it is, without

---

*This is a more controversial and complex issue than I can deal with here. It seems to me that one kind of evidence to pursue, aside from theoretical grounding and artistic evidence, is the history of copyright law and the culture surrounding *it*. Particularly suggestive is the recent movement, led by the pop-artist Robert Rauschenberg, for a "copyright" system in the visual arts. Rauschenberg's action was inspired by seeing a picture he'd sold to Robert Scull a few years before auctioned off by the collector for an amount which I believe was nearly 10,000% of its purchase price. From a Marxist standpoint, Rauschenberg's parting remark was most provocative: leaving to consult an attorney, the painter told Scull, whose fortune comes from owning a fleet of taxi-cabs, that he owed every artist in the place free cab rides!

critical fetishism, it is essential that we see it whole and within *its* history, from a vantage point informed by *ours*. Now,

> the life-process of society, which is based on the process of material production, does not strip off its mystical veil until it is treated as production by freely associated men, and is consciously regulated by them in accordance with a settled plan. This, however, demands for society a certain material groundwork or set of conditions of existence which in their turn are the spontaneous product of a long and painful process of development.[10]

If we take the making of art to be at once a kind of commodity-production, created for distribution under specific market conditions, and a kind of ideology-production, expressing and reinforcing those "specific market conditions," then what Marx says about historic process is particularly vital to the small corner of that process occupied by literary criticism. That is, only social experience eventuating in the free association he speaks of can fully demystify art in general or any work in particular. It seems a rather indirect sort of invitation to a revolution. Yet the most that criticism can do in the meantime is to reveal and examine the mystification, the way in which the present mode of making and studying art is an extension of the system's characteristic inversion of social and material relations.

An important part of this effort involves getting in touch with those elements of a critical response that are shaped by our own participation in history. It seems to me that the most positive steps in this direction—steps that have at least served to inject some vitality into departments of literature—have been made by Third World people and by women. In both cases, the existence of a movement for social liberation has made it possible for those of us still in the academy to recognize and express the consciousness informed by our condition. The flowering of black and feminist criticism—concentrating on writers and audiences that had previously been excluded from consideration, and reevaluating the monuments and attitudes of the dominant culture—is a welcome sign of life. But it has not always led to good criticism because, although it reflects that individual historic consciousness that I have been claiming is not purely subjective, it also reflects a very limited understanding of that consciousness as a part of history. As a result, critics who are struggling against the literary objectification their group has traditionally suffered participate in that objectification by talking about "black" and "woman" as if these were trans-historical categories.

In the area of feminist studies, where I feel best qualified to comment, a body of criticism has developed that is remote from the concerns of the movement for women's liberation and that is of limited usefulness to it. I think this has occurred because of the isolation in criticism of the category "woman" from the other historical forces and events with which it interacts, forces that have made the meaning and experience of "woman" anything but static and absolute. Such criticism succeeds to the extent that it asserts—often angrily and, to my mind, always refreshingly—that criticism does indeed have a gender. But it fails to the extent that it proceeds from there as if gender functioned as a natural, rather than a social category. Of necessity, it begins by recognizing sexism as a social constraint, but then it fails to examine the forces in a particular society that made the constraint take certain forms. Awareness of sexism provides a new way of looking at literature and the conditions it reflects, but that awareness is too often inflexible and unmodulated. Thus, most feminist criticism does not help us use literature to understand an urgent issue that literature is uniquely fitted to illuminate—the peculiar forms sexism has assumed in *capitalist* society.

Although my primary concern is with making critical analysis available to a living movement, I believe that criticism whose historical insensitivity makes it impossible for the movement to use it is not professionally useful, either. It acquiesces in the peculiarly ahistorical approach of what is supposed to be literary history and, like bourgeois criticism in general, treats the encounter with a work of literature as a confrontation between the self and an objective thing.

A criticism whose point of departure was the awareness of *class* as historical determinant could not wander so far from history. Those of us who work this particular critical vein have a tendency to speak as if all the material forces with which we are concerned were equivalent and presented similar problems; in our ideological shorthand, class, race, and sex seem almost to fuse into a single concept. In fact, the kinds of issues they raise as they begin to operate in criticism are different from one another and call for an overall analysis that can show how they function together. The reason I think a stance that recognizes the class nature of art and criticism is most likely to be faithful to the exigencies of history is that one cannot admit the validity of "class" as a category without also seeing it historically. Which may be why its validity is not often admitted and why the most massive and brutal attempts to deny the existence of an analytic category occur with respect to class. (I suspect, for example, that the majority of well-meaning academics who have been taught to consider proletarian culture and proletarian criticism as some doctrinaire aberration of the Depression era have no idea that there really is a proletariat and that it has an historic role as well as an historic definition.)

I called Third World and women's studies sources of the first liberating energies within the profession. This priority is no accident, but is closely linked to the history of social movements in this country, and also to the masking of class distinctions and class struggle that characterizes American political mythology. I do not believe that this is by any means a permanent situation—in society or in criticism. But I will be very much surprised if the next stages of proletarian struggle can be contained by the creation of chairs of Proletarian Studies in the bourgeois university.

What, then, do we do with the chairs we've already got and that some of us are sitting on? If human history really is the history of class conflict, and if that did not change just because Senator

McCarthy or the Sociology Department said it did, what does that have to do with literary history? With me "in" the sixteenth century and my colleagues "in" the eighteenth, the fourteenth, or the nineteenth? I think it means, above all, learning to ask new kinds of questions and putting the answers to use. For our own period, it means taking mass culture seriously—examining the art addressed to working people, the forms it uses, the myths it creates, the influence it exerts, and seeking a new audience for criticism among those people who are the chief actors in history. For the past, it means looking at the recognized masterpieces as historically alive: conditioned by historical forces, produced in specific material circumstances, serving certain interests and ignoring, threatening or repressing others. And it means considering how popular culture coexisted and sometimes overlapped with those monuments. Only in this way, I think, can we as interpreters of literature finally come to be *in* the twentieth century, rather than letting it roll over us as it moves forward to someplace much better.

NOTES

1. Louis Kampf, "The Trouble With Literature," *Change,* 2 (1970), 27.

2. *New York Times,* August 19, 1973, Section 2, 1.

3. Karl Marx and Frederick Engels, *The German Ideology* (1845-6; rpt. New York: New World-International, 1967), p. 15.

4. In this and what follows, I have been influenced by Christopher Caudwell's *Studies in a Dying Culture* (rpt., New York: Monthly Review Press, 1971), especially his essay "D. H. Lawrence: A Study of the Bourgeois Artist," pp. 44-72. As far as I know, however, Caudwell did not pursue his ideas to the conclusions I am advancing.

5. Karl Marx, "The Fetishism of Commodities and the Secret Thereof," *Capital,* Vol. I (1867; rpt. Moscow: Progress Publishers, n.d.), 77.

6. *Ibid.*

7. For another application of the concept of commodity fetishism to culture, see Meredith Tax, "Culture is Not Neutral, Whom Does it

Serve?'' in *Radical Perspectives in the Arts,* ed. Lee Baxandall (Baltimore: Pelican-Penguin, 1972), pp. 15-29. Tax emphasizes the alienation inherent in the production and consumption of art under capitalism and employs commodity fetishism as a way of explaining the elevation of that alienation into "an artistic creed, which becomes in its turn a critical dogma" (page 23).

8. Karl Marx, "Transformation of Surplus-Profit into Ground-Rent: Introduction," *Capital,* Volume III (Moscow: Progress Publishers, 1971), 633.

9. See, for instance, *Capital,* III, 759, where he refers to "works of art, whose consideration by their very nature is excluded from our discussion."

10. Marx, *Capital,* I, 84.

Criticism: Who Needs It?

Whenever you speak to a worker you manage to get it all
wrong: your choice of words, your tone, your jokes. I can
tell what a mountaineer is thinking even when he keeps silent, and I know what's on his mind even when he talks
about something else. This is the sort of culture your poets
should have given you.
                    —Schoolboys of Barbiana, *Letter to a Teacher*

Even Marxist criticism . . . implies an elite, even arrogantly
separate, audience. Anyone wanting to focus his life on
changing society is mad to put his energies into literary
theory and criticism.
—George Levine, *Politics and the Form of Disenchantment*

The electronic media do away with cleanliness; they are by
their nature 'dirty.' . . . But fear of handling shit is a luxury
a sewerman cannot necessarily afford.
                    —Hans Magnus Enzensberger,
                    Constituents of a Theory of the Media

THIS IS BUFFALO, New York, and who needs cultural criticism?
The question, so stated, invites a cynical echo in reply: Yeah,
who needs it? Meaning, "No one." Meaning, at least, "Not me."
But if such a question is to have more than rhetorical force and
evoke more than a stylized response, its components must be
granted an unprejudiced—and unironic—scrutiny. What is Buf-

69

falo, New York? What does it have to do with criticism? What, for that matter, is criticism? And what might it become?

I

Buffalo is the kind of city that an entertainer or a comic writer mentions to get a laugh. There are many such ''joke cities'' in the United States; in fact, when vaudeville and burlesque performers used to tour the country, every major city had a nearby joke-locale, and standard stories in the repertoire would be adapted to include a reference to it. But some major cities are joke-locales in themselves, and continue to serve that function in nationally-broadcast humor. These cities either have ''funny,'' often Amerindian, names, or are centers of heavy industry with predominantly working-class populations. What is supposed to be amusing about both conditions is their remoteness from the centers of Culture.

The Buffalo metropolitan area has a population of three-quarters of a million. Included in this total are the neighboring cities of Tonawanda and Lackawanna, which have the heaviest industrial concentrations—as well as unambiguously Indian names. (Lackawanna is *Buffalo's* joke city.) The principal places of employment are steel, chemical, electrical, auto and automotive-parts plants. There are several large flour mills and oil refineries, some furniture and clothing factories. The printing business has more than local impact; indeed, convenient to my discussion of culture, the *Reader's Digest* is printed in nearby Depew. The rest of the labor force is engaged chiefly in service occupations, especially in the public sector, and the State University ranks with Bethlehem Steel and General Motors as one of the area's largest employers. The current depression economy had a head start in Buffalo, which was once an important railroad center and a port for Great Lakes shipping. Its industrial decline paralleled the decay of those modes of distribution that were developed in the second half of the nineteenth century. Many factories have either closed down or escaped to sources of cheap labor, and those that remain have a smaller work force than formerly. The unemployment level, even as calculated by the government, is one of the highest in the country.

Buffalo's white working class is largely of Polish or Italian extraction, and hence mostly Roman Catholic. Other European ethnic groups are represented in smaller proportions, and there is also a substantial number of Blacks, some Puerto Ricans and Chicanos, and a considerable group of Native Americans. Although the area has been losing population for a generation now, as children of both the working class and the ruling class have sought a livelihood elsewhere, most of Buffalo's blacks and most of its intelligentsia have come here within the last fifteen years. The reasons are different. For the blacks, their presence was part of a more general migration to the industrial cities of the North, whereas for students and academics, it has to do with the State's purchase of the former University of Buffalo and the subsequent growth of that institution.

The centers of cultural life in this city—as in most of urban America—are the job, the family, the automobile, and the tavern. For working people, two of these, the home and the bar, are also the principal sites of culture in the narrower, aesthetic sense: they are places where people engage in activities involving "the arts," the chief of these being television and music. Movies—generally Hollywood products—are most often presented at "theater complexes" clustered in suburban shopping malls with four, five or six auditoria on the same premises. Spectator sports are another focus of cultural attention, and Buffalo fields professional teams in football, basketball, and ice-hockey. Participation sports attract a smaller, but still considerable, portion of the working-class population. Public parkland is low in acreage, poorly developed, and prey to every sort of encroachment on its grounds, from inner-belt highways to golf courses; indeed, the inner city's pleasantest landscaped walk is in the cemetery adjoining a major park, and, recognizing this contribution to community life, Forest Lawn's management provides brochure-guides to the flora and fauna of the place, as well as to its funerary monuments.

As for the other kind of culture, it is by and large the preserve of another kind of people. Buffalo's ruling class supports a fine-arts museum and a symphony orchestra of some national standing, and the University employs writers of great prominence. There is also a small professional theater troupe in town. None of these is shaped by the particular city in which it is based, or influenced by the kind of demographic or cultural generalizations with which I began this discussion. And their presence, in turn, has had almost no impact on the people whose lives I have been describing. The Buffalo Philharmonic does sponsor enthusiastic public-relations efforts, nurturing a personality-cult around the orchestra's young conductor, Michael Tilson-Thomas. (Lapel buttons can even be purchased that show a photograph of him conducting in his shirtsleeves, and bearing the motto, ''Thomas is Terrific.'') They advertise the orchestra extensively on local television, but they are not advertising the *concerts*. Most of the time, you have to consult the newspapers to find out what music is on the week's program. What the TV audience is told is that the orchestra as an institution is a valuable community ''asset,'' in that its renown reflects well on Buffalo itself. It is depicted as being the same kind of asset, in fact, as the professional sports teams, which represent the city in another cultural arena; Mr. Thomas is depicted as *his* team's star, a celebrity second only to football hero O. J. Simpson. The only difference is that the working people of Buffalo know what it is that O. J. does, and they know that supporting the local team means buying tickets to its games and cheering it on to victory. The ''support'' requested by the Philharmonic at the end of its commercial is a monetary contribution to help the orchestra ''Boost Buffalo'' and eradicate our collective image as a city of uncultured slobs. No concern is expressed about whether we *remain* uncultured slobs in the Philharmonic sense. Despite some free concerts at schools, prisons, banks (!) and other social institutions, the real cultural division remains almost absolute.

The State University Center is statutorily required to admit half its undergraduate students from Erie County, which means primarily from Buffalo and its suburbs. Nearly all these students are from working-class backgrounds, with a few from among the poor or from the families of small shopkeepers. The State University College, an upgraded normal school, draws even more of its student body from this population, as do the two-year community colleges and the various programs of "compensatory" higher education. There are also several church-related colleges in the area, many of whose students are local residents. Institutions like the ones in and around Buffalo graduate very few of what educators euphemistically describe as "future leaders," those destined to occupy positions of national and international power in business or government. They do train a portion of our upper professionals, small business owners, scientists, engineers, and middle-level managers, along with most of the country's schoolteachers, social workers and welfare functionaries, accountants, speech therapists, librarians, technicians, and health professionals other than doctors. In addition, they serve to filter out (as "unsuited" to further education) a sizeable percentage of the working-class youth who enter them; many of these students, after being kept off the labor market for a few years, enter it with no degree and no vocational qualifications beyond the recorded fact of having passed those years at an institution with the word "college" in its name.[1] One result of this phenomenon is the rising educational level of many workers in traditional blue collar occupations. The female labor force, particularly in clerical fields, has always included a substantial number of women who have been to college; the same situation is now observable for men, as well. According to an informal estimate, for instance, about 40 percent of the younger white men working at Bethlehem Steel's Lackawanna mill have some post-secondary schooling.

There is no evidence that the class basis of Buffalo's "high culture" audience has been altered in any way by these educational developments, and no one who understands the way "our" heritage of classical music, art, and literature is packaged for working-class students could possibly expect it to. Nor does the presence on campus of so many students of local origin seem to affect the prevalent animosity between town and gown. At elite universities, I have seen much community hostility directed towards the institution itself, in its capacities as landlord, urban-remover, research machine, and employer. In Buffalo, by contrast, it tends to be aimed at the students, principally those at the University Center, and more particularly at the 50 percent who are not natives of the area and who typically are (and more stereotypically perceived as being) from New York City and environs, middle class, Jewish, and culturally disruptive. For their part, the majority of these non-resident students and most of the faculty have made Buffalo *their* joke city, too.

Some miscellaneous observations may help to round out this picture:

A poet in the Vermont hills told me that Buffalo gets only 96 days of sunlight per year.

The nearest cosmopolitan city or cultural center is Toronto. It is 100 miles away and in another country.

The city's air and water are both polluted. Some of us drink only bottled spring water (which may, in turn, come from areas with dangerously high radiation levels in the soil). The local death rate from certain pulmonary diseases is the second-highest in the country.

Like most American cities that developed in the late nineteenth century, Buffalo has few trees on the streets other than elms. And, like most American elms, ours are dying from Dutch Elm

Blight and are gradually being cut down. Nothing is being planted in their place.

At one time, the city was noted for its attractively designed internal boulevards. It is now noteworthy for its absence of urban planning, its decaying inner-city neighborhoods, its deserted downtown area, and its unappealing *ensemble*.

Almost all television entertainment available in Buffalo is centrally produced at media headquarters in Hollywood. The *locally* produced programs with the greatest audience appeal are those that stage amateur bowling matches.

II

But what has all this to do with criticism? The question may arise from someone more interested in cultural criticism than in Buffalo, New York. As a certified expert in high culture and a resident of this city, I have been asking it myself, minus the irritation and with the terms reversed. What do the critical disciplines in which I was trained have to say about the culture that surrounds me? Fidelity to the letter of my training would have me answer, "Nothing." Fidelity to its spirit would keep me complacent about such insulation or feed me platitudes about universal truths and widely applicable methods. I am a specialist in European literature of the Renaissance period; my doctoral dissertation was about Ariosto, Tasso, and Spenser, and had an introductory chapter on Virgil. Before beginning work for the Ph.D., I did post-graduate study in art history, as well as in English. Had I pursued a conventional career pattern, I should, at the appropriate stage, have sought a job in a department of English or Comparative Literature that had a "slot" for a "16th-century man," either because the program in that area was being expanded or, more likely, because the previous occupant of the "slot" had expired, retired, resigned, or, most probably of all, failed to achieve tenure. As the new 16th-century "man," I might, these days, be allowed a wry chuckle at the sexual incongruity of that label, but I would not be expected to perceive any anomaly at their requiring such a person in Buffalo—or in Akron, Toledo, Oshkosh, or Walla Walla. The department "happened" to have an "opening" and that's where the university "happened" to be. Buffalo itself—or Akron, Toledo, Oshkosh, or Walla Walla— would, of course, be as much of a joke to me as to my colleagues.

It would be very easy, at this point, for my tone to become philistine, deriding the hermetic absurdities of my education, or sanctimonious, extolling my moral superiority to professional norms, or both at once. If I resist the temptation, it is out of a lively sense of my own shortcomings and those of the movements with which I identify. The social ferment of the 1960s gave rise to a critical reexamination of the academic enterprise, the scholarly disciplines, and the traditional curriculum. For those of us involved in the humanities, it became both possible and essential to understand the larger social functions of the institutions and how these informed what went on in the library and the classroom (as well as in the admissions office and the research lab). Our insights into the class nature of the arts and of criticism were translated into a counter-criticism and formed the basis of what we tried to communicate in our teaching. As long (and only as long) as there was a campus movement that compelled and nurtured our analysis and a student body whose own political experience helped make sense of that analysis, our work was not entirely futile.

Even when the student movement was at the height of its influence, however, the effort I have been describing had some evident limitations. Its strength was the strength of all New Left scholarship: it laid bare the bases and the operation of power, it "made the connections." Its weakness resided in the same characteristic of looking upward in the social structure, of relying for its political impact on revelation and exposure. In the literary realm, that exposure was accompanied by some attempt to expand the accepted view of what literature it was legitimate to study. Women writers joined blacks and other national minorities, as well as the authors of rock songs and proletarian literature, in a new canon. And with this enlargement necessarily came new definitions of literature itself and the uses to which it might be put. But, although such work does try to identify and build on the culture of oppressed people, it retains, nonetheless, a certain investment in the assumptions of high culture. It does not address itself to the leisure activities that *take the place* of art in the lives of most people, including most students. It does not provide students with critical instruments that they can apply to their other cultural experiences. And it does not speak intelligibly to anyone who lacks its own initial commitment to the subject.

But all this takes criticism as the point of departure—to the extent of personifying it and attributing to the artificial being so created the shortcomings of people like me. What happens if I return to the perspective from which I began, the cultural situation of Buffalo's working class? Some initial clues may be derived from consideration of what criticism means to the people of that class. The primary definition, of course, has nothing to do with culture. Criticism means simply a reproach or attack. It connotes commentary, to be sure, but negative commentary. If someone says to me, "My boss is always criticizing: my work, my attitude, even the look on my face," I do not assume that the objective observations tendered include praise as well as blame, or that they meet any of the analytic criteria applied to good cultural criticism.

It is only in a secondary meaning that the arts enter the common definition of the word. Newspaper reviews of cultural events—films, television programs, books, plays, concerts, and art exhibits—are "criticism" in this sense, and the journalists who produce them belong to an elite, inscrutable breed known as "The Critics." Something of the negative connotation inherent in the more usual meaning attaches to this one, too. Reviewer-critics are perceived as professional fault-finders, judging our mass entertainment by standards alien to that culture's true audience, and endowed with the power to destroy what they do not approve. And who needs *that?*

III

This impasse could stand as a conclusion, if the issue were as static as my outline thus far would suggest. And if it were, I should accept what one epigraph to this essay calls the arrogant isolation implicit in the content, subjects, and audience of Marxist criticism. After all, most working people don't understand the writings of Marx, Lenin, or Mao either. But participation in a social movement does not mean simply taking a certain position about the way things are; the kinesthetic metaphor is entirely apt, in fact, because the criticism I am postulating exists to serve the forces of change. Such criticism assumes that to be a radical does not consist in holding certain opinions, but in learning to make those views the basis of concrete social action.

Not everyone can read the classics of Marxist thought, but certain people who feel a need to understand their lives—their jobs, their alienation, their social relations at work and away from it, how things got this way and how to have an impact on history—do find their way to and through those books. But who reads Marxist cultural criticism? Mostly, I'm afraid, other Marxist critics, with the addition of some few academics interested in criticism itself as a subject and some few intellectuals interested in every aspect of the Marxist tradition. The difference is that the works of political-economic theory—however densely argued and clumsily translated—have reference at every point to the real experience of real people. The works of cultural criticism, generally speaking, do not.

The radical academic, who is both promoter and product of the educational upheaval of the Sixties, approaches the problem of making one's work relevant to the movement by saying, "I am a cultural critic. How can I use my skills to serve what I believe in?" I am increasingly convinced that this is the wrong question and leads inevitably to a condition of stalemate. We should be coming at the issue from the other end, asking questions like: What is wrong? How does it operate? What does it do to people? Who can change it? What are those people's sources of resistance and the obstacles to it? What forms has the struggle assumed and what forms should it take? This formulation sounds like the next thing to baby-talk, but that does not mean that the answer is simple or that any of its steps may be safely skipped. For to arrive at problems of culture and consciousness through such a process means that one perceives those questions very differently from the way they appear if one takes one's own professional definition as an inalienable fact of life and builds from there.*

When I say that this fundamentally political framework puts culture and consciousness in a new perspective, I do not mean that they necessarily assume a lower priority. They do lose the artificially inflated significance that any subject achieves in academe through the very fact that somebody is studying it. Similarly, the radical intellectual loses the facile comfort that comes from a false assurance of "relevance." But surely it does not deprecate the importance of any question to be exploring it because it is urgent, rather than because it is "interesting." And in trying to understand the nature of power in society, who holds it,

---

*None of this takes into account the situation of someone whose "radicalization" occurs *through* study of a discipline. It is certainly true that graduate education is intrinsically alienating and that alienation can lead to a searching evaluation of the traditional content of one's field, as well as the demoralizing process of one's apprenticeship in it. The contradiction between the truths one's research uncovers and the received doctrines of the profession can be even more of a revelation. Nonetheless, I do not believe that coming to consciousness through this process exempts anyone from the responsibility of examining her work in the light of a social vision that goes beyond that work.

who is oppressed by it, how it is maintained, what the oppressed
have going for them, and how they can get it together, one finds
that some of the most urgent issues are essentially cultural in
nature. Many of these have to do with the broad definition of
culture I was applying when I said that its principal foci in the city
of Buffalo were the job, the family, the automobile, and the
tavern. The problems of ideology and expression that occur in
regard to the more limited use of "culture" to signify artistic
pursuits are, however, an inseparable part of the larger definition.

In considering the sources of resistance and the barriers to it, it
is indispensable to examine the elements that work to shape
people's consciousness and the forms in which members of society express their consciousness. The commercial production and
distribution of cultural artifacts in the United States come close to
eliminating the distinction between art that people create and art
intended to appeal *to* them. (Which is sort of like eliminating the
distinction between cooking and eating.) This is why the term
"popular culture" is so confusing as to be almost useless as a
description; it may be used to describe the people's *own* cultural
forms, media addressed to the mass audience, or the cooptation
and packaging of the one through the modalities of the other.
Thus, although I shall be primarily concerned with the working
class as audience and the culture addressed to it, my doing so
does not deny the existence of an indigenous working-class culture or ignore the relations between that culture and the dominant
one.

A schema for cultural criticism coming out of my formulation of
questions about society itself would concentrate on the conflict
between people's ability to act collectively in their own interests
and the forces that impede their doing so. The role that ideology
in general and aesthetic culture in particular plays in this process,
the way art helps people to order, interpret, mythologize, or dispose of their own experience, is complex and often ambiguous,
but it is not impossible to define. My sense of priorities would

focus criticism, first of all, on examining the culture directed at the working class, the myths it creates about people, the situations and institutions in their lives, the world they live in. It would explore how those myths function in the media themselves and also in the popular consciousness. And it would do so in a way that made it useful to the same audience that the popular arts themselves are addressing. This is an intentionally moderate and matter-of-fact statement of how to proceed, but the kind of criticism it describes does not exist.

IV

Well, why doesn't it exist? I have called for a detailed and synthetic examination of mass culture, an exploration of its social influence, and a discussion of the results in terms accessible to a mass audience. What we have instead is an almost complete disjunction between the interpretation of specific items of mass culture, on the one hand, and the sociology of the media, on the other. This grotesque division of intellectual labor is reinforced by the fact that the close analysis of particular works is the province, by and large, of bourgeois critics, usually those with backgrounds in literature, art, or "folklore," whereas the sociological studies come from critics on the left, usually people whose training is in philosophy or the social sciences. As for the audience, the masses who actually go to the drive-ins, listen to the music, watch the television programs, both kinds of commentators seem equally willing to leave them to the tender critical mercies of journalists directly tied to the communications industry. For this reason, I think that both sides of the polemic, intrinsic criticism and social analysis, require further scrutiny.

Given the industrialization of education and, more generally, of knowledge itself, that has taken place in recent decades, it should come as no surprise that popular culture has attained near-respectability as a field of academic pursuit. Although elite universities have ignored it or relegated it to marginal status, other institutions have established entire schools and colleges that specialize in media criticism. Graduate degrees are granted by some of these programs, and dissertations on popular culture topics are also being accepted by traditional departments. Within these departments (as well as in special "media studies" or "communications" programs) "slots" for a "film scholar" or "media man" coexist with those for an "18th century," "Anglo Saxon," or "Greek sculpture" man. Such scholars publish historical and critical articles in journals read by other scholars in the field, and attend conferences where they deliver and listen to papers discussing the minutiae of their subject.

The hegemony of formalist doctrine in the interpretation of high culture has combined with the ponderous machinery of pedantic scholarship to create a deadly fashion. The conventions of popular genres are not perceived as phenomena with content, but as responses to the "influence" of other artists in the genre. Images become ends in themselves, rather than means, and are all the more seductive in that describing them requires the mastery of a new technical language; this fosters the illusion that labeling a conventional device is equivalent to comprehending its significance. Most media studies programs teach craft as well as criticism, which serves to keep them in touch with the reality of the arts and their practitioners, but, at the same time, enhances the tendency to understand and discuss those arts in almost purely formal terms. All the paraphernalia of structuralism, psychoanalysis, myth-criticism, and vulgar historicism become theoretical bases for this formal analysis, which is often accompanied by a consumerist obsession with the cultural artifacts themselves. (Although some literary scholars are also bibliophiles and many art historians collect visual art, most serious students in these fields cannot afford and do not necessarily wish for a relation with the work of art in its capacity as a marketable item.

Pop-culture scholars, motivated by the ephemeral nature of the objects they study and aided by mass production, are often "media-freaks" themselves. For private delectation or university collections, they accumulate old Disney comic books, tapes of 1930s radio serials, wartime cigarette ads, and so forth.)

The program of a learned society meeting in popular culture reads like a parody of a scholarly convention in art or literature. Approaches may range from the morbid seriousness of film criticism to the lighter-hearted excesses of rock and roll or TV studies, but the media scholar still makes a clear separation between himself and the "real," non-specialist, audience to whose tastes and interests the popular arts are supposedly directed. Outside the academy, interpretation of mass culture follows the modes established by the elite, though non-scholarly, publications addressed to informed consumers of high culture. Magazines of film criticism, for example, share both the format and the social assumptions of those art magazines addressed to gallery visitors and collectors.

At the other extreme, ideologically and conceptually, are thinkers of the Frankfurt School and their followers, whose principal concern is "mass society," and who view the production and consumption of the popular arts as a significant factor in that society. Whereas most popular culture scholars are exclusively involved with what is *there* on the movie or TV screen, the radio, the phonograph, the pages of the wide-circulation magazine or novel, these social critics are more interested in the audience and, by extension, in the phenomenology and influence of mass media. This means that they tend to move very rapidly from the specifics of any work to abstractions about the culture that produced it and that it helps to shape.

In contradistinction to the pop-cultists, who tend to fetishize and enthuse over the trivia—material or factual—of their subject, the social critics begin with the assumption that it isn't even intrinsically worthwhile. The introduction to *The Dialectic of*

Enlightenment, for example, contains what amounts to an apology for taking "the culture industry . . . more seriously than it would implicitly require."[2] It is the perceived tension between the two words in the phrase "culture industry" that necessitates both the seriousness and the apology, for, if that contradiction in terms is not acknowledged, the mass media are protected both as art and as enterprise. Horkheimer and Adorno argue that if the media, by their very nature, create what are supposed to be aesthetic images, they "accordingly embody truth," yet they can retreat into their commercial status to avoid taking responsibility for the absence of truth.

This approach is responsible for one of the chief limitations of such criticism. The demand that if something has claims as art, then it must be judged according to the values of art, which include the capacity to convey truth, is an excellent strategy for depriving mass culture of the rhetorical shelter permitted to a "real" industry under capitalism. But Horkheimer and Adorno apparently fail to recognize that it is only a strategy, and so become entrapped in the logical consequences of accepting the assumptions their challenge postulates. Although they acknowledge the class-bias and exclusivity that enables bourgeois art to hypostatize its own autonomy, they seem to admit that freedom as a fact.[3] Now, it is one thing to attack the dishonesty of the mass media by applying the notion that art is supposed to tell the truth; it is quite another to accept that high art *does* tell the truth, without examining all the problems and contradictions inherent in the view or, for that matter, in the idea of "truth" as it relates to the realm of creative expression.

Of course, if it is art, most popular culture is pretty bad art, and hence not "implicitly" worthy of serious attention. But, if it is art, it has its own conventions and traditions, which have to be understood as such, and cannot be shrugged off as simply "imitative" devices demonstrating a lack of imagination or an adherence to the cautious aesthetic of the marketplace. (Indeed, the conventions of art are social phenomena themselves and must be

understood as such.) By mystifying high culture—or, more precisely, by tolerating its self-mystification—the Frankfurt School
critics also romanticize the notions of "originality" and "creativity" in the arts generally, and particularly as reflecting an illusory
spirit of resistance if they are manifested in mass culture.
(Enzensberger, whose critical approach to the media comes
closer to the sort of realism I have been advocating, also tends,
rather surprisingly, to romanticize the concept of creativity and
daring in the popular arts and thus to exaggerate their social significance and potential.)

Sociologists of the media do not press the artistic claims of
mass culture far enough to begin analyzing its exemplars as works
of art; they are concerned with the conditions of production and
consumption that pertain to the popular arts as a social phenomenon. Observations of specific works are therefore replaced by
gross generalizations about their content (words like "violence"
have to cover an awful lot of ground) or about the nature and the
implications of their influence. It seems to me that this approach
is no less formalist, in essence, than the methods employed by the
"intrinsic" critics of popular culture. In ignoring the manifest
content of films, songs, TV shows and the like, even where this
content impinges directly on the content of actual experience,
they are clearly telling us that the media aren't really *about* their
own manifest content. What sociological critics think they are
about, instead, is laid out rather explicitly in these passages from
Horkheimer and Adorno's essay on the culture industry, subtitled
"Enlightenment as Mass Deception":

Films, radio and magazines make up a system which is uniform as
a whole and in every part. Even the aesthetic activities of political
opposites are one in their enthusiastic obedience to the rhythm of
the iron system. (Page 120)

Real life is becoming indistinguishable from the movies. The sound
film . . . leaves no room for imagination or reflection on the part of
the audience, which is unable to respond within the structure of the

film, yet deviates from its precise detail without losing the thread of the story; hence the film forces its victims to equate it directly with reality. (Page 126)

The entertainment manufacturer knows that his product will be consumed with alertness even when the customer is distraught, for each of them is a model of the huge economic machinery which has always sustained the mass, whether at work or at leisure, which is akin to work. For every sound film and every broadcast program, the social effect can be inferred which is exclusive to none but is shared by all alike. (Page 127)

[The housewife does find relaxation and escape in the movie theater] just as she used to look out the window when there were still homes and rest in the evening. (Page 189)

In short, mass culture is not about anything. It is about itself. I think I have heard that song before, and I did not like it the first time. Both content and audience are eliminated, in this perspective, from consideration as participants in the meaning of the event. As these quotations amply demonstrate, the authors either make no attempt to deny the social and economic situation of the media or they assume for them the kind of ahistorical autonomy normally implied by a formalist approach. When they discuss the influence of media process on the minds of people experiencing their leisure between periods of work, they are not ignoring what it means to be a worker in this society. Indeed, their analysis of mass culture at once depends on their understanding of the proletarian condition and contributes to our further understanding of it. Nonetheless, their concentration on the totality of the process and what it does to people leads only to further exploration of media *forms* and how they must necessarily entail certain psychological effects. From the point of view of criticism, this leads ultimately to the shallows of McLuhanism—surely the ideological antithesis of what Horkheimer and Adorno were trying to do. And, from the point of view of the audience, those masses depicted for us as sitting stolidly in the dark, transfixed by images on a screen, the implications are even more dismal.

Concentration on the phenomenology of mass-culture events, the action of the media on the consciousness of their consumers, has strong determinist overtones. If the starting point for criticism were the object itself, conclusions about how the audience takes it would, at least, have to be qualified: this kind of image, myth, theme, convention, especially if repeated often enough, *might* have certain effects on the people who are exposed to it. Anyone employing such an approach is forced to take account of modulations, subtleties, and variations of all sorts, lest the argument reduce itself to absurdity and self-destruct. (As did the controversial '50s thesis about some inevitable connection between violent or grotesque "comic books" and juvenile crime.) But the approach reflected in Frankfurt School criticism of mass culture explicitly takes a given medium as an undifferentiated whole whose impact is entailed in its very forms and modalities of presentation. The effects—at least on the benighted masses—are thus portrayed as inevitable results of certain cultural "causes," people's readiness to accept them that way being conditioned by the same system that shaped the product itself, in whose interests people and culture both work.

For example, sociologists of the media reject the characteristic argument of the culture industry that it cannot be held responsible for either the quality or the specific content of its offerings, since they merely cater to public tastes. In fact, the social critics maintain, the reverse is true, and "popularity consists of the unrestricted accommodation of the people to what the amusement industry thinks they like."[4] Although the ruling class claims that the reason mass culture consumers put up so little resistance to the industry's wares is that production standards were initially based on public need, "the result is the circle of manipulation and retroactive need in which the unity of the system grows ever stronger."[5] There is a certain respect for the people in all this, at least to the extent that it does not assume their present cultural "debasement" to be their original or natural condition. But even this bears out the sense, implicit in descriptions of what the media do to the audience, that the "manipulation" is mechanically and invariably successful, that the message of "retroactive need" normally and necessarily "takes." If full *response* is impossible within the media universe, where the mass audience is trapped and confined, then so is criticism. The consumers, seen from this perspective, cannot detach themselves sufficiently from the product they consume to make a judgment on the experience as a whole.[6] (Presumably, they really *are* what they eat!)

This position does have the virtue of consistency, for, if one pointed out that what social critics have to say about mass culture is expressed in an impenetrable style, through a series of constructs and categories incomprehensible to the members of that mass society their criticism describes and deplores, they would not deny the charge. It is only important to reach the working class with an analysis of the nature and the power of popular culture if one believes there is some point to this communication. What is at issue is not some metaphysical question of "faith" or "lack of faith" in the masses, but the process that would lead to either conclusion about the working class's capacity to act in its own interest.

Social critics of the popular arts believe that the influence of those arts is intrinsic to them and hence universal; individual members of the "mass" may decide that they like or dislike a particular film or TV show, but this does not mean that the discrimination they are exercising is critical, for it does not and cannot extend to the medium itself, which continues to exert the same power over them.* This line of argument goes on to affirm that it is precisely because they participate in mass society and

---

*The argument might even be advanced that the unpopularity of many new culture industry products is itself evidence of the conservatism of an audience all too well conditioned by its previous media experiences.

are victims of mass culture that workers are incapable of revolutionary action. In which case, why even attempt to tell them about "their" culture in terms they can understand and put to use? It is the inherent nature of popular culture, in short, as it affects its proper audience, that precludes meaningful criticism addressed to that audience.

V

I think it is of enormous significance that the U.S. working class watches television. Any mass culture theory or critical method that attempts to provide an alternative to either of the brands of formalism I have been describing has to start from this thesis. Unfortunately, "significance" is a word susceptible of serious misunderstanding. Its unexamined use might even place me among the detached observers of social phenomena, "university professors and academic writers, people whom the power elite has relegated to the reservations of what passes as 'cultural life' and who consequently have resigned themselves to bear the unfortunate name of cultural critics."[7] When I say "significant," therefore, I should make it clear that I do not mean that it is another useful, inanimate fact to explain "mass society." I mean that the role of mass culture in working-class life is significant *to the working class*. And, for this reason, it is significant to anyone contemplating the realities and possibilities of revolutionary social change.

A number of commentators have discerned the connection between the experiences of work and leisure in advanced capitalism. Mass-culture forms become part of the process of reproducing labor power in that they help condition the worker for the job. These forms are packaged and distributed in units defined by time, and one's consciousness as a consumer comes to keep pace with the rhythm of the medium. On American TV, for example, commercial announcements come at what are usually predictable—and frequent—intervals within and between programs. Many people wait for these times to use the toilet; this phenomenon is common enough to make it possible to determine a program's relative popularity by the abrupt decline in the water-supply level at the precise point when its commercial pauses occur! For this reason, a regular viewer of commercial television may undergo a certain discomfort while watching a lengthy program on public TV, where the only breaks are short ones between programs; subconsciously, the viewer is still waiting for the "commercial" before going to the toilet.

There is a real analogy, here, with the patterning of a worker's time on the job, or with the very definition of a job as the commodity labor-power sold in time-defined units. Nor does the similarity consist solely in a wry metaphor about how many hours a day—on and off the job—the boss controls our smallest bodily functions. The entire process of viewing television (or experiencing any other mass medium) represents an extension of work into "private life." The vital link is the control.

But this sort of analysis is both limited and defeatist. If the media, through their influence on consciousness, have established a continuity between the job and leisure-time, then it is of the greatest urgency that we understand that "leisure" experience in all its complexity. The subject of work under capitalism has been extensively studied by revolutionary theorists because it is clear that the social relations of production encompass the most brutal oppression of working people and also the means of overcoming it. There is no reason to assume that the behavioral and ideological control the ruling class wields through mass culture is any likelier to be one-dimensional than the power it exerts on the shop floor.

The history of the working class in recent times, its failure to respond like a collection of stupefied, consumerist robots to the events of those years, would suggest a far different hypothesis. In fact, there is every reason to assume that leisure experiences, like work experiences, have a dialectical nature. How else can we explain the restlessness, the refusals, the rebellion that constitute the other side of the contradiction? How do we interpret the rejection of the media by some of its intended victims? How do we understand the use of pop culture to express the liberatory aspirations of other consumers?[8] And what can we do to neutralize or even transform the undeniably destructive effects of mass culture?

My own work starts from the unstartling assumption that both media and daily life have content, as well as form, that they are specific, as well as general. You do a job and its name is machinist or file-clerk or assembler or housewife. It is true that you measure your labor in terms of time and take a part in social production. But it is also true that your job has its own specific patterns, its own collectivity or isolation, its own relations with coworkers and superiors. All these facts, which are particular, but not individual, contribute to shaping your consciousness, and entail a set of feelings and ideas about your experience.

You also watch television, and TV fiction shows you a great many people doing their jobs. It tells you what sorts of jobs people do and what sorts of people do them; what kinds of relations develop among fellow workers and what kinds between boss and subordinate; what boundaries exist between work and private life. It has developed a series of conventions for the portrayal of certain feelings connected with work—feelings like anger, hostility, or anxiety—and it has conventional patterns for the containment and resolution of those feelings.

Television has evolved a series of myths about the central aspects of daily life—sexuality, work, and family—and those myths intersect with life as we actually live it. As Enzensberger very aptly points out, a left critique that consigns all of this to the rubric of "ideological manipulation" is woefully inadequate and ultimately sterile; the complexity of people's response to seeing myths about themselves and their lives that they know to be untrue and yet accept as something beyond fiction cannot be so readily dismissed.[9] Yet the social influence is undeniable; the effect on the way people perceive their lives, and hence on what actions they are able to take, is incalculable. It seems to me essential to explore these myths and the life situations into which they are projected and to make the connections at least as intelligible to the viewers as the original television programs were. It is not a matter of simple "exposure," but of analysis, interpretation, synthesis—in short, of criticism.

The same question arises, of course, as occurred with regard to the study of high culture; if anything, now that the subject of the criticism is so immediate, it is even more incumbent on me to ask, "So what?" And the answer can hardly be sanguine. I have been discussing culture and work as if each person experiences them in isolation, outside of a social organization. And this model falls apart completely when I attempt to go beyond the atomized, individual situation to the collective action that could change the basis of power. In fact, once I begin to speak about working people as a *class* organizing into the self-realization expressed in that term, then the question of criticism also moves out of the sphere of the individual theorist and becomes a matter of political program. Until there is a working-class movement that can generate real social criticism, attempts at interpreting mass culture are bound to be fragmentary, misdirected, and elusive. But until that movement, in the course of its development, learns to look critically at cultural experience, it will remain trapped in the contradictions of that condition. This can be either a vicious circle or a dialogue since, at present, neither the criticism nor the movement is very far advanced.

Meanwhile, whenever I tell someone here in Buffalo—almost anyone who is not an academic specialist in media—that I am writing a critical book about television, the first reaction is concerned perplexity: "What's to write about *that?* Everybody knows it's just shit." One answer, I suppose, would be to say, "You watch it, don't you? What does that say about you?" I have found a different approach more valuable, though, for the work itself and for its future implications. I begin talking quietly about the book, the way it is trying to put together the pieces of what television tells about everyday life. It isn't long before I'm interrupted by the other person telling me I must have a chapter on this and be sure to include that and how they try to make us think. . . . They start helping me write the book they've just called a waste of my time, energy, and talent. And they provide the only trustworthy answer to my initial question about criticism: they show me, over and over, who needs it.

NOTES

1. The expanded functions and clientele of higher education since the Second World War are, of course, a national phenomenon, various aspects of which are addressed in Colin Greer, *The Great School Legend* (New York: Basic Books, 1972), Stanley Aronowitz, *False Promises: The Shaping of American Working Class Consciousness* (New York: McGraw-Hill, 1973) and Ivar Berg, *Education and Jobs: The Great Training Robbery* (New York: Praeger, 1970).

2. Max Horkheimer and Theodor W. Adorno, *Dialectic of Enlightenment,* trans. John Curry (1944; rpt. 1969 and trans. New York: Herder and Herder, 1972), p. xvi.

3. See, for instance, pp. 135 and 157.

4. Max Horkheimer, *Critical Theory,* trans. Matthew J. O'Connor, *et al.,* (1968; New York: Herder and Herder, 1972), p. 290.

5. Horkheimer and Adorno, p. 123.

6. I realize that there are important differences among the thinkers generally grouped together under the "Frankfurt School" label. I hope I am not caricaturing or slandering Adorno, Horkheimer, Marcuse, or any of their associates by this very general summary of a rich and complex set of ideas.

7. Hans Magnus Enzensberger, "The Industrialization of the Mind," in *The Consciousness Industry: On Literature, Politics and the Media,*

ed. Michael Roloff (New York: Seabury Press, 1974) p. 4. In context, this description is very much to the point, since it is part of an attack on Horkheimer and Adorno's term "culture industry," a concept that Enzensberger says reveals more about the social origins and the social functions of its users than it does about the phenomenon it is supposed to be labeling.

8. Some illustrations of what I mean may be found in Stanley Aronowitz's discussion of the way rock music embodies the liberatory aspirations of young workers (*False Promises*, Section 2) or in the article by "Wovoka" (*Radical America*, March 1975) about the connection of "Motown" music to the consciousness of black auto workers. I find both of these examples somewhat undialectical, in themselves, but they offer a refreshing corrective to the more common refusal to see this half of the picture at all.

9. Enzensberger, "Constituents of a Theory of the Media," in *The Consciousness Industry*, pp. 100–101. This is not intended in any way to discount the very real manipulation that goes on—much less the social power it represents.

PART TWO

Theory into Practice

Who's Afraid of A Room
of One's Own?

THE HUCKSTER congratulates me on attaining full humanity. Of course, I made myself ridiculous for a time back there, demanding equal rights and the vote, but now my emancipation is complete, and its badge, like a tiny torch of freedom, glows in my hand:

> You've got your own cigarette now, baby,
> You've come a long, long way.
> —Advertising jingle for "Virginia Slims"

Virginia Woolf's *A Room of One's Own* is forty years old this fall, and, by the deplorable sexual analogy that informs our culture, should be approaching the age of irreversible infertility.* But the experience of any woman who begins to inquire into her own condition at first recapitulates that of her predecessors, so that "for women writers, as for Negro, what others have said bears down on whatever they can say themselves."[1] New limitations have indeed given me the impatient feeling that our ancestresses "mismanaged their affairs very gravely," but in reopening her

*The original version of this essay was written in November of 1968. I revised it in January of 1970, and it was published in May 1972. Although I have tried to respect the historical integrity of the essay, I made some further revisions for this collection in June of 1977.

subject, Women and Fiction, I find, to reverse the analogy, that
Virginia Woolf's essay is still seminal and remains a logical starting place.

Although the cultural condition of woman has not changed in
substance, two areas that *A Room of One's Own* mentions only
incidentally—the realms of sexuality and politics—have seen the
emergence of some new possibilities, possibilities that could radically reshape more than our literature. I may not agree with that
other Virginia, the tobacco peddler, about how far my liberty has
already taken me, but if I had been alive when *A Room of One's
Own* was first published, the developments I discuss would not
have been part of my own formative experience. Virginia Woolf
speaks of straining off whatever was personal and accidental in
her impressions and so reaching "the pure oil of truth." The
experience of literature itself provides a standard by which to
measure the extent and effects of the changes that have already
occurred and those I believe are impending.

I

"No age," Virginia Woolf remarks, surveying the wealth of
written opinion on the Woman Question, "can ever have been as
stridently sex-conscious as our own." In an era of even greater
sexual candor, Woolf's notions of sex-consciousness appear
quaintly limited. She attributes male writers' preoccupation with
the subject and their new desire for self-assertion to a kind of
backlash, their defensive response to the militant struggle for
women's rights. It is true that the suffrage movement of the last
century was popularly identified with "free love." I think this is
only partially due to the movement's attack on traditional ideas
about "woman's place" or to the sexual liberation campaigns of
such radicals as Victoria Woodhull and Frances Wright. It is
more likely to have happened because mention of "woman"
evokes an immediate association with sexuality—almost despite

the context in which it occurs. (Göring used to say, "Whenever I hear the word 'culture' I reach for my gun." The analogy doesn't quite work if I were to say what most men reach for when they hear the word "woman," yet their response is equally reflexive.) Nonetheless, the sex-consciousness provoked by the struggle for suffrage was only rarely an explicit awareness of sexuality.

By contrast, the "revolution" in sexual mores that had only begun in 1928 makes our own period sex-conscious (even, to square the compound, self-consciously sex-conscious) in a sense whose principal focus *is* the bedroom. Permission to be unchaste has not freed women from the object-role we occupied when it was chastity that was the valued commodity. The standard is still imposed from without, and realization of one's femininity must still be achieved at the sacrifice of a fully liberated personality. Perhaps it is "one of the tokens of the fully developed mind that it does not think specially or separately of sex," yet the contradictory expectations women must live up to make such measured growth impossible. Fuller consideration of both the old chastity taboo and the contemporary ethic of free sex will perhaps illuminate our new double standard.

The most striking invention in *A Room of One's Own* is Shakespeare's gifted, doomed sister, who is frustrated and ultimately destroyed by the related limitations of sex and sexuality. Conventional notions of her social role defeat her as an artist, but it is her breach of the chastity taboo that is her final undoing. The poet Judith Shakespeare kills herself after her seduction and impregnation by Nick Greene, but the enforcement of chastity has already done its worst.

> No girl could have walked to London and stood at a stage door and forced her way into the presence of actor-managers without doing herself a violence and suffering an anguish which may have been irrational—for chastity may be a fetish invented by certain societies for unknown reasons—but were none the less inevitable. Chastity had then, it has even now, a religious importance in a woman's life, and has so wrapped itself around with nerves and

instincts that to cut it free and bring it to the light of day demands
courage of the rarest.[2]

Today, when it is equally damning to be considered "afraid of
sex" (that is, of sexuality), the courage required is far less, but in
either case women's sense of identity is still supposed to depend
upon sexual conformity.

Virginia Woolf is content to leave unexplored and unchallenged
those "unknown reasons" for the chastity fetish. But it is here
that the problem begins. According to one of Freud's most widely
accepted theories, the communal life of humanity had a twofold
foundation: "the compulsion to work, which was created by external necessity, and the power of love, which made the man
unwilling to be deprived of his sexual object—the woman—, and
made the woman unwilling to be deprived of the part of herself
which had been separated off from her—her child."[3] This is a
description of only one way of reconciling erotic drives with the
"reality principle." It is the mode characteristic of the stage we
may, with Freud, call "civilization," only as long as that term has
descriptive rather than normative value. For our ancestors experienced a number of social forms before the establishment of the
monogamous family, with its insistence on female chastity. In
fact, the earliest communities might not have survived if our
forebears had, as Freud suggests, so conflated the experiences of
loving and owning as to desire exclusive rights over the "object"
of love. "Mutual toleration among the adult males, freedom from
jealousy, was . . . the first condition for the building of those
large and enduring groups in the midst of which alone the transition from animal to man could be achieved."[4]

Only when property began to be individually owned and subject to inheritance was the assignment of children to particular
parents a necessity. As long as the value of the mother's work
entitled her to participate in such ownership, it was unnecessary
to be certain who was a child's father in order to assure its rights

of inheritance. But when the division of labor made the home the woman's sphere, while the realm that produced the wealth was the man's even if she worked in it too, property had to descend along the male line. Thus, Engels maintains that the overthrow of "mother-right," or inheritance via the female line, was "the world-historic defeat of the female sex" and the origin of male supremacy. "Monogamy arose out of the concentration of considerable wealth in the hands of one person—and that a man—and out of the desire to bequeath . . . [his] wealth to this man's children and to no one else's. For this purpose, monogamy was essential on the woman's part, but not on the man's."[5] It is not difficult to see from this how the same principle came to be applied to premarital chastity and how female virginity was reified into a commodity. Virginia Woolf herself accepts the whole sex–family–property relation when she speaks of the material deserts of the gentleman to whom the first "letter" in *Three Guineas* is addressed and defines his prosperity as consisting in "wife, children, house."[6]

It was in the Victorian period, when the Woman Question went public, that the contradictions in the female condition were most explicitly identified with both class and property. The dual functions of physical pleasure and material security were separated and assigned to different women. Frigidity in one's wife, interpreted as assurance of fidelity, was the safeguard of respectability, while seduction or rape of a lower-class woman provided the double enjoyments of sensuality and ownership.[7] Sexual availability and the concomitant capacity to enjoy it were hallmarks of lower-class women. This attitude is carried to an extreme and reduced to unconscious absurdity in the later novels of Henry James, where the unchaste woman is not a wanton servant girl but a society woman whose poverty is entirely relative, noticeable only in the rarefied circles in which she moves. For such women as Kate Croy or Charlotte Stant, their comparative poverty "not only accompanies sexuality, but appears to cause it."[8] Edith Wharton's *House of Mirth* makes this implicit causality more credible. Lily Bart has been forced by her dependent status to use sexual potential as a means of social advancement. But the increasingly compromising situations in which she is entangled are actually the result of her financial need and only superficially of the flirtations that are its symptom. Even where this link between poverty and unsanctioned sexual behavior is not so direct, some man's assumption of the *droit du seigneur* creates a classic situation in the English novel from *Pamela* and *Fanny Hill* on.

Now by 1928, it was no longer possible to objectify a "nice fresh servant" as completely as does the Victorian author of *My Secret Life* when he describes the class as "ready, yielding, hot-arsed, lewd, and lubricious." Nor was it possible to make corollary generalizations about the virtue and unresponsiveness of "ladies." But more than a trace of the attitude remains in Virginia Woolf, as she discusses the widening opportunity for a young woman novelist to observe and describe "the courtesan, the harlot, and the lady with the pug dog." A female writer, she acknowledges, is better fitted than any man to portray these women, but even with the best will in the world, we are not yet ready for her to do so. For some time to come, the writer "will still be encumbered with that self-consciousness in the presence of 'sin' which is the legacy of our sexual barbarity. She will still bear the shoddy old fetters of *class* on her feet."[9] The italics are mine, but it is Woolf who takes it for granted that the difference between a woman who is sexually selective and one who is not is a matter of class.

Well, there, you might say, is one substantive change wrought by the Sexual Revolution—a social pattern so radically altered as to justify leaving off the inverted commas around the word revolution. At first glance, this is certainly true. It is no longer possible to use considerations of class status to draw any conclusions about a particular woman's capacity for sexual enjoyment or the likelihood of her indulging it. In another sense, though, chastity remains as much of a class *determinant* among women today as it ever was. I first realized this by considering a rather bizarre but entirely apt model. A friend (male and black) was describing how, as an isolated civil rights worker confined in a Southern jail, he did serious political work among his fellow prisoners. The focus of his story was the interest he was able to arouse among men whose initial attitude toward him was overtly hostile. As he spoke, I recalled similar stories about prisons that became schools of political action—in Ireland, in Algeria, and increasingly, in our own country. I began romanticizing my own future as a politically aware convict. As I write, I am awaiting trial for two political crimes that could earn me fifteen months behind bars.* For a brief moment, I rather relished the image of myself at the House of Detention, or Bedford Hills, helping to define the inmates' awareness of our oppressed condition and focus my sisters' anger. But almost before I began, I felt there were barriers to a sense of sisterhood, barriers that gave the word itself an unfamiliar flavor that even "brotherhood" does not have.

I tried to analyze the obstacles that might prevent me from sharing a basis of trust with other imprisoned women—most of them prostitutes. There is a difference, and it is based ultimately on sexual behavior. My "respectability," or their probable reaction to it, is the only seemingly insuperable barrier. At best, I

---

*In 1968, I had two charges pending, carrying a maximum total sentence of fifteen months. I began revising the essay in 1970 just after New Year's Day, by which time one of those charges had been dropped, the other settled by plea-bargaining with a fine and a permanent record of my fingerprints. Before the month ended I faced two more charges and the possibility of 60 days in jail; that time I got probation. I have not been arrested since. This history says something about the high energy of the period in which my first feminist essay was written, but a great deal more about the issues of sex and class with which I was trying to grapple in it. In the '70s, as it has become somewhat less likely that "respectable" women like me will be imprisoned, American prisons have indeed become schools of political action, with a seriousness and dedication that make my adventurist fantasies seem wholly frivolous. Nonetheless, it is never inappropriate or exaggerated to imagine oneself as a political prisoner and to prepare to meet that experience with honor.

would benefit from a kindness that says, "You're a 'nice' girl; you don't belong here." At worst, I would be playing a missionary's role and would deserve a missionary's martyrdom. But what really creates this frontier that women themselves police? Education, of course, and my being a teacher. My "idealism" might get in the way, too, since I'd be in jail for what might look like an esoteric *and freely chosen* offense. But I did not opt to be an activist any more than a prostitute has selected her profession. Objective conditions—the same objective conditions— determined both our "choices." Our common situation as women and our shared circumstances might, in the long run, provide grounds for unity that are more persuasive than any divisions among us. But it is interesting that I had even a momentary hesitation and that the word "sister" retains an uneasy ring. The mystification surrounding our sex is so compelling that a woman who is convicted of a "crime" and imprisoned is far more degraded than a man in the same position. It is this same mystique that made me think that the apparent gap between me and my sister inmates would be created by my "respectability," a quality that is defined by the Man, but that women are all too ready to enforce.

My own chastity is at best a relative matter, consisting principally in the exercise of a veto power. What makes the difference—and would continue to do so in a place where no man appeared for weeks on end—is how men treat me, as contrasted with how they treat prostitutes. Or how one *would* treat us if he were present. My self-respect does not depend on some notion of my fancied superiority to other women, but it does to some extent depend on being respected by others. And of course the way others treat you derives in large measure from your own expectations. Mother always said that girls who cheapened themselves lost all self-respect. And so they do—if not in the way she meant it.

Virginia Woolf, musing on the female condition, says, "I

thought how unpleasant it is to be locked out; and I thought how it is worse perhaps to be locked in.'' My little fantasy about prison life makes her metaphor rather uncomfortably concrete, but still true to the double imprisonment resulting from actual incarceration and from the social condition of women. We are supposed not to like—or to trust—each other, and the basis for our antipathy is our purportedly permanent competition for a mate. The greatest mutual suspicion exists, however, among women with different life styles, where that is a matter of sexual behavior. It has usually been women who maintained the distinctions and created the bitterness, but never we who ordained the system. A couple of generations back, I would have been relegated to the class of whores and excluded from the company of suburban housewives. Now I have a greater latitude—men have made it possible for me to be unchaste and remain in the category of ''good women.'' But although membership has shifted, the categories themselves remain, and my ''freedom'' does nothing for the women still excluded by male fiat from the ranks of the ''respectable.''

As I reread what I have written, I realize that I have been playing with the connotations of ''class'' and ''caste.'' It would be more exact, though clumsier, to say that sexual behavior both constitutes and reflects the material conditions that underlie a class analysis. Unexamined use of the concepts of caste and class does not much illuminate what remains a vexed question among women trying to define our situation. Yet it is important to consider how these terms can help describe it.

When Virginia Woolf says that class makes the world of sexual ''sin'' unfamiliar to her, she is literally correct in that her economic status protects her from having to earn her living as a prostitute. But her class identification is precarious and, as an attribute acquired by association, it differs from the usual factors through which economic relations determine class. In *Three Guineas,* she speaks about the shared ''background'' that would appear to place her in the same class as her male interlocutor. But there is a gap between them that she at first perceives as a difference in privilege, signaled by her having to use an awkward formula to describe herself. "Our ideology is still so inveterately anthropocentric that it has been necessary to coin this clumsy term—educated man's daughter—to describe the class whose fathers have been educated at public schools and universities. Obviously, if the term 'bourgeois' fits her brother, it is grossly incorrect to use it of one who differs so profoundly in the two prime characteristics of the bourgeoisie—capital and environment."[10]

For this reason, one tendency among present-day feminists is simply to make class coextensive with sex. Theoretical justification for this position is sought in such observations as Engels's that "the first division of labour is that between man and woman for child breeding . . . I can add: The first class antagonism which appears in history coincides with the development of the antagonism between man and woman in monogamous marriage, and the first class oppression with that of the female sex by the male."[11] But coincidence is not identity; it is because the institution of slavery appeared simultaneously with the monogamous family and in response to the same economic conditions that the relation can be made. Only by analogy can a class description be applied to the family, in which, because of their respective relations to production, the husband is the bourgeois whereas his wife represents the proletariat.[12] To rely on this, however, is once more to elevate metaphor to the status of argument.

At one point, Virginia Woolf goes so far as to address the educated British male as a member of an opposed class: "Your class possesses in its own right and not through marriage practically all the capital, all the land, all the valuables, and all the patronage in England. Our class possesses in its own right and not through marriage practically none of the capital, none of the land, none of the valuables, and none of the patronage in England."[13] Woolf comes closer here to a materialist definition of class than many who depend on citations of Marxist texts, for she recognizes control of the means of production as the basis of oppressive power. A contemporary Radical Feminist position correctly defines all women as oppressed, but does not take into account that, while those few who own the wealth are men, most men do not control any of it. In material terms, it is insufficient merely to allege that all men benefit from a system of male supremacy, and if we are not to use materialist standards, why bring in a term like "class" at all?

The question of caste arises when we acknowledge that women can acquire a class affiliation from their fathers or husbands and that this identity is functional. This "secondary" affiliation shapes our lives to the extent that Virginia Woolf could, after all, afford to be a writer and not a streetwalker. When Lenin speaks of "women . . . worn out in petty, monotonous household work, their strength and time dissipated and wasted, their minds growing narrow and stale, their hearts beating slowly, their will weakened," he specifically exempts the pampered ladies of the bourgeoisie "who shove onto servants the responsibility for all household work, including the care of children."[14] Yet his description of the psychological effects of women's work is closely echoed in Virginia Woolf's description of the lives of bourgeois women deprived of the privileges of "their" class. As for the exercise of power, she believes that "the daughters of educated men" are at a real disadvantage. "Not only are we incomparably weaker than the men of our own class; we are weaker than the women of the working class. If the working women of the country were to say: 'If you go to war, we will refuse to make munitions or to help in the production of goods,' the difficulty of war-making would be seriously increased." But economic conditions deprive working women of the freedom to exercise this imputed power. This kind of mutual misapprehension—attributing to some other class of women the power one feels deprived of—is one factor that serves to divide women.

Many American women today who are themselves educated

and who, by paternity or marriage, are "middle class" hold jobs and receive salaries that are definitely "working class." Their primary identification is with their acquired status, even when they perceive the frustrating contradiction they are acting out and when they suffer its cultural and material consequences. Among working women, a similiar tendency creates an artificial "class" barrier between clerical employees and those who do factory or domestic work. On a level that is personal as well as economic, there is mutual envy and suspicion between women who are "free" to be exploited on a job and those who are "free" to stay home and be oppressed there. For a vulgar Marxist analysis, the factors of status and group identification simply contribute to false consciousness; class is determined by the individual's relations to production. But because a woman's relation to social production is often at one remove, we must consider very carefully what other elements constitute the *material* basis of women's lives.

It is in this sense that forms of sexual behavior create material barriers best understood as class-based. Engels claims that "among women, prostitution degrades only those unfortunates who fall into its clutches; and even these are not degraded to the degree that is generally believed. On the other hand, it degrades the character of the entire male world."[15] On an abstract moral plane Engels may be right, but the transformation into social norm of the economics underlying monogamy has a far more degrading and divisive effect among women. This conflict has a class nature and, as the most cursory glance at "our" literature reveals, is one of the most enduring divisions among women. Yet, I have sisters who are prostitutes; no man who buys a woman is my brother.

Lenin himself perceived the ways in which all women share a common condition: "We hate, yes hate everything, and will abolish everything which tortures and oppresses the woman worker, the housewife, the peasant woman, the wife of the petty

trader, yes, and in many cases the women of the possessing classes."[16] An unexamined "class" division among women becomes
like any artificial contradiction imposed upon members of a subject group so that they cannot see that their true interests are
identical. Black and white workers, male and female workers, in
this country have been so divided as, historically, were white
workers of different ethnic backgrounds. Withdrawing sexuality
from the realm of material considerations and accepting it on its
own terms is the only way we can liberate ourselves from destructive isolation. And it is the only way the whole race can
begin to realize its full erotic possibilities.

But what does that mean, "sexuality on its own terms"? The
erotic dimension of freedom leads to consideration of the other
side of the coin, the new morality that is supposed to have liberated me and that has at least allowed me to indulge myself sexually and retain my social standing. What the Sexual Revolution
has actually done is to establish a new bartering system, on the
premise that one kind of freedom can only be won at the sacrifice
of another; fulfillment "as a woman" (orgasm, childbearing,
motherhood) is made to substitute for, and is seen as qualitatively
different from, fulfillment as a person. The new rules owe a great
deal, of course, to Freudian theories and prejudices. Freud attributes the fundamental female conflict to the "momentous discovery which little girls are destined to make," recognition of
their own natural inferiority to males because of their lack of a
penis. Psychic difficulties arise as a result of the two-phase sexual
life that women lead, because, as they mature, their focus is
supposed to move from the clitoris (a truncated "masculine"
organ) to the vagina; the first phase thus "has a masculine character, while only the second is specifically feminine."[17] Two
different kinds of orgasms are purportedly experienced in the two
zones: clitoral orgasm is immature, reflecting adherence to one's
innate masculine qualities, the masculinity complex, and the undeveloped male organ; vaginal orgasm is the reflection of mature

femininity. According to Marie Bonaparte, intellectual rejection of this two-orgasm descriptive model is also symptomatic of that pathetic "claimant" [of male privilege], the "clitoridal" woman.[18] They do get us coming and going!

Freud does not, as far as I know, explicitly recommend that women interpret acceptance of femininity as acceptance of a passive *social* role, but he condemns all female efforts to formulate another role. I say "condemns" advisedly, because his strictures do not stop with merely stigmatizing certain behavior as reflecting the castration complex, but rather develop into normative statements. Thus he says, "behind the envy for the penis, there comes to light the woman's hostile bitterness against the man, which never completely disappears in the relations between the sexes, and which is clearly indicated in the strivings and in the literary productions of 'emancipated' women."[19] (Freud's setting off of "emancipated" is rather like the promiscuous know-nothing use of "so-called" but in this case it is ironically apt; there is indeed no such thing as an emancipated woman.) It does occur to Freud that males also are convinced of the superiority of having a penis and that the oppression of women has something to do with male fear of castration, but he quickly dismisses the idea.

Similarly, he does not consider the ways in which culture reinforces the woman's initial sense of being permanently without something very important. Freud apparently cannot credit that any of the freedoms and privileges of human (that is, masculine) life have intrinsic as well as symbolic value. A little girl may want to be a boy because it seems to her that boys and men have better lives than girls and women; even if it were the castration complex, theirs or ours, that has given the male his dominant role, it could also follow that to someone who envies that role, possession of a penis is symbolic of *it* and not vice versa. In any event, we are "bitter" and again our bitterness has no content; it is only the continuation of our first reaction to not having a penis.

The most distressing thing about the Freudian attitude is that it disarms criticism by asserting that female attempts to take issue with the theory are merely further demonstrations of the castration complex. Freud anticipates arguments in favor of the male masculinity complex from women analysts and their male colleagues with feminist views, but says that it is "quite natural that the female sex should refuse to accept a view which appears to contradict their eagerly coveted equality with men." Worse yet, the utilization of one's mind to dispute Freud's arguments shows "masculine" aggressiveness and competitiveness. Again, arguments have no content, only form. And "the use of psychoanalysis as a weapon of controversy can clearly lead to no decision."[20] In short, don't show *him* any evidence—particularly if you're a woman and can't be "objective" about the implications of the penis envy theory.

Freudians are thus quick to see the castration complex in female "literary productions" with a positive thrust of any sort; they shake their heads like Virginia Woolf watching the Manx cat and marvel that "it is strange what a difference a tail makes."[21] A woman I know mentioned Carolyn Heilbrun's perceptive *New York Times* review of Mary Ellmann's *Thinking About Women* to her analyst; in it, the reviewer alludes to Freud's responsibility for our present predicament. "She is obviously," snapped the doctor, "a typical neurotic spinster with a castration complex." Since Freud also "freed" us from some of our guilt about sexuality, a new norm of the fulfilled woman appears, such that one can "see" not only penis envy in some women's intellectual efforts but also perhaps frigidity, homosexuality, or virginal frustration. The fact of one's writing in a critical way is often "proof" enough—if one's sex life were all right, one wouldn't need to do so. An extreme (but not isolated) case of this attitude is reflected in a female listener's letter to a radio film-reviewer. Addressing her as "Miss," which she clearly considers an insult in itself, the listener remarks, "I assume you aren't married—one loses that nasty, sharp bite in one's voice when one learns to care about others." Altruism is obviously the result of a satisfactory sex life. "Mrs. John Doe and her sisters who write to me," says the broadcaster,

> seem to interpret Freud to mean that intelligence, like a penis, is a male attribute. The true woman is supposed to be sweet and passive—she shouldn't argue or emphasize an opinion or get excited about a judgment. Sex—or at least regulated marital sex—is supposed to act as a tranquilizer. . . . [In this sense, popular Freudianism goes] beyond Victorianism in its placid assumption that a woman who uses her mind is trying to compete with men. It was bad enough for women who had brains to be considered freaks like talking dogs; now it's leeringly assumed that they're trying to grow a penis—which any man will tell you is an accomplishment that puts canine conversation in the shadows.[22]

So we are freer to enjoy sexuality but jeopardize our capacity for enjoyment if we try to do anything else as well. Which may explain why the Sexual Revolution is not only a failure but is neither essentially sexual nor a revolution.

In this regard, even considerations of what "free" sexuality might be like reflect a kind of blind spot where women are concerned that makes their projections rather hard to visualize. Herbert Marcuse, for instance, speaks of such freedom as involving "not simply a release but a *transformation* of the libido: from sexuality constrained under genital supremacy to eroticization of the entire personality. . . . The free development of transformed libido within transformed institutions, while eroticizing previously tabooed zones, times, and relations, would *minimize* the manifestations of *mere* sexuality by integrating it into a far larger order, including the order of work."[23]

I fail to see how the social oppression of women can be made consistent with *anyone's* discovery of the liberated Eros in a nonrepressive society, but so it must remain as long as meaningful work for women is interpreted simply as "competition" rather than unalienated production. Marcuse's study ignores this question, which could lead to the comfortable conclusion that when he speaks of a new mode of being for humanity he means all of us. A volume, however, that is subtitled "A Philosophical Inquiry into Freud" must not remain silent if its author rejects one of the good doctor's principal assumptions. As it is, I am uncertain whether I am allowed to imagine myself as part of that potentially free humanity about which Marcuse is so eloquent. Marcuse foresees the release of homoerotic as well as heterosexual feelings, without mentioning women's place at all, or, on the other hand, giving us the sense that we are so completely and necessarily involved in his new structures that it would be superfluous to speak of us separately or specifically. (Virginia Woolf found Woman almost entirely absent from the pages of history and thus felt bewildered as she read. I often fail to recognize myself in psychological or philosophical works in which Woman appears, yet when she is not present at all I sometimes feel like a tactless intruder.)

Freud himself, while encouraging women to live a fully mature (that is, vaginal) sex life, would question our fitness for the broader range of experiences Marcuse postulates, not only because we should eschew self-assertive competition but also because we cannot maintain a moral standard established by and for men. We in the West have a long (though by no means unchallenged) history of maintaining that women have souls and thus have the same degree of final responsibility as men. Our culture has an ambiguous tradition with regard to the relative corruptibility of each sex, and makes some allowances for weakness, but does not apply a double standard to ethical expectations. Freud, however, suggests that "for women the level of what is ethically normal is different from what it is in men." His reasoning is that in boys the Oedipus complex is destroyed by the castration complex, whereas in girls it is preceded and caused by the castration complex. This means that girls lack incentive to destroy the Oedipus complex, with devastating results:

Their super-ego is never so inexorable, so impersonal, so independent of its emotional origins as we find it in men. Character traits which critics of every epoch have brought up against women—that they show less sense of justice than men, that they are less ready to submit to the great exigencies of life, that they are more often influenced in their judgments by the feelings of affection or hostility—all these would be amply accounted for by the modification in the formation of the super-ego which we have inferred above. We must not allow ourselves to be deflected from such conclusions by the denials of the feminists, who are anxious to force us to regard the two sexes as completely equal in position and worth; but we shall, of course, willingly agree that the majority of men are also far behind the masculine ideal and that all human individuals, as a result of their bisexual disposition and of cross-inheritance, combine in themselves both masculine and feminine characteristics, so that pure masculinity and femininity remain theoretical constructions of uncertain content.[24]

Here again, as in the case of possible feminist disagreement with his analysis of penis envy, Freud puts into operation a kind of psychic Uncertainty Principle intended to discredit objections. His logic reminds me of the old Jewish joke about the two neighbors who go to court over a broken vase, which ends with the defendant's lawyer trying to prove conclusively "that Schwartz never borrowed from Weiss the vase, that it was cracked when Weiss lent it to him, and anyway he returned it in perfect condition."[25] For if we point out that many women are no more unjust or emotional than many men, a Freudian can always fall back on the master's notion of human bisexuality. The important thing to remember is that the weaker side, the one functioning on the lower ethical level, is the feminine one, so that a woman's strengths come from the masculine admixture in her personality, while a man's flaws are from the presence of feminine traits in his.

In this instance, too, Freud ignores the effects of cultural expectations on character. The weakness and emotionalism of women is encouraged—sometimes we are even taught to use it as a weapon—whereas that of men is suppressed. We are taught to have different ideas about what constitute the great exigencies of life and to respond accordingly. Intuitive judgment is regarded as our natural substitute for reason, and we are brought up to rely on it.

Although I have cited his writings so often, Freud himself is not the culprit we are up against. His ideas are simultaneously a product or symptom of a cultural evil and a force to justify and perpetuate it. But he and his followers have offered women immense and fraudulent sexual rewards for embracing and (womanlike) rearranging all the dollhouse furniture on which Nora Helmer slammed that door.

II

Which brings us back at last to literature. Freud takes it as evidence of his theories that women have been assigned certain traits "in every epoch." We know this, of course, from what men have written about women. And the whole point of *A Room of One's Own* is, after all, that for most of that time women had no literary voice of their own. We do not know how they lived, let alone what they would have considered their own dominant characteristics and those of their men. Even in our own time, a serious female writer delineating a masculine failing is likely to be accused of almost everything but attempting to speak the truth. Woolf mentions her astonishment "when Z, most humane, most modest of men, taking up some book by Rebecca West and reading a passage in it, exclaimed, 'The arrant feminist! She says that men are snobs!' " They are not ready to listen to us, but how often, since finding our tongues, have we had something significant to say about men?

English literature, in the engaging person of Virginia Woolf's Orlando, turned female sometime in the eighteenth century, when the novel became a potent literary force. For the purpose of speaking about a room of one's own is precisely that women writers, confined for both subject matter and a work-space to the common family sitting room, chose the novel as the most appropriate literary medium. And the novel has consistently attracted a wider female audience than any other genre. Our greatest nineteenth-century novelists, Jane Austen and the Brontës, bring women characters to a kind of prominence different from any they previously enjoyed. They have almost nothing to say about men, however—flattering or deprecating—because the male as such was almost an unknown quantity to them. (I say "as such" because they obviously were aware of certain types that exist in the ranks of both sexes.) Mr. Darcy, Mr. Rochester, and Heathcliff—the ones who spring most readily to mind—all represent similar solutions to the problem of depicting a hero. If he is defined a priori as "remote," it is already attractive to the romantic mind, and it becomes unnecessary to put him into quite as many situations that would reveal his creator's ignorance about him. If this sounds flippant, it nonetheless makes more sense than dismissing all such figures as a maiden lady's Byronic masturbation fantasies.

Consider, too, these authors' other male figures. Edgar Linton and St. John Rivers are halfhearted constructions, not merely in contrast to the brooding heroes of the books in which they appear, but also because it is impossible to see around the particular literary functions they serve to a full range of human qualities. They are quite as inscrutable as their dark, brooding rivals, but embarrassingly inadequate without the cloak of mystery the others wear. The men good enough for most Jane Austen heroines to marry are similarly undistinguished, especially when measured against the women they eventually win. Her male figures, whether good or bad, are caricatures, what an earlier age would have called humor-characters. Two exceptions, one in each category, are Henry Crawford and Henry Tilney. Crawford is the most interesting man in Jane Austen, but he is also unbalanced, inconsistent, poorly motivated, and hard to believe in. Tilney, although not a fully developed character, is perhaps the one male portrait the novelist could fill in from her own experience: I strongly suspect that the hero of this novel in which three important brother-sister pairs occur was modeled on the author's own brothers.[26]

I have separated George Eliot from the other three "famous names" with whom Woolf classes her. I did so in part because I could not make the same generalization about her experience of men. More important, I think her male characters should be considered with those of later women novelists. It seems to me that writers as different from each other as George Eliot, Edith Wharton, Doris Lessing, Mary McCarthy, and Virginia Woolf herself succeed with two principal types of men, the womanish and the weak. (And I do not mean to identify these two qualities.) In general, if one had to form a conception of man from his appearances in women's writings, he would turn out a spineless creature, one who needs mothering and whose weakness is yet more sadistic than overt strength. It is the element of sadomasochism, in fact, that puts relationships these women depict in quite another tradition from the Erring-Male-Set-Straight-by-Good-Woman myth that recurs from Dante through Louisa May Alcott to Johnny Cash. This cruel, weak man, whom every woman recognizes as a genuine and familiar type, does not appear in the novels of male authors until quite recently and then as an antihero. Even so, he is treated from a masculine point of view, and we are shown his sufferings rather than what he does to others.

Women novelists not only introduced this man into our literature but have been almost obsessed with him. I can only speculate about some of the reasons for this preoccupation. Is it possible that such men are especially attracted and appealing to women who are free enough of their socialization to become writers at all? The parasitic dominance of Doris Lessing's men, for example, could not be fruitfully exercised over a woman who was *not* gifted and "independent." The woman novelist may, because of those very characteristics that make her a novelist, have even more (extraliterary) experience of this man than the rest of us. Furthermore, being able to put him in a book gives her more definitive control over the situation than she is likely to have in life. Literary treatment of such a character is also a form of protest against a tradition that prepared one for almost anything in a lover but this preponderant type. I don't mean to imply that a woman's creation of literature is an aberration whose symptoms may be deduced from consideration of particular works; the corollary to such a clinical approach is to discard the specific work once we have determined the "ailment" it points to. What I do think is important is that, as Simone de Beauvoir expresses it, even our greatest women writers "in men . . . comprehend hardly more than the male." That is, they are reacting to their experience, and their reactions have a common imbalance. In this sense, it is worthwhile for the reader who wishes to know what to make of a widespread male character-type to inquire about its real and fictional antecedents. Such inquiry may also help explain why female novelists have failed to direct their attention to the full range of masculine possibilities.

But what of women in fiction? Have novelists of their own sex added to the range of types or the dimensions of personality presented by men? An answer requires first of all some consideration of male writers' portrayal of women. Virginia Woolf says that between the reader and a female character an obtrusive figure always blocks the view, the figure of the masculine "I." Women do dominate the scene, however, in the writings of some men; the problem is how they do so, whether the author, in showing us what goes on in his heroine's mind, is showing us anything like the mind of an actual human female. As I look for examples to help answer this question, I am amazed at how many writers have chosen to evade it by externalizing the psychological situation, using "objective" images that convey the pattern or content of a woman's thought without actually entering into it. The experi-

ences of Emma Bovary and Anna Karenina, to name two eminently successful literary creations, are realized for us in this
way.

In the fiction of Henry James, women are more delicately cali-
brated instruments for the reception of impressions than men—
more so, at least, than any man who is represented as being an
active *and sexually potent* participant in events. His women's
special sensitivity is reflected in an awareness of social or moral
nuances so fine as to be unobserved (in fact, unimagined) by the
average person. Although I cannot quite imagine James saying,
"Isabel Archer—*c'est moi,*" he does give the impression of
strong identification with some of the women he writes about. We
so readily see the author himself as the archetypal asexual James-
ian observer that there is a tendency to say that he "doesn't
count." But however little he may have counted as a man, he had
never had the sexual or psychic experience of being a woman;
there is no reason why someone of James's temperament should
find it easier than other men to imagine what it would be like to be
female in a given situation. (Indeed, the only comparison that can
be made along this line is a negative one with the self-consciously
masculine novelist who is so uneasy about his virility that he feels
it threatened by even attempting such an identification.) Despite
the acuteness of James's observations, he does not give his
women a wider scope than those who are less perceptive about
female psychology. They are still principally shown, as Virginia
Woolf claimed most female characters are, in their relations with
men.

The question of the author's identification with his character
suggests the peculiar problem of point of view. Very few first-
person narratives are related by a character whose sex is not the
same as the author's. The necessity, in such a case, of delving
into a mind of such different configuration from one's own, and of
having fewer ways of masking one's ignorance about it, has kept
most writers from making the attempt. Almost all the instances I
can think of are, for one reason or another, rather special cases.

There are the epistolary novels of the eighteenth century, some of which involve the author in psychologizing. Although the novelist does have to adopt the persona of a woman, the letter form still provides some measure of protection, for the most prolix letter writer is holding something back, presenting herself as a character. Moreover, the role assigned such young women as Pamela and Clarissa is not simply exaggerated; it is mythic. A diametrically opposite archetype is embodied in such figures as Fanny Hill (whose narrative is still nominally epistolary) and Moll Flanders. These characters serve their purpose by being women as men wish them to be, not guides to the feminine psyche. To my mind, keener psychological penetration is demonstrated in the letters from women in *Les Liaisons dangereuses,* for these characters—however distinctly "typed" they are—do have as much independence and vigor as the men whose epistles alternate with theirs. The alternating male-female point of view, even when less ambitious, is rarely this successful. Mark Twain's "Diary of Adam and Eve," whose whole point is to demonstrate something about comparative psychology, is an embarrassing failure constructed of platitudes veneered with wit and culminating in a genteel, domestic truism. Another case, Cesare Pavese's *Among Women Only,* succeeds precisely because the female narrator does not pretend to reveal anything about psychology but rather to make a point through the flat recital of events. The tone of the novel is deliberately colorless, and the dominant mood of its characters is alienation. As long as alienation is his subject, it is no *more* ambitious for Pavese to assume the voice of Clelia than, say, for Camus to assume that of Meursault. Another problem is that of the female in a stream-of-consciousness narrative as practiced by Faulkner or Joyce, but here again the identification is incomplete and the narrator, far from being individuated by the author's use of her point of view, is actually *generalized,* mythologized.

Much masculine investigation of women's minds is of this formulaic sort. Speaking as a psychoanalyst, Theodor Reik says,

"Why do we men not understand women even though they give us so much material by which to know them? We see them, we hear them, we even smell them, but all this is not enough because we can never be women. We always conclude that women understand men, but men don't understand women. It is one-way traffic."[27] But the heart of Virginia Woolf's objection to male domination of literature is not that female psychology is unexplored but rather that so much experience is omitted, women being present in books almost exclusively as the lovers of men. She is delighted to find in a young woman's first novel the typical line "Chloe liked Olivia," because it opens up a whole new realm of literary possibility. Friendship, particularly of the special sort shared by those who work together, is a relationship entirely neglected by men writing about women. It is only partly male ignorance of women's self-contained culture that is responsible for this neglect. More often, it is cultural bias about women's relations with one another: we "don't like" each other and we don't, of course, have work of the kind that provides meaningful experience with one's colleagues. (For some reason, men do not regard women at the village well or the city laundromat as colleagues who share a job.) The typical male assumption is embodied in the remark that arouses Reik's professional chuckle: "She is an exceptional woman. She is beautiful and warm. Even women like her in spite of her qualities." Another of Reik's patients says, "I would like to meet a young woman who is not an exception. Most women I know say they are not like other women, they are exceptions. I would like to know a young woman who says she thinks and feels just as women do." But despite the irritation that certain women provoke in us, I suspect our constant competition is more legend than fact. The goal that Virginia Woolf ironically articulates, "the development by the average woman of a prose style completely expressive of her mind," is not calculated to place the woman writer in an elite position with respect to the rest of her sex—nor yet to make a freak of her. Self-hatred does work to give some women desperate confidence in their uniqueness; but for each one who speaks of herself as an exception, there are many of us who are outraged when men tell us how free we are of the stereotyped sins of our sex. (It never occurs to them to alter the stereotype, and they cannot understand why we are not flattered by being exempted from it.)

Despite Chloe and Olivia, Virginia Woolf was perhaps premature in her belief that women were now truly able to expand their literary horizons. She speaks of being free to explore new subjects, almost free from bitterness about the female role or about men. "She wrote as a woman," says Woolf of her composite young novelist, "but as a woman who has forgotten that she is a woman, so that her pages were full of that curious sexual quality which comes only when sex is unconscious of itself." The typical novel of which Virginia Woolf speaks is meaningfully entitled *Life's Adventure,* but in inventing it she spoke too soon. Literature follows history, it does not shape it, and the predicament of women has not allowed us to forget our sex or even to write without awareness of the Woman Question. The women of whom we write are still struggling to define themselves *as* women; life's other adventures are inevitably encompassed in this experience. Not to write about it would be a betrayal of our condition.

For a woman to write about a female character's search for herself does not necessarily mean that she is concerned with social problems or with feminist ideas. Our modern novelists have been less interested in public conditions and limitations than with their personal effects. In fact, as Simone de Beauvoir observes, women writers "do not contest the human situation because they have hardly begun to assume it."[28] Self-definition, for a woman, still means self-definition in relation to men. Thus, authors of their own sex have limited fictional women almost as narrowly as have men to their role as the lovers of men.

Doris Lessing has expressed her dismay that *The Golden Notebook* is read as a novel about sexual relations or even as a feminist work. She apparently intended it to reflect an entire epoch in intellectual history. But to depict such an epoch through the experiences of a woman is, because of the nature of our society, to give it the coloring of sexuality. To entitle one segment of the novel "Free Women," however ironic the term, and to view relations between the sexes so candidly, is merely to reinforce this interpretation. Or perhaps the "personalism" (Beauvoir calls it narcissism) drilled into the behavior of women is such that "the woman writer will still be speaking of herself even when she is speaking about general topics."

The novels of Colette show a more realistic appreciation of the way that sexuality is always dominant in female identity. Colette's women are not restricted to a single age or type and their decisions are often concerned with an entire life-pattern. But sexuality is always at the heart of the story, whether the subject is adolescence, loneliness, lesbianism, or sympathy with nature. When Annie in her admittedly slight novel *Claudine s'en va* determines to leave her husband, the reflection of what is in her mind and what she will become is far more vivid than when Ibsen's Nora walks out or James's Isabel decides to stay. And in a more fully realized work like *The Vagabond*, Colette's examination of the meaning to a woman of isolation, work, jealousy, independence, and revived love is both passionate and remorseless. Yet in *Break of Day* the writer herself suggests another, more paradoxical reason for preoccupation with sexual relationships:

At no time has the catastrophe of love, in all its phases and consequences, formed a part of the true intimate life of a woman. Why do men—writers or so-called writers—still show surprise that a woman should so easily reveal to the public love-secrets and amorous lies and half-truths? By divulging these, she manages to hide other important and obscure secrets which she herself does not understand very well. The spotlight, the shameless eye which she obligingly operates, always explores the same sector of a woman's life. . . . But it is not in the illuminated zone that the darkest plots are woven. . . .

We are so accustomed to *defining* women as enclosed space that
the desperate need for privacy, for that room of one's own, is
articulated only rarely. The woman writer, says Virginia Woolf,
has her scope limited to a cramped but always public territory.
Colette adds that within that territory she exhibits what appear to
be secrets so as to preserve the real secret. The lives of women
are so public that many feel they have no secrets to protect, aside
from the false "feminine mystery" that puts us outside the
bounds of *human* psychology. Colette seems almost to be making
coy reference to that kind of mystery, when actually she is speaking of a much more profound need to pull back and try to establish
an independent self. A powerful paradigm of this urge occurs in
Pavese's *Among Women Only,* where everyone crowds into a
single (female) life and feeds on it. Brought up where there is no
spatial or moral privacy for women, the young Rosetta has to rent
a room in an elegant hotel in order to attempt suicide.

The question of how much is revealed appears at first to be a
matter of "characterization," since so often the woman writer's
only subject is herself. Simone de Beauvoir maintains that most
women who write do so in order to charm, and that the selective
self-revelation of women's literature is analogous to stripping
oneself naked as a form of passive seduction. Women writers
"suppose that . . . it is sufficient for expression, communication,
to show what one is." The complaint most commonly leveled
against women's fiction is that it takes a narcissistic view of private life and thus concentrates on "boring" details of clothing,
person, and surroundings. Yet even if the superficial aspects of
domestic-sexual life were the sole subject of women writers, their
contribution to literature would be a leavening realism. Virginia
Woolf lists the great heroines of Western literature with their
monumental scale and moral extremes, remarking on the disparity between their larger-than-life fictional quality and the oppressed existence of actual contemporary females. "A very
queer, composite being thus emerges. Imaginatively . . .

[woman] is of the highest importance; practically she is completely insignificant." Yet, however overwhelming the stature of
the Clytemnestras and Lady Macbeths, a good case can be made
for their inability to initiate a whole action. They do not act, but,
like women writers, they react. Less heroically polarized ladies of
bourgeois fiction, when the novelist is herself a woman, are freer
to act. In this sense, their autonomy is much greater, although the
scope of their actions is more limited. Female characters, as well
as female authors, come into their own in the novel.

I discussed earlier some positive reasons for women writers'
apparent restriction to the personal universe or viewpoint. One
need only allude to the areas of experience from which women
are excluded to comprehend the negative arguments. As Virginia
Woolf constantly reiterates, it is impossible to describe commonplace events one has not seen or participated in. Even her
own relative freedom to travel across London unescorted in a
public conveyance and lunch alone at a restaurant could not have
been enjoyed by her nineteenth-century predecessors. As some
man is always ready to point out, the best of them made a literary
virtue of those restrictions; but some other man is equally ready
to deride the "feminine" touch in modern novels that continue to
describe the heroine's costume and coiffure now that both she
and her creator are free to experience more important things on
that bus. A Jane Austen would have used her opportunity well,
and we should certainly be exposed to no more recitals about the
sprigged muslin and pelisses of her young ladies than we are while
they are restricted to Bath or Highbury. But she would still be a
woman riding that bus, and that fact continues to shape what she
experiences, how she transforms it into fiction.

Marie Bashkirtsev, quoted in *The Second Sex,* said that in
order to be a true artist, she needed "liberty to go walking alone,
to come and go, to sit on the benches of the Tuileries Gardens." I
am sure this must seem an extravagant excuse for failure—and
the "proof" is that woman has done so little now that she has that

freedom. The problem is that she can go for a walk, sit on a park bench, but not in such a way as to transcend her sexual identity, much less apprehend whatever lies beyond that.

> Culture must be apprehended through the free action of a transcendence; that is, the free spirit with all its riches must project itself toward an empty heaven that it is to populate; but if a thousand persistent bonds hold it to earth, its surge is broken. To be sure, the young girl can today go out alone and idle in the Tuileries; but . . . [the street is] hostile to her, with eyes and hands lying in wait everywhere; if she wanders carelessly, her mind drifting, if she lights a cigarette in front of a cafe, if she goes alone to the movies, a disagreeable incident is soon bound to happen. She must inspire respect by her costume and manners. But this preoccupation rivets her to the ground and to herself.

So the woman writer whose plot calls for her to take her heroine walking in the park would draw upon what she knows it is like for a woman to walk in the park. Whether or not she decides to expose the heroine to a "disagreeable incident," all her own experience has made her aware of her body, carriage, and clothing on such a walk, and some of that is likely to carry over into what we are told about the heroine.

These "disagreeable incidents"—do men know just how destructive they are to a woman's sense of herself as a person? How intrusively they remind her that her notions about love, work, respect are illusions or are granted her on male sufferance, since her very presence on the street is a sexual act and an implicit challenge? It occurred to me that even Virginia Woolf on an omnibus was exposed to this possibility of insult, this hint of danger. She could not be "just" a brilliant novelist observing a segment of London life; she was also a piece of female flesh experiencing it. And that had to be part of how she perceived whatever happened to her. My own grandmother used to take a streetcar to her job in a sweatshop. She was free to earn her own miserable living, free to travel alone. Because she spoke no English, she always carried a hatpin to protect herself from the men who pressed close to her to provoke "disagreeable incidents." I have always wondered why the hatpin has become, in family tradition, a substitute for language; what on earth could she have *said* had she all the verbal skill of a Virginia Woolf? For each of us, any escape from the domination of gender is brief and illusory.

I should not like these observations to be so vulgarized that I seem to be saying that female novelists concentrate on physical descriptions because of their encounters with strange men in the street. The "disagreeable incident" is only one element in the sexualization of women's whole life and psychology, for almost everything in our experience is translated into sexual terms. Thus the woman writer's tendency to make relations with men her principal subject is a symptom of the same condition that is also responsible for her notorious attention to superficial detail. Mary McCarthy's essay on "The Fact in Fiction" presents a convincing argument about the realistic "information" that novels contain. At one point, she refers to a novel's "documentation" as feminine. Her theory can be usefully related to Virginia Woolf's thesis that the novel is a uniquely appropriate feminine genre; my idea about the sexualization of women's experience is simply a further restriction added to those she adduces to show why women writers write novels. It also helps explain why, if the novel in general is a vehicle for material facts, those written by women dwell on one category of facts: the environmental details that are descriptions or extensions of our own bodies.

In discussions of Women and Fiction, it apparently becomes impossible for many commentators to separate feminine style from feminine subject matter. Mary Ellmann's *Thinking About Women* supplies a great many examples of critics who use sexual analogy to describe both the way women write and the things we write about. They even use it to comment on the laudable absence of these "feminine" habits if they cannot find them where the stereotype insists they should be. And it is always useful as a slur. Wolcott Gibbs, for example, discussing his own editorial idiosyncrasies, says, "I suffer . . . seriously from writers who divide quotes for some kind of ladies' club rhythm, 'I am going,' he said, 'downtown,' is a horror. . . .'' It *is* a horror, but it bears no discernible relation to that other male bugaboo, the women's club. What it does sound like is a parody of James. But James's ''femininity'' is normally seen as a matter of subject, not style; Geismar describes him as ''perhaps . . . the greatest feminine novelist of *any* age, the artist who brought the domestic realm of a Jane Austen, say, to the edge (if no further) of world literature.''[29] Apparently, it needed a *man* to take it even that far! Yet the very existence of the ''Jacobite'' cult among male critics belies the notion of the domestic scene as the exclusive province of women writers or readers. What is meant by the domestic realm in this case, anyway, if not that of relations between the sexes? And, although our culture has made that very nearly women's only interest, it has never been only we who were interested in it.

Feminine style remains an elusive notion. In *A Room of One's Own,* Virginia Woolf makes a great point of the ''man's sentence'' and how uncomfortably the great women writers of the last century used it. Jane Austen alone, she believes, was able to laugh at that sentence, transcend it, and thus develop a perfectly good, serviceable sentence of her own. But what makes it a ''woman's sentence'' aside from the undeniable fact that Jane Austen was a woman? The blurred distinction between style and subject is brought out when the same notion is applied to Dorothy Richardson in Woolf's *Contemporary Writers,* where she states that the difference between the ''psychological sentence of the feminine gender'' in the hands of male and female writers is in Richardson's molding of the sentence to explore a woman's consciousness. ''It is a woman's sentence, but only in the sense that it is used to describe a woman's mind by a writer who is neither proud nor afraid of anything that she may discover in the psychology of her sex.'' But then, as Mary Ellmann points out, ''the only certain femininity is in Dorothy Richardson's subject.''[30]

I have similar impressions from my own experience. When I was an undergraduate, a woman who was very confused about both sex and literature suggested I read the fiction of Anaïs Nin because she writes "like a woman." I found the first book I tried very tedious, not because her style was particularly "feminine," but because of her protagonist's self-conscious hold on neurosis and on conventional female stereotypes. When I castigated my classmate for inflicting this experience on me, she explained that she hadn't meant that Anaïs Nin writes like a woman, but from a distinctly feminine standpoint, a very different thing indeed. On the other hand, a teacher in a "creative writing" course once told a female student to read Grace Paley "because she writes like a man." That one really puzzled us, and the only partially satisfactory explanation we could come up with is that she is straightforward, though not particularly naturalistic, about the pleasures of sexuality. (That is, she writes *as* a woman!) Which means that we are outgrowing a little of our protective hypocrisy. But there is surely nothing that reflects her gender (or that contradicts it) in the shape of Paley's sentences.

Developments in the Sexual Revolution should have made it possible for the first time for female novelists to supply a woman's "style" and viewpoint about heterosexuality. No man, one would think, could do a very accurate job of describing what it feels like for a woman to have intercourse with a man, and the subject is certainly germane to concern with defining the female condition. But women have concentrated more often on the inward aspects of a sexual affair. I am not arguing that women should strike back at men by objectifying them in dirty books as oppressive as those written by and for men; but not all explicit descriptions of sexuality are dirty and women have not given us such descriptions. In Doris Lessing and Anaïs Nin, we encounter characters who are self-conscious about their femininity, "superior" women whose nerves are very close to the surface. These women have extensive sexual experience, but we learn about what goes on in their minds, mostly in regard to the whole relationship and not its specifically sexual side. Lessing accepts the implications of so doing, rejecting not only mechanical male formulae but nearly all descriptions of sexual scenes. "Women," she claims, "deliberately choose not to think about technical sex. They get irritable when men talk technically, it's out of self preservation: they want to preserve the spontaneous emotion that is essential for their satisfaction." And this emotion is to be apprehended in terms of Freudian mystification:

> A vaginal orgasm is emotion and nothing else, felt as emotion and expressed in sensations that are indistinguishable from emotion. The vaginal orgasm is a dissolving in a vague, dark generalized sensation like being swirled in a warm whirlpool. There are several different sorts of clitoral orgasms, and they are more powerful (that is a male word) than the vaginal orgasm. There can be a thousand thrills, sensations, etc., but there is only one real female orgasm and that is when a man, from the whole of his need and desire, takes a woman and wants all her response.[31]

At the other extreme is Mary McCarthy, whose depiction of sexual scenes is almost invariably ironic. She is detached and clinical, as one must imagine her characters themselves are, and even a pleasurable experience is described in an alienated way. Sexual experience that is more than technically successful and that accompanies feelings of warmth and love arouses the same reticence in McCarthy as in Lessing.*

For the most part, we have left it up to men to define women's sensibility in this as in other areas—with predictable results. Women who read Joyce are naturally impressed with Molly Bloom's soliloquy in the overall structure of *Ulysses*. But it is normally men who think of Molly's sexuality as defining a female

*The decade that has passed since I first wrote these words has produced a great deal of explicit female writing about sexuality. Most of it—and certainly the most realistic material—has to do with the sexual inadequacy of either men or women. Interviewed on television when *Fear of Flying* was at the height of its success, Erica Jong pointed out that she could hardly be said to have written an erotically stimulating book when her major male character is unable to sustain an erection a great deal of the time. (It may be culturally significant to note that Jong's actual phrase "can't get it up half the time," was bleeped out, although, earlier in the same program, an "erect phallus" stood uncensored.)

type that is realistically as well as mythically recognizable; to a woman, she is only an archetypal male fantasy of woman's inner life. Despite my recourse to this notion of woman as men wish she would be, I do not believe there are very many female characters in literature that are deliberately constructed as fantasy-ideals for male readers. Outside of pornography, where the females are no more than stylized orifices, fictional women are not created to provide imaginary lovers for the men who read about them. It is my general impression, in fact, that men do not realize fiction in that way, that they rarely encounter a lady in a book with whom they "fall in love," or liken a woman they meet to some literary heroine. Women do this constantly—at least adolescent girls do, and adult women without much literary sophistication. The hero, in these cases, is always the same, the masterful Byronic figure, never that weak man in search of Mother who is fully and credibly delineated in modern novels written by women. In young girls, it is a phase, and when they outgrow it they remember more of *Wuthering Heights* than the dominating personality of Heathcliff. But the subliterary works intended for older women supply a continued need that I imagine is the nearest many of these readers get to masturbation. Our grandmothers gasped over *The Sheik,* with its overtones of romantic rape, long before Valentino gave the word flesh. And our mothers reacted the same way to Rhett Butler.

On the next lower level, however, there is no pornography written by or for women, and even the milder sexual titillations appeal to our narcissism or our aspirations rather than to more outgoing impulses. After all, a sexy woman appears every month on the cover of *Cosmopolitan* as well as *Playboy.* I think there is a whole range of popular literary forms that cater in this way to culturally induced fantasies. What men seek in those forms— detective, Western, and adventure stories, as well as pornography—is a confirmation of the virile ideal, an identification of themselves as master. What women seek is the force that we are educated to believe will act upon our "natural" passivity and bring it to life, fertilize our incompleteness, and give us an identity, much as the sperm is depicted as bringing life from an otherwise inert ovum. In pornography, the man is master in fact, not merely "masterful" as in confession magazines or light romances. But his dominance is necessarily exercised over a being without personality, whose "fulfillment" is in total reification. Women do not identify with such a figure, and it is not part of our fantasy life to reverse the politics and make of ourselves the monstrous master a distorted system recognizes as Man.*

I find confirmation of this, rather than an exception, in *Story of O,* whose author's pseudonym is female and whose "heroine" degenerates (as the ideogrammatic name "O" itself implies) into undifferentiated femaleness. This femaleness is defined as total abdication of personal and sexual autonomy, degradation of both flesh and spirit. In an introductory note, André Pieyre de Mandiargues discusses the way the book ends. O, depilated, chained, and wearing an owl mask, is in the final scene "exposed to public scorn: the display of a body which is no longer anything but an object, flouted beneath the plumage, offered to the first comer. Then: death. Inevitably; woman, through the decline of her flesh, having become pure spirit." The mystic arithmetic is faulty here: he says you degrade and then subtract the flesh and what is left is pure spirit. But what makes him think there is any *spirit* left?

All the commentary I have read about this novel is by men and follows the lead of Jean Paulhan in describing it as the absolute apotheosis of female sexuality and the fulfillment of our darkest fantasies. I can hardly imagine its arousing any woman sexually; women who read it tend to consider it mildly disturbing, but even our revulsion is impersonal, political, not of that overwhelming

---

*The recent publication—in Nancy Friday's *My Secret Garden* and *Forbidden Flowers*—of what are supposed to be typical female sex fantasies serves to underscore these speculations. The dominant theme in the fantasies, which have been edited with so heavy a hand as to share a single voice, is narcissism. The masochistic fantasies do not even approach the depths of pornographic writing for men, and there is no sustained fantasy of female sadism.

sort that might reveal some correspondence of O's experience with one's own secret wishes or fears. (I recall Colette's story about herself at age fourteen, fainting when she read Zola's description of labor pains in a volume that had been forbidden her. Or an eighteen-year-old of my own generation who fainted in the office of the doctor teaching her to use her first diaphragm. We are so conditioned that certain natural truths do indeed make us sick, but everything that makes us sick is not, for that reason, the truth.)

I believe a case can be made for Pauline Réage's being a man, none for "her" being a woman. As Paulhan acknowledges, O is a masculine fantasy. Addressing the author, he says:

> That you are a woman I have little doubt. Not so much because of the kind of detail you delight in describing—the green satin dresses, wasp-waist corsets, and skirts rolled up a number of turns (like hair rolled up in a curler)—but rather because of something like this: the day when René abandons O to still further torments, she still manages to have enough presence of mind to notice that her lover's slippers are frayed, and notes that she will have to buy him another pair. To me, such a thought seems almost unimaginable. It is something a man would never have thought of, or at least would never have dared express.[32]

Female authors, the argument runs, observe and report on details of dress and appearance. I have acknowledged that and attempted to explain why it continues to be true when both real and fictional women should have more engrossing subjects on their minds. But precisely because this preoccupation is recognized as part of the feminine value-system, it is subject to imitation and even to parody. Pavese, who comes much closer to depicting woman's world than to assimilating her thoughts, has mastered that habit without the standards that inform it. In an early scene of *Among Women Only*, the female narrator describes a character's slipper-satin dress as "worth more than a lot of words." A few chapters later, Pavese has Clelia tell us about a gathering of shal-

low young society people and affected artists: "Then Momina
arrived. . . . Her gloves alone were worth more than the whole
studio." But Paulhan's argument about Réage is more intricate; it
is not merely her trick of observation that is "feminine" but the
self-effacing ability to notice homely details, details relating to
how she can serve, at such a moment. He uses the book's thesis
about female nature as if it were a proved fact. For surely if Réage
is a woman that detached remark about the slippers is meant
ironically.

Paulhan goes on to reveal why it is so important for him to
believe that the creator of such a bizarre lapse into domesticity is
female:

> In her own way O expresses a virile ideal. Virile, or at least mas-
> culine. At last a woman who admits it! Who admits what? Some-
> thing that women have always refused till now to admit (and today
> more than ever before). Something that men have always re-
> proached them for, that they never cease obeying their nature, the
> call of their blood, that everything in them, even their minds, is
> sex. That they have constantly to be nourished, constantly washed
> and made up, constantly beaten. That all they need is a good mas-
> ter . . . that we must, when we go to them, take a whip along. Rare
> is the man who has not dreamed of possessing Justine. But, so far
> as I know, no woman has ever dreamed of *being* Justine. I mean,
> dreamed aloud, with this same pride at being grieved and in tears,
> this consuming violence, with this voracious capacity for suffering,
> and this amazing will, stretched to the breaking point and even
> beyond.

In short, the supreme masculine fantasy is for the woman to
confess that all of it is really *her* fantasy. And that it is not some
aberration, but the unconscious female norm. But which of us is
so acute and yet so self-destructive as to pander to this particular
male fantasy? To be able to do so demands an unimaginable
combination of meretricious intent and freedom. We are not that
blindly generous to the madness of others, nor is any of us that
free.

III

Once again, I catch myself using the word "freedom" in a paradoxical sense. The only way to escape this and to bring this essay to a close is to speak in political terms. In *A Room of One's Own,* Virginia Woolf comes very close to it, but the solutions she hints at are restricted by their idiosyncratic nature and their class bias. I suspect that the impossibility of developing a program from her poetic statements has contributed to the work's acceptance. It is just what a romantic plea for freedom should be: eloquent, stirring, and ultimately ineffective. But Virginia Woolf was not wholly satisfied with beautiful language. At least, she felt the need to reopen the Woman Question ten years later and report new, essentially political conclusions.

The resulting volume, *Three Guineas,* has never been as widely read or as well liked. Critics tell us that in this work Virginia Woolf allowed her bitterness at the female condition to distort and overcome the lyric power demonstrated in *A Room of One's Own.* E. M. Forster says that although "feminism inspired . . . the charming and persuasive *A Room of One's Own,*" it is also responsible for what he considers her worst book, "the cantankerous *Three Guineas.*" Carl Woodring is the rare male commentator who apparently relishes the clever blending of earnestness and irony that marks *Three Guineas.* But he destroys the force of his observation by claiming that the author offered the second of her three guineas "to help the daughters of uneducated men enter the professions. The insistence on uneducated fathers, as a way of giving civilization a fresh start, is as shrewd as the financial manipulations of Keynes.[33] But there is no such insistence; the contribution actually goes to those daughters of educated men who make up the "class" with which Virginia Woolf identifies and whom she just as accurately describes as the daughters of uneducated *women.* The difference between the sexes remains a considerable one, after all, and this misreading makes one rather wonder at Woodring's earlier contention that the argument of *A Room of One's Own* "was already obsolete" when it was written.

The real difference between the two feminist essays has nothing to do with a subject gone stale or, as Forster suggests, with "grumbling from habit." Rather, it results from a deepened awareness that makes Virginia Woolf's feminism, that "peculiar side of her," the force that ultimately alters her entire social outlook. Consideration of the politics of both works reveals a developing analysis and points the way to future strategies.

The fundamental insight of *A Room of One's Own* is that psychological and cultural oppression of women is the result of economic dependency. Thus, possession of the requisite five hundred pounds a year—bequeathed, or earned by one's wits—is to her the *sine qua non* of creative life. Advocating that some women have the opportunity to earn that five hundred pounds means at best a limited extension of privilege. She does not stop to consider that women's poverty is an essential part of an entire system, or what would happen to an economy based on profit if all adults had remunerative jobs. Extending privilege without sex bias but within a small class also means giving a few women a stake in maintaining the system. Virginia Woolf acknowledges, with Lady Lovelace, that the price of empire "was mostly paid by women." She recognizes that it was women's contribution to the war effort after 1914 that finally won them some independence, and that "if they were again dependent upon their fathers and brothers they would again be consciously and unconsciously in favor of war."[34] Yet, although deliberately rejecting that party, she aligns herself with the masters of empire when she exults that "no force in the world can take from me my five hundred pounds."

In *A Room of One's Own,* Virginia Woolf presents her central perception about women's need for fiscal independence as something different from politics. The speaker tells of the bequest that she received around the time women were granted suffrage in

England: "Of the two—the vote and the money—the money, I own, seemed infinitely the more important." Despite its relative insignificance to herself, Woolf apparently believed that since the enactment of suffrage women were, in fact, politically emancipated. At that time, she did not take the next step and recognize how meaningless are formal political rights in an unfree economic system. The later work, *Three Guineas,* does link economic and political questions. The author discusses the power bourgeois women now have, apart from the old whorish "influence" of the salons.

> For some reason, never satisfactorily explained, the right to vote, in itself by no means negligible, was mysteriously connected with another right of such immense value to the daughters of educated men that almost every word in the dictionary has been changed by it, including the word 'influence.' You will not think these words exaggerated if we explain that they refer to the right to earn one's living.

Once again, Virginia Woolf leaves unexplained a social "mystery" that she is very close to penetrating. For there is no reason to be surprised that economic and political power are related. *Three Guineas* implicitly recognizes this fact whenever its author looks beyond male "attitudes" to the material sources of power. Women now have the opportunity to earn their living; why do so few succeed in attaining financial success and the social influence that accompanies it? Clearly, it is because ours is not a system in which much power is wielded by those who earn their living. In their own right, women still own almost none of the means of production and reap almost none of the profits. Thus, they exercise little power, and only briefly does Virginia Woolf toy with the notion that things would be better for women if there were a female automobile manufacturer to scribble a check and endow, say, a college for women. One woman's elevation to the ranks of privilege could do nothing for the rest of us; even her influence, the writing of the check, could not open the way to the next lower rung of privilege to many women. For under capitalism, there is only so much material power to be had, and those who have it hold on to it. As Virginia Woolf knew, they protect what they own in the name of God, Law, Nature, and Property.

> Behind us lies the patriarchal system; the private house, with its nullity, its immorality, its hypocrisy, its servility. Before us lies the public world, the professional system, with its possessiveness, its jealousy, its pugnacity, its greed. The one shuts us up like slaves in a harem; the other forces us to circle, like caterpillars head to tail, round and round the mulberry tree, the sacred tree, of property.[35]

Virginia Woolf thus arrives at an analysis of her condition and identifies the enemy precisely as a Marxist would. She does it without abandoning her own social identity, but as a means of elucidating it.

On the question of work, Virginia Woolf is less clear. Because her subject in *A Room of One's Own* is the cultural condition of woman, she speaks of the freedom to work at artistic creation. And because that work does not necessarily produce the requisite income, she mentions earning five hundred a year by one's wits. In *Three Guineas*, the subject is wider, and therefore she speaks about women's place in the professions. As the author constantly reiterates, however, we cannot judge or even describe what we do not experience. So, although she knows the drudgery of working merely to eat, she cannot write of what meaningful, unalienated work might be like.

According to *A Room of One's Own*, in a hundred years women "will take part in all the activities and exertions that were once denied them. The nursemaid will heave coal. The shop woman will drive an engine." (In short, the class system will remain absolutely static.) This is to some extent an attractive image of the future, since the existing division of labor is one cause of both the economic and the psychological oppression of women. Virginia Woolf has it backwards, however, when she claims that making these exertions available to women will mean that womanhood is no longer a "protected occupation" and that we will begin to die off earlier than men. Actually, the idea of having female coal heavers and engine drivers represents freedom from the mystique of feminine frailty, a mystique that Virginia Woolf herself apparently accepts. Moreover, it is a continuation of precisely that phenomenon that brought so many women (and children) onto the labor market in the first place, the technological advances that made brute strength less important in production. When people exist to serve production, rather than production existing to serve them, the labor of women and children is degrading and inhuman. The tragedy of the woman driving an engine and heaving coal is not that she will stagger exhausted to an early grave; rather, it is that she shares both the exploitation and the alienation of the men who do these jobs.

Theodor Reik remarks complacently that "a woman's life is tragically interrupted or even finished when she renounces the desire to please others by her appearance and begins to neglect her looks. A man's life is tragically interrupted or even finished when he renounces work, whether manual or intellectual."[36] It will feel good for women not to have our identity so tied to sexuality, to be able to define ourselves in terms of work, too. But it will be better still when the work itself has meaning. When the process of production exists for the people who do the work, "the fact of the collective working group being composed of individuals of both sexes and all ages must . . . become a source of humane development."[37]

But how can production be for the benefit of the workers while it is for the profit of the owner? How can there be jobs enough for all when maximum profit is the goal of production? That profit depends on the existence of both a marginal labor force and an untabulated army of domestic workers who are "paid" indirectly with the wages from *their husbands'* productive work. "The emancipation of women and their equality with men are impossible and must remain so as long as women are excluded from socially productive work and restricted to housework, which is private."[38] As for the socialization of domestic labor, it is Virginia Woolf and no dialectical materialist who suggests that the state provide "a wage . . . to those whose profession is marriage and motherhood." Addressing a man of the educated class, she tells him:

> If your wife were paid for her work, the work of bearing and bringing up children, a real wage, a money wage, so that it became an attractive profession instead of being as it is now an unpaid profession, an unpensioned profession, and therefore a precarious and dishonored profession, your own slavery would be lightened. No longer need you go to the office at nine-thirty and stay there till six. Work could be equally distributed. Patients could be sent to the patientless. Briefs to the briefless. Articles could be left unwritten. Culture would thus be stimulated. You could see the fruit trees flower in spring. You could share the prime of life with your children. And after that prime was over no longer need you be thrown from the machine on to the scrap heap without any life left or interests surviving. . . .[39]

She attributes society's inability to execute this scheme to the exorbitant amounts spent for what we have since learned to label "defense." But what is it that our armies defend, if not property? Who profits materially from war and the preparation for war? And how is "the state" to pay wages for housework until we all own the means of production in common and state policy is an expression of our ownership?

Virginia Woolf's researches into the comparative poverty of women were prompted, she says, by her visit to Oxbridge. It is the marked contrast between the spacious richness of the men's foundations and the beef-and-prunes atmosphere of Fernham, the women's college, that made her ask why women are poor. The university stands for a whole world of leisure, elegance, and luxury that *A Room of One's Own* treats as essential to the creation and perpetuation of art. The university is the bastion of that "intellectual freedom of which great writings are born," and the important fact about it in *A Room of One's Own* is that in recent times almost all the great writers of England had "procured the means to get the best education England can give."

But whereas *A Room of One's Own* is a book about money, sex, and culture, *Three Guineas* is a book about money, sex, and power. In the later work, the important facts about the university are that "the great majority of men who have ruled England for the past 500 years, who are now ruling England in Parliament and the Civil Service, has received a university education," and that "an immense sum of money . . . has been spent upon education in the past 500 years." These facts lead her to recognition of what the university is really about, whom it really serves, and thence to rejection of the entire ruling class culture *A Room of One's Own* is so ready to embrace. She envisions, instead, a new kind of institution, one that will foster neither the old culture nor the system whose vehicle she now perceives education to be. In this experimental environment, there is to be no opulence, no museum hush, no permanent decoration.

Next, what should be taught in the new college, the poor college? Not the arts of dominating other people; not the arts of ruling, of killing, of acquiring land and capital. . . . The poor college must teach only the arts that can be taught cheaply and practised by poor people; such as medicine, mathematics, music, painting and literature. It should teach the arts of human intercourse; the art of understanding other people's lives and minds, and the little arts of talk, of dress, of cookery that are allied with them. The aim of the new college, the cheap college, should be not to segregate and specialize, but to combine. It should explore the ways in which mind and body can be made to co-operate, discover what new combinations make good wholes in human life. . . . There would be none of the barriers of wealth and ceremony, of advertisement and competition which now make the old and rich universities such uneasy dwelling-places. . . .

[Artists and scholars] would come to the poor college and practise their arts there because it would be a place where society was free; not parcelled out into the miserable distinctions of rich and poor, or clever and stupid; but where all the different degrees and

kinds of mind, body and soul merit co-operated. Let us . . . found
this new college; this poor college; in which learning is sought for
itself; where advertisement is abolished; and there are no degrees
and lectures are not given, and sermons are not preached, and the
old poisoned vanities and parades which breed competition and
jealousy. . . .[40]

Thus Sir Leslie Stephen's snobbish daughter, detached "from the
working-classes and from Labor," she whose "attitude to society
was . . . aloof and angular," paints for us the People's University. But "reality" intervenes in her dream, the reality of higher
education as a channeling mechanism for bourgeois society. The
college Virginia Woolf depicts can only flourish in a society where
competition is not a norm and where learning and culture are
valued because of what they contribute to the common good, not
how they bolster existing power and profit. In short, the People's
University is the cultural focus of a free, socialist society.

A free, socialist society—does Virginia Woolf say *that*? Well,
no. I can underline her radical analysis of social inequality, her
radical vision of a new world. I can point out the close parallels
with classic Marxist views. But I can't distort Virginia Woolf into
a revolutionary. Her strategy for change has built into it not only
defeat but resignation to defeat. That is why it is appropriate to
re-examine that strategy and see what new possibilities forty
years of history have opened to us. Forster admits that as a man,
and an elderly one, he is unfit to judge Virginia Woolf's feminism.
"The best judges . . . are neither elderly men nor even elderly
women, but young women. If they . . . think that it expresses an
existent grievance, they are right." Recent experience shows that
they—that we—still do. Our differences lie in how we believe the
grievance can be redressed.

Virginia Woolf's solutions are never collective, however much
she may talk about social problems and the number of people they
affect. She denies Walter Bagehot's claim that most women "are
utterly destitute of the disciplined reticence necessary to every
sort of cooperation. Two thousand years hence you may have

changed it all, but the present women will only flirt with men and quarrel with one another." It is clearly not up to women to make drastic changes in themselves, individually, before changing the system that is responsible for their present "defects." Yet in her own most radical proposals Virginia Woolf is suggesting precisely the same kind of isolated reform.

In *Three Guineas,* she elaborates on the idea of the "poor college" and then, when reminded of the goals of existing colleges, simply "drops out." Action consists in refusing to support institutions that serve a corrupt and vicious system—a withdrawal that is personally cathartic, perhaps, but socially useless. Similarly, a request for contributions to an organization promoting peace and freedom is countered by the vision of an Outsiders' Society made up of "educated men's daughters working in their own class—how indeed could they work in any other?—and by their own methods for liberty, equality and peace." Despite her own arguments, Virginia Woolf is not convinced that the Woman Question crosses—at times obliterates—class lines. And what are women's own methods? The enemy and his institutions are again clearly labeled, for the Outsider "will bind herself to take no share in patriotic demonstrations, to assent to no form of national self-praise; to make no part of any clique or audience that encourages war; to absent herself from military displays, tournaments, tattoos, prize-givings and all such ceremonies as encourage the desire to impose 'our' civilization or 'our' dominion upon other people." She believes that the "psychology of private life" warrants her conviction that this use of indifference would help materially to prevent war. "For psychology would seem to show that it is far harder for human beings to take action when other people are indifferent and allow them complete freedom of action, than when their actions are made the centre of excited emotion."[41] In short, the Outsider is to accept her status as Outsider and work a new kind of "influence" upon the war-makers of her "own" class. She is to re-enact Lysistrata as psychological drama.

To do this means to work for change within the isolation of individual female lives; to acknowledge and depend on the power of those who rule; to refuse reinforcements from the ranks of other oppressed groups. By contrast, in this eighth decade of our century, all women's liberation organizations, whatever their political orientation, seek to destroy the private, individual battlegrounds that have so long assured defeat for women's struggles. All reject the ruler's definition of ourselves and our movement, as we reject the legitimacy of his authority. All perceive the analogy between our own situation and that of other oppressed people. Our entire program is based on these differences between our perspective and that of Virginia Woolf.

A similar evangelical note distorts Woolf's description of what our oppression has taught women, our "vocational" education at the hands of "poverty, chastity, derision and freedom from unreal loyalties." Women, she says, must turn these great teachers to advantage and refuse to be separated from them. Thus, practice of poverty means earning only enough to live on independently; chastity means refusal, having earned that much, to sell one's brain for the sake of money; derision means rejection of "all methods of advertising merit," preferring obscurity and censure to praise and fame; and freedom from unreal loyalties means ridding oneself of pride at belonging to a nation, a religion, a family, an institution, or a sex. (She says nothing of class pride.) To be sure, these are the qualities that go into making a fighter for freedom. But developing them does not in itself constitute liberation. The oppressed can find the sources for freeing themselves in the identity shaped by oppression, but, again, that is not the same as being free. Once more the note is one of self-purification rather than social action.

The trouble with taking the next step, with proposing collective solutions, is that it leads to the problem of collective means. So long as the struggle for liberation is kept private, there is no political reason to wrestle with the issue of violence. Virginia Woolf, who passionately hated war and killing, points out that "scarcely a human being in the course of history has fallen to a woman's rifle; the vast majority of birds and beasts have been killed by . . . [men] not by us."[42] It's a beautiful record. Women are only now awakening to question whether it may not also be the means of our enslavement. For if we accept the principle that the oppressed must be the vanguard of a revolution, and if we acknowledge the rhetoric of women's oppression, then how can we let someone else fight for our freedom? And knowing as we do how women have always had to relate to those in power, how can we expect to coax, to legislate, to seduce that power away? How can we participate now in a movement for liberation as it educates and takes limited action—only to drop out when the action escalates? The women who realize that the next struggle for freedom includes us have already enlisted as soldiers in an army we have yet to build. But we have accepted this responsibility with sorrow, not exhilaration, for we have no tradition of *machismo,* of the "fine, manly character" inculcated by war. I don't think women are in danger of developing our own *machismo* cult. If we become soldiers in the next revolution it will be because without that we never can be free. And without us, it would not really be a revolution.

Finally, in the strategy of sexual liberation, there is sexuality, the almost unmentioned realm in both of Virginia Woolf's feminist books. Andrew Sinclair, in *The Emancipation of the American Woman,* deplores the initial tolerance women's suffrage leaders showed for Victoria Woodhull's free-sex movement, a tolerance inspired by no more than the humane feeling that this time it would not be *women* who destroyed the sister who broke sexual taboos. The nineteenth-century radicals were premature, says Sinclair; they "demanded physical freedom outside marriage too soon." Society's unreadiness for this liberation delayed the granting of political rights to a movement associated with "free love." Actually, the free-sex enthusiasts may have come closer than the suffragists to naming the enemy. They recognized sexual repression as a form of tyranny and the monogamous family as the institution of oppression. The failure of the early feminist movement was not that "free-lovers" held back suffrage, but rather that the mainstream dismissed their arguments and clung to the campaign for civil rights. Those rights are valuable, but alone they failed to alter the real material basis of women's lives, a basis in which economics and sexuality are inextricably linked. Norms of sexual behavior are different now, but it still remains for us to liberate sexuality from notions of ownership, competition, and domination. In the process of revolution, we have to reinvent love.

A Room of One's Own concludes with an exhortation about the resurrection of "the dead poet who was Shakespeare's sister," in language finer than any I can muster to frame my disagreement. Virginia Woolf speaks of all of us living with the famous five hundred pounds and rooms of our own, with the habit of freedom and the courage to live fully human lives, saying that if we do so, then the poet will finally rise from among us. But she never really means *all* of us and she cannot explain how we each— separately—put on the habit of freedom. The poet, she maintains, "would come if we worked for her, and . . . so to work, even in poverty and obscurity, is worth while." This is itself poetry, but it also embraces private martyrdom and self-effacement, with no clear notion of how that individual austerity will lead to the desired advent. It is self-interest that should make us work, not merely for the conditions that will at last allow a female poet to be a poet, but for the liberation of all people, on which that poet's freedom finally depends. If we do so, who can tell what poetic energies will be released from our ranks to take their part in remaking human life?

NOTES

1. Mary Ellmann, *Thinking About Women* (New York: Harcourt, Brace & World, 1968), p. 199.

2. Virginia Woolf, *A Room of One's Own* (1929; reprint ed., New York: Harcourt, Brace & World, Harbinger Books, 1957), p. 51.

3. Sigmund Freud, *Civilization and Its Discontents* (New York: W. W. Norton & Co., 1962), p. 48.

4. Friedrich Engels, *The Origin of the Family, Private Property and the State* (Moscow: Foreign Languages Publishing House, n.d.), pp.54-55.

5. Ibid., p. 123.

6. Virginia Woolf, *Three Guineas* (1938; reprint ed., New York: Harcourt, Brace & World, Harbinger Books, 1963), p. 3.

7. In *The Other Victorians* (New York: Basic Books, 1966), Steven Marcus points out the pervasive Victorian identification of sexual domination with capital and with class domination. The same pattern appears throughout "our" literature, but only in nineteenth-century England did, literature define both sexual and social categories so rigidly.

8. Maxwell Geismar, *Henry James and the Jacobites* (Boston: Houghton Mifflin Co., 1963), p. 6.

9. *A Room of One's Own,* p. 92.

10. *Three Guineas,* p. 146.

11. Engels, *Origin of the Family,* pp. 106-7.

12. Ibid., p. 121.

13. *Three Guineas,* p. 18.

14. Clara Zetkin, *Lenin on the Woman Question* (New York: International Publishers, 1934), p. 19.

15. Engels, *Origin of the Family,* p. 123.

16. Zetkin, *Lenin on the Woman Question,* p. 17.

17. Sigmund Freud, "Female Sexuality," in *The Complete Psychological Works of Sigmund Freud* (London: The Hogarth Press and The Institute of Psychoanalysis, 1957), Vol. 21, p. 228.

18. Marie Bonaparte, *Female Sexuality* (New York: Grove Press, 1965), p. 7.

19. Sigmund Freud, "The Taboo of Virginity," The Psychology of Love, III, in *Complete Psychological Works,* Vol. 11, p. 205.

20. Ibid.

21. *A Room of One's Own,* p. 13. I am wrenching the line out of context, of course, but that is a proper Freudian procedure.

22. Pauline Kael, "Replying to Listeners," in *I Lost It at the Movies* (New York: Bantam Books, 1966), p. 206. Kael's qualification about marital sex is necessary because a "free" sex life can also be suspect: "When a woman has a succession of short-lived sexual affairs the suspicion arises that the woman unconsciously wishes to be a man." (Theodor

Reik, *The Many Faces of Sex: Observations of an Old Psychoanalyst* [New York: Farrar, Strauss, & Giroux, Noonday Press, 1966], p. 116.)

23. Herbert Marcuse, *Eros and Civilization: A Philosophical Inquiry into Freud* (New York: Random House, Vintage Books, 1955), pp. 182, 183. Italics are his.

24. Sigmund Freud, "Some Psychical Consequences of the Anatomical Distinctions Between the Sexes," in *Complete Psychological Works,* Vol. 19, pp. 257-58. Both citations are from this passage.

25. Nearly a year after using this story to epitomize Freud's reasoning process, I was delighted to discover that he himself cites a version of it as a "piece of sophistry which has been much laughed over." (*Jokes and their Relation to the Unconscious* [New York: Norton Library, 1963], p. 62.)

26. The young Austens' pleasure in satirizing literature is preserved for us in Jane Austen's Juvenilia. Similarities in tone between the sister's *Love and Freindship* and the brothers' essays in *The Loiterer* have often been commented upon. James Austen is the author of a letter from "Sophia Sentiment" (*Loiterer,* No. 9) which discusses the mandatory content of "Novels, Eastern Tales and Dreams," while Henry Austen wrote the catalogue of stylistic devices appropriate to such ventures (No. 59). As I read these attempts, however, it is not the exaggerations of *Love and Freindship* I hear, but the somewhat matured ironies of Tilney himself. Henry Tilney is revealed to us principally through these opinions of his, and it is very likely that what little we see of his actions and character is drawn from the novelist's two brothers, whose views are so much like his own.

27. Reik, *Many Faces of Sex,* p. 102. I wonder about this "understanding" that women are supposed to have—even when we are neither psychologists nor novelists. How much of what is called understanding is the masculine demand for essentially maternal attentions? How much is the subject's ceaseless, wary observation of the master she has to please?

28. Simone de Beauvoir, *The Second Sex* (New York: Bantam Books, 1961), p. 669. Subsequent quotations from Beauvoir are passages in the same chapter.

29. Geismar, *Henry James and the Jacobites,* p. 49.

30. Ellmann, *Thinking About Women,* p. 172.

31. Doris Lessing, *The Golden Notebook* (New York: Ballantine Books, 1968), pp. 214-16.

32. Jean Paulhan, "Happiness in Slavery," in Pauline Réage, *Story of*

O (New York: Grove Press, 1967), pp. xxiv-xxv. The next passage cited is also from this page of the introductory essay.

33. Carl Woodring, *Virginia Woolf* (New York: Columbia University Press, 1966), p. 9.

34. *Three Guineas*, p. 36.

35. Ibid., p. 74.

36. Reik, *Many Faces of Sex*, pp. 75-76.

37. Karl Marx, *Capital*, Vol. I (New York: International Publishers, 1967), 490.

38. Engels, *Origin of the Family*, p. 266.

39. *Three Guineas*, pp. 110-11.

40. Ibid., pp. 34-35.

41. Ibid., p. 109.

42. Ibid., p. 6.

Woman under Capitalism:
The Renaissance Lady

IN GRADUATE SCHOOL my major field was something called the Renaissance; the more I learn about my subject, the more puzzling this title seems. Its initial force was clearly chronological, providing us comp. lit. students with a category analogous to— though somewhat broader than—those of English literature, which was neatly divided into centuries, each of them a recognized "field" of literary investigation. But there was no agreement about the boundaries of the Renaissance perceived as a period of time, so most specialists added to the rough estimate of inclusive dates (and 1300 to 1600 *is* pretty rough) some generalizations about characteristic cultural modes. Is "the Renaissance" the name of an intellectual movement, then? Well, no, at least not just one and not consistently. Or is it a definable artistic style? Well, sort of, but not, of course, occurring as early as changes in philosophy and ideology and, in any event, developing at a different pace in each art form. Besides, we speak of history as if people lived in "the Renaissance," but no one lived in Mannerism or the Baroque, so it *must* have been a period. . . .

Do I exaggerate? Only in attributing a kind of ingenuousness to the inquiry that I know it did not possess. My teachers and my fellow students knew a great deal about the subject and they approached the question of definition armed with that information and the conclusions toward which it seemed to point. There was a remarkable integrity in the terms and manner of the exploration. Yet we continued to use the phrase and the concept of "the Renaissance" quite as if there were a commonly accepted view of what, when, and even whether it was. Deriving from our own observation, as well as from scholarly tradition, the sense that somewhere back in there something happened, we confused what happened in books with what happened outside them and were left with the Renaissance as a category rather uneasily suspended between the history of expression and the history of events.

The reason I begin my exposition with this rather exotic problem is that it points up the difficulties faced by anyone attempting to understand the way literature interacts with social reality. The particular issues I am exploring demand a sensitivity to these relations that is suppressed by the way the discipline perceives itself and defines the question. The history that was considered appropriate "background" for the student of Renaissance literature emphasized the acts of the mind, other events—wars, revolts, economic crises, voyages of exploration—being portrayed as the response to those acts. Calling the period the Renaissance, even while acknowledging that no one knows if it was actually a period, a cultural force, or a style designation, enhances this distorted vision of history. It reflects the kind of unexamined idealism that names an era according to its dominant ideology, as if that set of ideas had an autonomous life of its own and, although itself innocent of a social basis, were able to motivate events in the historical world.

In this sense, the Renaissance takes its place in idealist history right between the Age of Chivalry and the Age of Puritanism, and a false sense of all three categories informs the accepted view of women in the period. I was taught that somehow (there are always a great many "somehows" when you think that human relations and institutions come about because of ideas which, themselves, come out of nowhere in particular) the Renaissance represented a period of emancipation for women inserted between the restrictions of chivalry and the stringencies of puritanism. Evidence for this emancipation is sought in the careers of several aristocratic ladies who patronized the flourishing visual and literary arts and who followed or, often at one remove, participated in the great movements and debates of Humanism and the Reformation.

But the most important source of support for the assumption that a period of temporary emancipation intervened at the stage of European history designated by the term "Renaissance" is, of course, the literature of the time. The strong and independent heroines of Shakespearean comedy are seen as reflections of a new strength and independence on the part of women in Elizabethan England. Similarly, the women warriors of heroic poetry are viewed as only partially symbolic reflections of the virago, the purported dream-girl of Renaissance Italy. Literary and historical interpretation, then, appear to chase each other around in a not very enlightening circle, a circle that began to constrict about me as I attempted to understand the nature and content of women's experience in the period and the connections between that experience and certain contemporary poems.

The specific problem from which I started is the function of lady knights in the sixteenth-century romance epic. Ariosto's *Orlando Furioso*, Tasso's *Jerusalem Delivered* and Spenser's *Faerie Queene*, poems whose composition and publication span almost the entire course of the sixteenth century, all include at least one female warrior character. Unlike the Amazons who are their military models, these heroines also play a part in love stories, for they share both the ascribed character and the sexual destiny of more traditional women. Each of the ladies takes part in repeated battles for a cause she considers holy; but the military life is a far from uncongenial choice, and each of them also indulges in the more casual fights that engage the attention of a knight errant. They are also first-rate warriors and normally vanquish their male opponents without difficulty. Each of the three principal heroines eventually encounters and duels twice with a man who is her predestined lover, defeating him in the first contest and narrowly losing the second time around; male and female are therefore equally matched in military prowess. Two of the couples fall in love and marry. In the third case, Tasso's Clorinda is mortally wounded by Tancredi, but dies after receiving Christian baptism at his hands, so that an equivocal promise can be made about their reunion in heaven. (Marriage, in any event, is very much on Tasso's moral agenda, although he cannot bring himself to give any of the love stories in his masterpiece this particular happy ending.) The two couples who do marry— Ariosto's Bradamante and Ruggiero, Spenser's Britomart and Arthegall—live to found great ruling houses; in fact, they become the ancestors of the very families for whom the poets were working.

Now, a dynastic marriage for love is almost a contradiction in terms, and it was certainly an ideological innovation—as was the notion of love based on equality between the sexes, much less equality demonstrated through military combat. Yet here are some diplomatically aware court poets saying to their ruling-class patrons, "Your ancestors accomplished certain glorious, pious deeds; and, what is more, you are descended from a couple that married for love on the basis of an equality proved in battle." How and why did this become a suitably politic—and political— compliment, and how was that compliment related to other themes and issues in the heroic poems?

I was taught that the way to interpret this new and apparently radical idea was to place it in its history—where that was understood to mean tracing the literary origins of the phenomenon. In the case of the sex equality/love-marriage theme, this meant studying, first, the conventions of twelfth-century courtly poetry, in which the troubadour lover depicted himself as a suppliant knight in the service of a lady to whom he attributed the powers of a feudal suzerain, sometimes even addressing her as "my lord." Marriage was never the issue here, for that was an institution concerned with the acquisition and consolidation of dowered land, the supervision of household production, and the assurance of a legitimate succession. Whether or not the lady in the poem was sexually available—and her most frequent courtly stance was unapproachability—the love celebrated by the troubadours had an adulterous force. Nor was sex equality part of the scheme, for the woman was (rhetorically) situated above her lover in status and power. However artificial, this elevation of the beloved lady provides one of the first sources for her "emancipated" role in the later romance epics, as does the application of chivalric imagery to the experience of love. If actual twelfth-century conditions ever entered academic discussion about the courts of love, it was as a basis for arguments about whether the Provençal legal system and the prolonged absence of Crusader husbands really gave women the kind of temporal power that was implied in the language of courtly poets (the consensus was that they did not).

In the next century, the process was continued by the Italian poets whose collective label comes from the "sweet new style" practiced by its members. They retained the attitude of helpless adoration for a highly placed and inaccessible beloved, but eliminated the chivalric metaphors. Proportionally more emphasis was given to the effects of love on those who possessed "the gentle heart," which is to say the ennobling capacity to love at all. Again, my education devoted almost no attention to the differences between feudal Provence and the urban communes of Italy, a country where feudalism had never taken root. Of course those young Florentines would find feudal rhetoric alien to their experience and, equally naturally, those sons of the new bourgeoisie and petty bourgeoisie would be seeking out new definitions of nobility, finding it, unsurprisingly, in the personal, not the inherited, qualities of worthy individuals. The true love that made one a true noble could hardly remain the adulterous though unconsummated passion that the troubadours sang. The lady was now understood to belong not to a higher class but to a higher spiritual order (especially if she happened to die in mid-sonnet-sequence); hence, love for her, experienced in the mind and soul, eventually lifted the lover above fleshly concerns and toward God. In the works of Dante, whose contemporaries perfected this mode of experience, there appears the most developed example of a love that begins with a desperate but essentially earthly passion and that leads the subject upward to "the love that moves the sun and the other stars."

Petrarch, writing in the fourteenth century, continued and advanced the conventions that shaped the beloved woman into a guiding angel. Both his theme and his language stressed the contradictory nature of an earthly love whose reward was or might be spiritual salvation. It was this tension, embodied in his characteristic antithetical conceits, that was adopted by hundreds of followers and imitators among sonneteers up through the time of the heroic poems I am exploring. Marriage remained the concern of a world quite separate from that in which the intricacies of love were expressed. The beloved—Dante's Beatrice, Petrarch's Laura—was probably married, and the poet might also have a wife, but that had nothing to do with poetry.

The final element in the chain of literary antecedents is the influence of Neoplatonic thought. (What that revival had to do with the growing prominence and ideological requirements of a new class was also, need I add, left unexamined.) The Platonic ladder of love, with its eventual transcendence of the body and its progression to truth through the apprehension and love of beauty, was eminently adaptable to the ideology evolved by the Italian poets. In a Christian framework, however, the homosexual assumptions of Plato's scheme had to be suppressed and the same ideas applied to relations between the sexes. Since Platonic love presupposes that one loves a person equal or superior to oneself, the prospect emerged of a woman's being so perceived.

One of the most influential popularizations of the ideas expressed by Plato in the *Symposium* occurs in Castiglione's *Book of the Courtier*. Significantly, this early-sixteenth-century work also includes the advice that the good courtier ought only to pay his amorous addresses to a lady who is available and eligible for marriage; this passage occurs in the context of other practical suggestions, distinct from the theoretical Neoplatonism with which the book concludes, but the two levels of reasoning are not meant to contradict one another. Spenser, writing in a similar vein toward the end of the century, adapts the Petrarchan tradition to produce a series of sonnets, the *Amoretti,* whose goal is the loving matrimony celebrated in his *Epithalamium*.

These were the phases of the literary tradition as my education presented it, and this self-contained progression thus represented the developing "history" of the idea I was studying. For the three heroic poems themselves, further sociological analysis was in order. The military combat was interpreted as an exceptionally forceful symbol of a new equality between the sexes—an equality subsisting in life as well as in poetry—and the reflection of an emerging norm of marriage for love. This view was reinforced from three different directions: what is known about the great ladies of the Renaissance courts, the standard histories that tell us how the virago was admired and what high status she and her sisters were granted, and our own historical experience, where love-marriage is indeed the accepted social norm. It took some years before I learned to see through each of these sources of authority to another way of approaching the issue.

The argument that relies on the status of exceptional women is, of course, the easiest to dispose of. Increasing leisure for upper-class women, particularly for those who did not reside year-round on landed estates, was a feature of the times; it led to somewhat wider educational opportunities, assuring literacy in the vernacular, at least, and, in a few cases, extremely high levels of intellectual and scholarly attainment. The matter of women's leisure was to become a critical material and cultural force with the further consolidation of the bourgeoisie. In the sixteenth century, however, the impact was barely beginning to be felt; its influence on the intellectual life of women affected only a minority within an already small privileged class. Of that cultivated minority, only a handful were able to combine humanist achievement with social position in such a way as to become a cultural force in their own right. And it was by historical accident that a few of *these* women—most notably Elizabeth and Mary Tudor—also held political power.

But any reading of the three romance epics that insists on their foundation in social history must of necessity take a broader view of society and recognize the extent to which the relative emancipation of the great patronesses was entirely atypical. Moreover, if love-marriages in the heroic poems are alleged to represent a trend toward love-marriage in contemporary society, it should be recalled that the class of intellectually elite women was least likely to have the freedom to marry according to the dictates of the heart. Not even those who consider the careers of Isabella d'Este or Vittoria Colonna significant for the history of women in general would claim that these ladies were able to marry for love or lived according to values that prescribed such a marriage. Indeed, the increasing dominance of a cash economy in this period led to inflation in the dowry market; the size and strategic importance of the dowry increased, and the payment was likelier to be in cash or marketable real estate than in family-held land. Marriages not only continued to be arranged, but were arranged and sometimes even consummated when the parties were very young. The poems thus become harder than ever to read if we have to understand the female independence they depict as realistic, but the love-marriages as merely symbolic; you cannot have it both ways.

It is in running the second source of historical authority to earth that one encounters the problem of circularity, in a fine illustration of the logical fallacy called "begging the question." Graham Hough's study of Spenser is widely read, not only for the insights it provides on its principal subject but also for its chapters on Ariosto and Tasso.[1] Discussing Bradamante, the female warrior in the *Orlando Furioso,* Hough says she is as brave and effective as a man, in fact, the perfect virago. He refers to Burckhardt's classic work of historical interpretation for the information that this ideal was "much cherished in the Italian Renaissance."[2] But what is the source of Burckhardt's "historical" assertion? If we consult *The Civilization of the Renaissance in Italy,* it turns out that the argument about the virago as a Renaissance ideal relies to some extent on the few notable ladies, but *primarily* on the poetic evidence of Ariosto and his predecessor Boiardo![3]

When all such material is set aside because its several parts cancel one another out, there remains very little independent evidence to support the conventional wisdom about an historical "breathing space" for women in the Renaissance period. The arguments have not been examined critically because assumptions that were being tentatively formulated in the literature of the sixteenth century have become the commonplaces of our own society. In the heroic poems it was suggested—though not for the first time in Western literature—that love was an appropriate motive and forerunner of marriage. Obstacles to love-marriage, particularly in the form of venal parental objections, were to be deplored and, if possible, overcome. In later fiction, a corollary proposition also came to be accepted: that it was wrong to marry for any reason other than love. This essentially literary norm eventually became a precept by which Western society as a whole was supposed to be conducted. When certain values become ingrained in a culture it is not easy to recognize that they have not always been present; in this case, although most people are aware that love-marriage is a relatively modern concept and practice, we do not examine its origins or its connection to other aspects of social change. It is precisely the persistence and power of the idea that make it an essential one to pursue and understand.

In my own work on the women warriors, I reached a point where many common assumptions were called into question by the dearth of credible evidence. The delicate interaction between social and literary values that I was taught to perceive in the character and fate of the lady knights had turned out to be a figment of critical imagination. A clean start was indicated, one that would take account of a different kind of history and thus make it possible to grasp the poetic myth in a different way. As I began this effort, I realized how naïve my previous approaches to that myth had been. In the course of my graduate training, much energy had been devoted to understanding the theory of allegory with its four levels of composition and interpretation, yet the allegorical content of my three heroic poems, at least insofar as they involved the women warriors and their role, had been reduced to an almost mimetic function. That is, I had been taught that female knights, equality, love, and marriage in the epic must stand for the status of women, love, and marriage in contemporary history. In postulating that it might not be so simple and seeking another sort of explanation, I learned that I had allegorical form, as well as history, on my side.

II

The first requisite was to look at the poems as a whole, without losing sight of the single theme that initially engaged me. (All three poems are not only extremely long, but contain a multitude of characters and incidents and are narrated through an overlapping structure of shifting perspectives and uncompleted episodes. Moreover, all are in some measure allegorical. Looking at them "as a whole," therefore, is not an easy task to encompass.) From this perspective it is apparent that, despite their dependence on earlier sources for plot, theme, and style, *Orlando Furioso, Jerusalem Delivered,* and *The Faerie Queene* constitute a unique tradition. Their adaptations of old themes and modes are deliberate and purposeful, and the use to which those modes are put is directly related to the ideological intentions of the romance epic.

That awkward term "romance epic" is in itself an index of the problem's scope. If it designates a separate literary genre (or "kind" as the sixteenth century would have said), the three poems under consideration are its only unambiguous examples. All three borrow from medieval romance a characteristic subject matter that unites the themes of love and war around a central chivalric motif. Their sprawling design and discontinuous method of narration are also traceable to this source. Yet in their organization and direction, the poems also owe much to what is called secondary or literary epic, that is, to works that serve the political and national functions of epic poetry but that do not derive from a native oral tradition; they are, in short, epic poems that some literary person sat down and wrote, as contrasted with those that have been collectively made, handed down, and developed through a culture. Virgil's *Aeneid* is the prime formal model for Ariosto, Tasso, and Spenser in their work.

Like Virgil, each of the three sixteenth-century poets was

working for a particular ruler—Spenser for Queen Elizabeth, Ariosto and Tasso for two successive generations of the House of Este in Ferrara—and had a poetic intent connected with this employment. On one level, glorifying the deeds of the patrons' ancestors was simple courtly flattery. It served as an argument for legitimacy, as well, for the poet pointed out that the patron had inherited not only the status of ruler but also the ability to rule. In tracing the line of Augustus back to Aeneas, Virgil is also making another kind of case for Roman rule and for the particular ruling clan to which the Emperor belonged. Aeneas was a Trojan prince who escaped with a small band of refugees when his city was destroyed by the Greeks at the climax of the Trojan War. He saved what was best of his civilization and merged it with that of Italy in founding what was to develop into Rome. Descent from the Trojans—always a somewhat problematical, if not entirely legendary, legacy—became, for Virgil's contemporaries, one more proof of Rome's imperial rights, for, through Aeneas, the mandate of Troy and its glory were inherited by her Roman successors.

Then Rome fell in its turn, as did two medieval formations that bore the title of Holy Roman Empire, and in the Renaissance period the mandate of Troy was once more vacant, by now rendered all the more valuable by the experience of the Roman *imperium*. For the sixteenth-century poet, demonstrating his own patrons' descent from the Trojan exiles could combine with the other themes of ancestral merit to consolidate their claim to the vacant *imperium*. Thus, *Orlando Furioso* takes place at the time of Charlemagne, whose supporters the young paladins are. The two lovers, Bradamante and Ruggiero, are descended from Troy—indeed, Hector himself is Ruggiero's ancestor—and their relation to Charles's Holy Roman Empire and their Emperor's crusade against the invading Saracens adds to the patrimony of the couple's Este descendants. (Ruggiero himself begins the epic on the Saracen side, his religious and political conversion forming one of the turning points in the plot.) Tasso's scene is the First Crusade, and he shows us several members of the House of Este making noble contributions to that effort; although direct descent from any of his heroes is impossible, since he allows no major characters to marry, Tasso is most explicit in pointing out the exemplary nature of these acts to his own patron, on whom he is urging a new crusade. *The Faerie Queene* has an Arthurian setting, and that national strain in the Tudor lineage is assured along with the Trojan background, which comes in via that Brut from whom the British Isles purportedly received their name.

The three poets were not the only ones of their contemporaries to try to win a mythopoeic security for their employers through the legend of Trojan origins. Ronsard's *Franciade* invents yet another scion of Aeneas (one Francus, no less) who founded the eponymous country and its present dynasty. The difference lies not only in the poetic quality of these efforts, but also in their overall political seriousness. Ariosto, Tasso, and Spenser were not satisfied, any more than Virgil was, with diplomatic flattery of a prince or his forebears, nor even with proving Ferrara's or England's right to imperial status. They were also concerned with helping their prince and their state to deserve that right. Hence, a great deal of direct advice is included in the poems—sometimes fitted in through the Virgilian tactic of attributing to the ruler political virtues, sentiments, and practices that the poet wishes he or she would acquire. (Only Tasso dares make use of a severely admonitory tone as well, lecturing the Estensi on the proper conduct of state.) More often the advice is oblique, occurring within the narrative itself, where questions about the best way to order the polity and to govern are paramount.

The dynastic theme is thus connected to larger political issues, on the one hand, and to love-marriages and female knights, on the other—a set of relations that suggests the possibility of a further connection between the ideas represented by the woman warriors and the poems' overall political thrust. One function of the military motif dominating all three poems is to provide a narrative equivalent for the state. In this sense, full participation of certain women in the poems' military aspect brings them into the state without having to involve them in any realistic machinery of government. The overriding metaphor of chivalry, reinforced by the traditional romance structure and content, also serves as an ideological cover. Use of the motif reflects little nostalgia for the bygone days of medieval warfare, not even in Spenser's conscious archaism. Rather, the chivalric motif makes it possible to present ideas that are new and to some degree radical under the protective coloration of a familiar literary convention and, what is still more important, of familiar social patterns. The new positions are gradually brought in and rendered unthreatening through the pretense that they are really just the same good old ideas after all. Many of these new conceptions are represented by the women warriors, and their presence in the chivalric episodes armors them in acceptable convention.

In fact, the code of chivalry was originally devised as a structure of essentially masculine values; that is, it formalized relationships and habits of thought belonging to a sector of feudal experience that was exclusively male terrain. Marx and Engels effectively demonstrate that the ruling ideas of any epoch "are nothing more than the ideal expression of the dominant material relationships, the dominant material relationships grasped as ideas."[4] From this perspective, chivalry may be understood as an "ideal expression," an expression in terms of ideas of the material relationships that constituted feudalism. Metaphorically it was an entirely apt figure for a system whose fundamental economic and political institutions all had their military aspect. The same system that established the pattern of land tenure also entailed the interlocking private armies that challenged and defended those property rights. The military structure was thus basic to feudalism, since it was the way that land, the primary means of production in the system, was acquired, secured, and added to.

Therefore, a cultural situation developed in which many facets of social life were conceptualized through the use of a military metaphor. For instance, juridical and even international disputes might be settled by single combat between two champions of the respective sides. It does not matter how often this practice was actually resorted to (for it is clear that regular judicial trials and full-scale wars continued to occur) but rather that contemporary ways of thinking made it possible for individual combat to become a normative model for human intercourse. The chivalric code, which was both a social and a literary formation, is the expression of this norm.

I referred earlier to the way courtly poetry applied the central fact of feudalism, the class relationship between lord and vassal, to the situation of the troubadour-lover and his beloved. In much the same way, the chivalric metaphor applies to social experience a set of concepts derived from the world of warfare. Other "ideal expressions" of feudal conditions—embodying, for example, the social frameworks of hierarchy and collectivity—may be found in painting, sculpture, architecture, and urban planning. But in literature, broadly defined, it was the military relations that were most frequently translated into the realm of ideas.

This meant that a great deal of cultural expression was carried out through reference to a side of life that did not have much room for women. Under feudalism, women participated in all aspects of production. Their work was likely to be sex-specific, and to that degree there was a division of labor by gender as well as by class, but there was as yet no separation of men and women into different sorts of workplaces, dominated by fundamentally different social relations. Thus, the most glaring sex division of labor did not occur between the home and the field, workshop, or marketplace, but between all of these locales and the field of battle. A woman's place might be in any or all of the first four sites, but it stopped short of the military sphere, where male imagery, as an expression of the male presence, therefore dominated.

Conceptually, the medieval state was understood in absolutist terms that recall the categories of chivalric metaphor. As in a contest between two champions or, for that matter, a game of chess, there was an array of forces perceived as diametrically opposed, with the outcome to be determined by what was seen as a military contest. This generalization holds true despite the fact that the central government did not exercise broad control, since much of what we would think of as state power was held by large landowners other than the monarch. And the law was perceived as standing above both king and state. The center of a medieval treatise on government was likely to be "good government," the proper conduct of kingship, and the categories were typically approached with a certain rigidity. Qualities deemed requisite for ruler and polity alike were those that were exalted by chivalric tradition, which means that the state itself, to the extent that the modern term has any meaning in discussions of earlier processes, was seen as having a masculine character.

With the transition from feudalism to capitalism, marked changes took place in social and constitutional structures. At the same time, both the state and the theory of the state became the subject of serious intellectual inquiry, so that these changes in superstructure are not difficult to trace. Emerging capitalism demanded of the state modes of operation that could assure continued development of these economic trends. This meant governmental units that were territorial, eventually national, a military force in the pay of that public sector, international relations that fostered exchange and credit, advanced diplomatic techniques, a centralized civil bureaucracy with specialized departmental tasks, businesslike methods, permanent records and, perhaps the most basic requisite for an essentially bourgeois state, "the rise of sentiments favorable to the moral autonomy of political behavior."[5] That is, further capitalist expansion necessitated a cli-

mate of opinion that perceived the state as having its own interests and that saw it as free to act in defense of those interests
without anachronistic moral constraints. The tension of values
implicit in this process reflects a conflict within the economic
sphere as well, for there, too, the older ethical systems condemned or at best failed to sanction some of the most lucrative
activities of the new moneymakers. The state was at once the
sphere in which these social conflicts were expressed, and a participant in them.

Development of a public bureaucracy in the sixteenth century
meant that matters of state depended increasingly on an office
rather than an individual. But centralization of bureaucratic
power was an outgrowth of the same development that led to an
increasingly centralized kingship. Government itself was an interaction between the prince's highly personal leadership and an
effective, nearly autonomous bureaucracy. Within that system,
as in any bureaucracy worthy of the name, departmentalization
was the keynote. As the ruler, in principle, became less specialized, government offices became much more so. And the tendency extended to the area of international relations. Diplomacy
became a full-time occupation, with the ambassador being regarded as a specialist or expert in the field. His services,
moreover, were no longer owing in principle to the collective
welfare of the Christian commonwealth, but were openly devoted
to the interests of his own state. This attitude was not yet
nationalism—for the national state was still a long way off in
Italy, where the modern view of diplomatic service was first
refined—but it was definitely secularism.

The political ideal articulated by both realistic and utopian
theorists in this period is balance between or among qualities,
classes, economic sectors, religious interests, and political states.
Balance is also a concept invoked by modern commentators in
their descriptions of the successful manipulations of personal
monarchy. Historians of the period also have frequent recourse to

the notion of flexibility in descriptions of diplomatic and bureaucratic maneuverings of princely style. Balance and flexibility were the qualities needed in the bourgeois state and in those who would direct its course. (Indeed, the two categories, government and leadership, were often fused, as sixteenth-century theorizing attributed to the state a moral autonomy that amounts to sheer literary personification.) But flexibility and balance were precisely the characteristics absent from the masculine absolutes of the feudal state. They were regarded as feminine qualities and this is where the women came in.

The human elements demanded by the state's new priorities correspond almost exactly to the stereotype of female nature prevailing in this period. Thus, for example, the theory of psychology that identified certain natural properties with the four "humors" held that, although both sexes had all four represented within them, female temperament was dominated by the cold and dry humors. Although "masculine" heat generated ardent activity and achievement, it also, for this very reason, led to exaggerated and hasty activity, whereas the greater coolness of the female conduced to greater flexibility. Beyond this dubious physiology, the social virtues of a lady were understood to include qualities variously denominated "love, the desire to please, kindness, pity or helpfulness."[6] Once more the emphasis is on a personal flexibility that can bring private and public demands into a new balance.

In the heroic poems of Ariosto, Tasso, and Spenser, the lady knights are the means by which a principle that the culture perceived as female is introduced into the state. The *Orlando Furioso,* through the functioning of Bradamante and Marfisa, the women warriors, presents a sort of redoubled double standard. Parallel to the conventional double standard requiring sexual chastity of women while permitting men a greater latitude, Ariosto, who both deplores and applies that standard, creates another duality that requires men to adhere to the rigid morality of chivalric life but allows women greater ethical innovation. Ruggiero, Bradamante's lover and Marfisa's twin, flounders about in the toils of this contradiction. In the first part of the poem he is caught in a conflict between love and lust, where his sexual faithfulness is repeatedly tried and found wanting. Later on, once his fidelity is assured, there arises a more serious conflict between love and what he perceives to be his duty, where "duty" means unwavering and unexamined loyalty to an obsolete chivalric code. By contrast, the singlemindedly faithful Bradamante cannot be faulted as to chivalrous conduct, either, but wherever a conflict does arise between the demands of love and those of duty, she places herself unhesitatingly in the service of her love—which also means that of her historic and dynastic role. Marfisa reflects an even greater shift in values. An admirable but often comic figure, she is the most hotheaded of knights, always ready to settle any question by a good fight and always prepared to see questions of chivalric honor in any issue that arises. Yet it is she who learns, like a good Renaissance statesman, to apply the diplomatic art of compromising honesty in the service of a "higher" political and personal expediency.

Tasso's Counter-Reformation vision does not tolerate any such compromise, yet his sanctified polity is also changed by the addition of qualities belonging to his female characters. Because the military realm unites all the concerns of Tasso's world, the poet does not often digress to scenes unconnected with the Crusade itself. Thus, Erminia and Armida, respectively a virgin princess and a sexually aware court lady, participate in the military campaign and live out their love stories within its boundaries quite as much as does Clorinda, the only one of Tasso's heroines who is actually a soldier. All three are Saracens, an ethnic and religious identity invariably linked, in *Jerusalem Delivered,* to a lack of emotional restraint. But, whereas this unrestrained character is the undoing of male Saracens, conversion makes it possible for the two conventionally feminine ladies to bring strong emotion, tenderness, even passion, to the rather austere Christian culture represented by Tasso's Crusaders. In the act of conversion, Clorinda, Erminia, and Armida all have to submit to male domination, yet their conversion and their character also have an impact on the masculine society they are entering. Moreover, since Tasso's theme is the restoration of holiness to human society, the women's conversion places them at the poem's ideological center.

For Spenser, balance is an explicitly articulated philosophical ideal and, in his allegory, is best expressed in equilibrium between male and female forces. Within the state, therefore, as in all other social and spiritual constructs, the female principle is essential for that balance and is most clearly and consistently embodied in the character of Britomart, the lady knight in *The Faerie Queene*. What is never clear or consistent, however, is whether Britomart should be interpreted as representing the female part of the requisite sexual balance or whether she contains both elements within a psychology defined as androgynous. More directly than either of his Italian forerunners and models, Spenser incorporates new, fundamentally bourgeois ideas into the fabric of his allegory by dressing them up in deliberate archaisms of language and concept. And for this ideological deception, the women were essential.

III

The question that comes to mind is how they got away with it. It was not *women* the early modern state required, but a principle, a set of qualities that the contemporary culture defined as feminine. The contradiction between woman as an historical being and woman as a conceptual entity was sharpened by events in both spheres, for the same social forces that were degrading women's equality as producers also inspired new concentration on the female as an intellectual instrument. This was by no means the first or the only period in which there was a conflict between the actual status of women and their symbolic function: as Virginia Woolf points out, "woman pervades poetry from cover to cover; she is all but absent from history."[7] What is more difficult to understand is how, in a time of historical ferment, marked by the general weakening of women's position, as well as by a certain level of philosophical, theological, and political controversy about the woman question, it was possible to confine the symbolism I have identified to the literary and theoretical realm.

One source of the answer is in the multiple levels of allegory. I do not believe that I have exaggerated the connection between the changing nature of the state in the sixteenth century and the character attributed to the female sex. It would become a distortion of reality, however, if I claimed that this political symbolism were the women warriors' only function in the romance epic. Pointing out that the rise of mercantile capitalism did not signal a period of emancipation for women means denying that the independence manifested by the epic heroines and the love-marriages the poets arrange for them have a mimetic intent. It does not mean that the themes that seem to have to do with women are entirely unrelated to the experience or the expectations of contemporary women. The allegorical mode makes it possible for more than one set of correspondences to be suggested by the same character or incident. Thus, an interpretation that relies on the "feminization" of the state under the growing hegemony of the bourgeoisie can coexist with an interpretation that assumes that these poems do have something to do with women's lives and the values that controlled them.

The poets' approach to love-marriage is the focus of confusion. Marriage for love is a frequent and admirable event in the romance epic. I have argued that it was not the prevailing ethic or custom in sixteenth-century Europe. Subsequently, however, it did become the dominant position on the issue in literature as in social life, the one that continues to shape our consciousness. For this reason, it is tempting to take the idealist position and assume that the love-marriage theme arose spontaneously in the Renaissance period and that its prominence and recurrence in literature gave rise to its gradual acceptance as a value by which people actually lived and Western society was organized. I believe, on the contrary, that examining the historical and material origins of our culture's view of love and marriage also leads to an understanding of why the theme arose in sixteenth-century poetry before it could be realized in contemporary life.

By the sixteenth century, the transition to a new mode of productive life was well under way. Although students of political economy do not agree about the precise stage the transition had reached, they are generally in accord about the decline of feudal institutions.* The cash market was becoming the dominant economic force, in agriculture as well as in commodity production and exchange. Wage labor was increasingly the norm in country and city alike, and farm rents were increasingly payable in cash. Moreover, management of the land according to essentially capitalist principles meant enclosure and engrossment, with a consequent shift of land use to purposes that were no longer labor-intensive. The predictable result was that masses of former agricultural workers were thrown off the land and either became homeless wanderers, liable to execution for vagabondage, or migrated to the growing towns; the survivors' descendents eventually formed the basis of the urban working class.

Although these conditions apply most precisely to England, many of the same social results were visible in Italy. Except for those sections of the South and of Sicily that the Normans had conquered, feudalism never achieved much of a foothold in Italy. The heritage of the Roman system placed the countryside very

---

*Those who acknowledge the existence of feudalism, at any rate. It is becoming fashionable to deny the viability of "feudalism" as an historical construct; I suspect this has something to do with the long-standing reluctance of bourgeois scholars to come to terms with *capitalism* as a construct.

much under the economic and political influence of the towns, even in those places where agriculture was the principal source of income. As those towns changed from medieval communes to centers of bourgeois commerce and territorial government, the pattern of domination that kept rural production at the mercy of the new cash economy was already established.

Under feudalism, as in earlier systems, there had been a general division of labor according to sex; within the economy of a particular household or farm, certain tasks were generally restricted to women and others to men, while some were appropriate for members of either sex. The jobs that were considered women's work tended to be directly concerned with the household: not only cooking, cleaning, laundry and child care, but production of cloth and clothing, basic nursing, care of cows and production of dairy products, kitchen gardening, soap and candle making, care of chickens and their eggs, and so on; even an upper-class woman, who did not engage in this work herself, normally was in charge of those in her household who did, so that "housewifery" could mean either application of the requisite skills or exercise of supervision. My list of the functions entailed in this occupation is not exhaustive by any means, but it should serve to demonstrate the material importance of the work normally assigned to women in the maintenance of an economy that was in essence domestic.

As cash became the principal means of exchange and men's work was performed for cash wages, a separation of economic functions or spheres was superimposed on the existing sex division of labor. Thus, women's work continued to be performed in, for, and about the house and outside the prevailing cash market. Men's work, by contrast, took place outside the household and within the cash system. A man might work for wages or hire others to work for him, but in either case his wife, daughters, perhaps his sisters, his mother, and other female relations, as well, did *their* work in the unpaid domestic sector. (It is not my intention to gloss over the gross social differences between the male entrepreneur and the male wage-earner; I merely mean to point out that they are participants, albeit antagonistic ones, in the same economy.)

Women's household work, as socially necessary as ever, became increasingly marginal to the economy. This resulted in a real loss of equality, though not of power, since women's economic contribution had never given them access to political power. The erosion of economic equality, though, had important cultural effects that bear directly on the literary theme of love and marriage. It should be understood, first of all, that the household remained as an economic entity. Dowries and marriage settlements did not disappear in the urbanizing society of early capitalist Europe; indeed, they became increasingly important. The family was still a necessary institution for material survival. And one economic function, that of consuming, was to expand considerably, as some of the items in my list of the feudal housewife's tasks were transformed into purchasable services or goods. (It is easy for a twentieth-century person to overestimate this last function; actually, most of the jobs I mentioned continued to be performed at home through the nineteenth century and, in rural areas, well into the twentieth.) The housewife's job itself did not change with the advent of capitalism or even with the industrial revolution. What changed was its status in the overall system.

Despite the persistence of all these functions, women's economic position was degraded by their removal from the center of the economy. And the household's status as an economic unit was increasingly deemphasized in people's cultural understanding of it. "Family" came to mean a system of personal relationships, rather than signifying those relationships in their proper framework, the institution I have designated by the term "household." In an urban cash economy, moreover, a smaller number of individuals made up the network of relationships that constituted

174SEX, CLASS, AND CULTURE

the family. And within this sphere, the heterosexual couple, its material basis denied, gained importance as an emotive entity. Men's work relationships, to the extent that management could control them, were being stripped of all affect, and work was defined as the place where human feeling was not. Meanwhile, as home was increasingly defined as the place where business was not, it was forced to be the one place where love was. Clearly, however, the establishment of this norm had different effects in the lives of women than in the lives of men.

Overcoming whatever obstacles to fulfillment-through-love might be set up by the world of business became the essential theme of bourgeois fiction. Often it was expressed through parental opposition to a love-match. (This approach is adumbrated near the end of *Orlando Furioso,* and its inclusion has offended the critics' sense of decorum ever since.) As long as the interests of capitalism continued to be served by the family, the institution could be made to serve a new ideological function along with its material one. Indeed, the ideology of the loving couple as the foundation of a domestic haven could serve to strengthen and support the household's economic function, especially insofar as that function involved the rearing of the next generation and the shelter of those for whom there is no room in the wage labor system (which, under capitalism, has meant at various times women, children, or the aged).

The ideology of family love effectively controlled women so that their economic contribution remained unrecognized. This is not to say that love, because it has an ideological basis, is imaginary or invented, but rather to point out that the heterosexual love relationship and the institutional forms by which it is expressed are not static categories existing in nature. They have a foundation in history and they change as historical imperatives change. When a woman says she loves her husband, she is not necessarily deluded, foolish, or lying; but if she says she is leaving him because she no longer loves him and their marriage is therefore meaningless, she is making a statement bounded by the ethical and cultural assumptions of our particular time in history, when love is supposed to be the basis of a meaningful marriage. And if she says that she does all the housework because she loves her family, she is seeing herself, her relationships, and her feelings as something unique and private, not as a part of history. Housework is socially necessary labor; it has to be done; and institutionalization of love ensures that a woman who doesn't want to do housework will feel guilt for failing at love, not at a job.

But all this was well in the future; the transition to the capitalist mode was a gradual one. If a conclusion can be drawn from the drastic increase in dowry size in the sixteenth and seventeenth centuries, it is that there was a difference between the immediate and the long-range effects of the cash economy. In the short term, introduction of capitalist modes meant treating the domestic establishment as if it were a business enterprise that must be made to "pay" directly. This pattern changed with the heightened ideological need for a family based on private emotional ties and supposedly remote from the standards of commerce. The new ideological and material goals of marriage could then be complementary as long as the latter were explicitly denied.

In the sixteenth century, even this reconciliation was a long way off. The love-marriage theme in the heroic poem is an initial response to conditions that were still relatively undeveloped. And the theme itself remains undeveloped, with Ariosto ignoring the fact that the love-marriages he proposes are an innovation, Tasso unable to achieve a resolution, and Spenser, the most socially abstract of the three, the only one who posits a whole cosmology around the idea of heterosexual love and the generative process. The social and class pressures that were bringing new sexual values into being were also—and rather more rapidly—effecting changes in the process and the concept of government. Looked at from this point of view, the political and the sexual themes are not distinct; rather, they are different aspects of the same problem. Understanding this congruence and, more generally, the history of love-marriage as an idea provides insight that is essential if we want to analyze the historical forces that are acting on the present-day family and develop a social movement with an operative strategy for liberation.

NOTES

1. Graham Hough, *A Preface to the Faerie Queene* (New York: Norton Library, 1963).
2. Ibid., p. 29.
3. Jacob Burckhardt, *The Civilization of the Renaissance in Italy* (rpt. New York: Random House, 1954), p. 294.
4. Karl Marx and Frederick Engels, *The German Ideology*, Part One (rpt. New York: International, 1970), p. 64.
5. Garrett Mattingly, "Some Revisions of The Political History of the Renaissance," in *The Renaissance: A Reevaluation,* ed. Tinsley Helton (Madison: University of Wisconsin Press, 1964), p. 11.
6. Ruth Kelso, *Doctrine for the Lady of the Renaissance* (Urbana: University of Illinois Press, 1956), p. 16.
7. Virginia Woolf, *A Room of One's Own,* (rpt. New York: Harcourt, Brace, 1957), p. 45.

Why Marry
Mr. Collins?

=====================================

IT IS A TRUTH universally acknowledged that Miss Charlotte Lucas married for material gain. Assembling the facts presented by Jane Austen in *Pride and Prejudice,* we learn that Charlotte, eldest daughter of Sir William Lucas, is twenty-seven years old and has never been handsome. Although a woman of good sense, she has not quite the "elegance of mind" that characterizes the two elder Miss Bennets. No one has offered for Miss Lucas and her prospects are not very bright, so when Mr. Collins, the estranged cousin on whom Mr. Bennet's Longbourn estate is entailed, proposes to her on the rebound from Elizabeth Bennet after an assiduous three-day courtship, she accepts. Since it is a truth no less universally acknowledged that Mr. Collins is a schmuck, the conclusion about Miss Lucas's motives inexorably follows.

But anyone leaping to this conclusion is ignoring some of Jane Austen's hints about who Charlotte Lucas is and what social distinctions mark her off from the Miss Bennets, and also denying the complexity of women's material position by assuming opposition, rather than identity, between the cultural aspect and the property aspect of marriage. And to miss all this means missing some of what the novel has to tell us about class, love, money, and marriage—which are, after all, the great subjects of *Pride and Prejudice*. Much can be learned from comparing Miss Lucas's situation to that of other young women in the book, exploring the implications of that situation for the social stratum in which the action takes place, and examining the historical changes that were influencing the class and family structures of English society. Through this process, though by no means incidentally, it also becomes clear why someone would marry the otherwise entirely resistible Mr. Collins.

One of the central themes of the nineteenth-century English novel is the enormous cultural, intellectual, and spiritual distance between the landed gentry and the bourgeoisie—that is, between those who make their money from land and those who make it from money. Viewed from the outside, and despite all the arguments weighed up on behalf of this distinction, the differences and their significance appear almost entirely fictive. Indeed, Raymond Williams maintains that a hypocritical effort to depict the countryside—land, people, and culture—as being despoiled and exploited by invaders from the city rather than by its own landed classes has pervaded Western thought and literature since antiquity. Although the dates of the supposed transition are constantly pushed forward, the idea that the good old ways on the land died within one's lifetime, so that the very old people one knew as a child could remember the thoroughly golden time, is part and parcel of the myth delineated by Williams.[1] Nonetheless, it is surely not his intention to ignore the fact that there really was a transition from feudalism to capitalism which had enormous impact on agricultural production, on village life, on domestic labor, and on the balance between city and country. One phase of that massive revolution in the material grounding of English society happened within Jane Austen's own time, with traumatic effects on the class about which she wrote. The conservatism of *Mansfield Park*, a later novel that is ultimately a hymn to the landed gentry and its way of life and a defense against threats to that class from aristocratic, commercial, or urban elements in the social order, is rooted in Austen's reaction to the menace of rapid cultural change.[2] In *Pride and Prejudice,* by contrast, written a number of years before and conceived still earlier, Jane Austen is a restrained but exact social revolutionary, accepting a coequal hegemony of gentry and bourgeoisie and upholding the daring, fundamentally bourgeois notion that human worth is not a matter of birth but of individual merit, of culture.

Who *are* the people in *Pride and Prejudice?* Jane Austen brings most of her major characters onto the scene neatly ticketed as to class, profession, income (or, in the case of a single woman, expected marriage portion), and what she calls "mind," a fusion of ethical and temperamental qualities. Only Mr. Wickham, who presents himself in a false light and about whom conflicting opinions are current among his acquaintance, is not introduced in this way by the omniscient third-person narrator. But the labels affixed by Austen are not always easy for twentieth-century readers to understand.

Among the characters presented in the novel, Mr. Darcy's family is at the top of the social scale. His mother, sister of the redoubtable Lady Catherine DeBourgh, was a Lady Anne Fitzwilliam, daughter of one earl and sister of his successor. We know she is from the upper nobility, because the title "Lady," followed by a woman's first name, is assigned to the daughters of earls, marquesses, and dukes, remaining their appellation if they marry a man of lesser rank and add his last name. The precise level of the peerage is specified for us because Colonel Fitzwilliam, Lady Catherine's other nephew, is described as the younger son of an earl.[3] Jane Austen takes this kind of social distinction for granted and it probably creates little difficulty, even today, for her British audience. But when the social universe of a novel has so many unfamiliar features, it is hard to separate those aspects—like entailed property, marriage settlements, titles of nobility—that are common reference points or definitions in that society from those that are specific to this author's work and are part of her thesis. The alien elements also create obstacles to our understanding of how the world of Jane Austen and the women she wrote about was transforming itself into a set of material conditions much closer to our own.

Both Fitzwilliam sisters have married well, although Rosings, Lady Catherine's home, has less beautiful grounds, is less impressively situated, planned, and decorated, and is less imbued with the sense of humane culture—"real elegance," in Jane Austen's lexicon—than Mr. Darcy's Pemberly. Darcy has an annual income of some £10,000, which implies an inheritance worth £200,000, his younger sister has a dowry of £30,000 (Wickham didn't attempt to elope with her for motives of revenge alone, much less out of lust). Darcy's income derives principally from the rent-rolls of Pemberly. Since this way of making money is somehow different from mere vulgar business, he has only contempt for "trade" and those who engage in it.

Nonetheless, he is friends with Bingley, and considers Jane Bennet, with her "low" (which is to say, bourgeois and petty-bourgeois) connections, an unsuitable match for that easygoing young man. As we know from his introduction as tenant of Netherfield Park, Bingley has yet to purchase an estate and establish himself as a member of the landed classes. Indeed, so relaxed is his attitude toward matters of status that, as Jane Austen suggests, once settled on the rented estate, he might leave it to his son to buy the land that will make the Bingleys gentry. At the end of the novel, we learn that marriage to Jane Bennet has actually provided the impetus for such a purchase, since Netherfield proved too near her family for the young couple's comfort. Bingley is a "gentleman" in his sentiments and his good instincts, if not yet in his property. He engages in no profession or business himself, but the original family fortune came from trade. It is his sisters who are most eager to erase that stigma by ignoring its existence, by marrying into the landed classes (the elder sister, as a result, has a husband of "more fashion than fortune," while

Miss Bingley, as we know, wants Darcy for herself and Georgianna Darcy for her brother), by holding Bingley's purchase of an estate as their "darling wish," and by deriding the Miss Bennets' connection with an uncle who lives in Cheapside.

That uncle is, of course, Mr. Gardiner, who, as one must keep reminding oneself, is Mrs. Bennet's brother. His existence is mentioned for the first time in the passage that describes the Bennets' "situation in life," which is to say, their social and economic position. Mrs. Bennet, daughter of a Meryton attorney, has two siblings, the "vulgar" Mrs. Philips and another, who does not appear in person for some chapters and is simply characterized as "a brother settled in London in a respectable line of trade." As Mrs. Bennet, her sister on the scene, and her younger daughters proceed to expose themselves to the contempt of Miss Bingley and Mrs. Hurst, there is no reason to suppose that the uncle in Cheapside, whose degrading business looms so large in their snobbish bill of particulars, is anything but the crass "cit" who would aptly complete our picture of the family's maternal line. When the Gardiners arrive to spend Christmas at Longbourn more than one-third of the way through the novel, we are deliberately disabused of this notion: "Mr. Gardiner was a sensible, gentlemanlike man, greatly superior to his sisters, as well by nature as education. The Netherfield ladies would have had difficulty in believing that a man who lived by trade, and within view of his own warehouse, could have been so well-bred and agreeable. Mrs. Gardiner . . . was an amiable, intelligent, elegant woman. . . ."

It is not just the absent ladies of Netherfield who would be surprised at Mr. Gardiner's being so gentlemanlike, but the reader, who has come to expect by now that bourgeois status and poor breeding are synonymous. The character of Bingley's sisters, who want to conceal their bourgeois origins and who, despite their claims to "accomplishment," are neither cultivated nor truly well mannered, does nothing to challenge this supposition. But Lady Catherine, with neither the cultural nor the social attributes of a gentlewoman, and the Gardiners, who are amply endowed with them but remain "in trade," make it clear that birth and personal value are by no means identical. Jane Austen never abandons the ideal of the gentry in *Pride and Prejudice,* or calls it by some other name, but she makes its boundaries flexible enough to embrace real worth, in whatever class she may locate it.

Mrs. Gardiner gives wise and compassionate advice to her nieces, and, when Lydia is removed from the shack-up with Wickham prior to their hasty marriage, she adds moral advice as well. But, whatever her youngest niece may think of her "preaching," Mrs. Gardiner is not all gravity. Her first responsibility on her arrival in the country is to regale the ladies of Longbourn with the latest fashion news. On a higher level, she shares Elizabeth's taste and her appreciation for style—whether they be reflected in the eschewing of romantic pretensions or in delight at the lovely grounds of Pemberley. Both she and her husband are readers, sharing too an unaffected love of good scenery and of pleasant society. Mr. Gardiner also enjoys fishing, a sport entirely in keeping with his image as a nature lover and a contemplative man. Unlike Mr. Bennet, who was born to his rank and certainly possesses the "quick parts" and intellectual culture of his class, both Gardiners also have a strong sense of family responsibility. They never emerge as full characters in their own right, but Jane Austen spares no effort in conveying that we are to think of them as fine, fine people.

Mr. Darcy, when he encounters them exploring the grounds of Pemberly, certainly thinks so, and the language in which his attitude is summarized proves most revealing. He asks Elizabeth

> if she would do him the honour of introducing him to her friends. This was a stroke of civility for which she was quite unprepared, and she could hardly suppress a smile at his being now seeking the acquaintance of those very people against whom his pride had revolted in his offer to herself. 'What will be his surprise,' thought she, 'when he knows who they are? He takes them now for people

of fashion.' . . . That he was *surprised* by the connection was evident; he sustained it, however, with fortitude, and, so far from going away, turned back with them and entered into conversation with Mr. Gardiner. Elizabeth could not but be pleased, could not but triumph. It was consoling that he should know she had some relations for whom there was no need to blush. She listened most attentively to all that passed between them, and gloried in every expression, every sentence of her uncle, which marked his intelligence, his taste, or his good manners.

Indeed, the Elizabeth Bennet who sees no indictment of George Wickham in the revelation that his father was the late Mr. Darcy's steward is fully vindicated by this meeting. Wickham is not a bounder because his father served the gentry rather than being of it. He is a bounder because he prefers to live by and for his own pleasure, at the greatest cost to others, instead of following a respectable profession and a decent line of conduct. Similarly, Mrs. Bennet and Mrs. Philips are not silly and superficial women because their father was a Meryton attorney, but because they have not made use of any but the most trivial opportunities that came their way. Their brother had natural gifts beyond theirs and, as a male, far greater possibilities of cultivating them. Jane Austen leaves us in no doubt, however, that it was in the two sisters' power to improve themselves had they been able to fix their minds on anything beyond appearances. Mr. Gardiner is not a gentleman *despite* his business any more than Mr. Darcy is one simply because he is a great landowner.

Yet it is important to stress that the terms of judgment remain entirely unaltered. Darcy takes the Gardiners for "people of fashion," that is, for members of his own class. And, although Jane Austen may adumbrate a smooth transition or a gradual eradication of the boundaries between different segments of the possessing classes, they are *not* "people of fashion" who move in "good society." Nor do they aspire to be. The social definitions remain fixed, although the elements that will force an eventual change are already present in the social fabric. In this regard, it should perhaps be noted that the Gardiners, although their role in the novel is primarily instrumental, have one of the few happy marriages that Jane Austen depicts in any of her novels and one that appears to be built on a foundation of both affection and equality between the partners.

Mr. and Mrs. Bennet's material situation is as different from all this as are their relations with each other. By most definitions, Mr. Bennet is a gentleman. He lives on inherited land that brings in £2000 a year, and he possesses a cultivated literary taste. His moral standards are informed and correct—in fact, gentlemanly—but his behavior to those around him often falls short of the civility that should accompany such standards. His wife is not a gentlewoman by birth, breeding, principles, or manners. Her father, the Meryton attorney, left her £4000. We learn later, in the discussion of Lydia's unfortunate marriage, that £5000 are set aside by the Bennets' marriage contract for the daughters' dowries and support of Mrs. Bennet's eventual widowhood. Most of that is presumably her own inheritance. Her sister, the Aunt Philips who obligingly keeps open house so that her nieces may meet and flirt with the officers, has also married an attorney, their father's clerk and successor. There is no mistaking the social distance between these two branches of the family, despite their connection and present intimacy. We are told of Mrs. Philips that she was "too much in awe of Mr. Darcy to speak comfortably in his presence, yet, whenever she *did* speak, she must be vulgar. Nor was her respect for him, though it made her more quiet, at all likely to make her more elegant." When Elizabeth Bennet asserts that there is no disparity of station between herself and Darcy ("He is a gentleman; I am a gentleman's daughter; so far we are equal"), she is stating the truth, but not the whole truth, and that arrant snob, Lady Catherine DeBourgh, can come back immediately with the reminder that she is not the daughter of a gentlewoman as well.

At the same time that we learn the value of the Bennet estate, we learn that it is "entailed, in default of heirs male, on a distant relation." None of Mr. Bennet's children is a boy, and only males can inherit an entailed estate; Longbourn will pass to Mr. Collins upon the decease of its present owner, who describes his heir with bitter accuracy as the man "who, when I am dead, may turn you all out of this house as soon as he pleases." Assuming that a son would be born to them, keeping Longbourn in the direct line and providing for his sisters out of the estate, the Bennets had always been unthrifty in their habits and lived up to their income. The result, with no son forthcoming, is that the principal of £5000 is all that will be left for Mrs. Bennet and her five daughters.*

Most important, there is nothing the Bennets can do to assure a more secure future for their daughters. Marriage is the only fate the Miss Bennets can hope for, their beauty and charm serving a compensatory purpose measurable in pounds sterling. What is otherwise in store for them upon their father's death is a spinster's life with their insufferable mother, supported by an annual income of £50 each per year. From this perspective, it is no small thing that Mr. Collins plans to make amends to his cousins by marrying one of them. Stupid and pompous he may be, but his offer, on the material plane, is valuable nonetheless.

The case is rather different for Charlotte Lucas. A member of the local bourgeoisie who had made "a tolerable fortune" in trade, Sir William Lucas had been knighted during the period of his mayoralty, at which point he had foolishly and inappropriately taken on the life style of the landed gentry, retiring from business

---

*That this doesn't add up to much of a dowry for each girl is amply attested by figures provided in other Jane Austen novels, as well as in *Pride and Prejudice* itself. The Miss Dashwoods of *Sense and Sensibility* are comparatively poor, with £10,000 for the three of them to share with their mother, whereas the young lady whom the perfidious Willoughby marries has £50,000. Emma Woodhouse, described as "handsome, clever, and rich," has £30,000, but when she refuses Mr. Elton, he goes off to Bath, confident that if he cannot win her, there is always "Miss Somebody-else with twenty or with ten." Indeed, the encroaching new Mrs. Elton brings him "so many thousands of pounds as will always be called ten." *Mansfield Park*'s Lady Bertram, at the time of her marriage to the baronet, was judged by her own uncle to be some three thousand pounds short of deserving a matrimonial prize clearly entitled to a portion of £10,000.

and from Meryton. Jane Austen is ironic about this transformation of tradesman into gentleman, pointing out that, once retired,
"he could think with pleasure of his own importance, and, un-
shackled by business, occupy himself solely in being civil to all
the world." But, although she portrays him as a silly and preten-
tious man, full of repeated references to his presentation at court,
she grants that, in respect to behavior, the area of gentlemanly
conduct wherein Mr. Bennet himself does not live up to the ideal
of his class, the transformation seems really to have taken: "By
nature inoffensive, friendly, and obliging, his presentation at St.
James's had made him courteous." The "tolerable fortune" is no
longer growing. Perhaps Sir William has even been foolish
enough to dip into the principal. But his property, as the profits of
bourgeois enterprise, is his to dispose of as he chooses, with no
regard for the obsolete and hobbling processes of entailment. He
has sons, but this does not mean he must deprive his daughters
and leave everything to one male heir. Moreover, his property is
presumably in invested monies, and the same kind of damage
would not result from dividing it up as from cutting up a landed
estate. The Lucases are decidedly not rich. Mrs. Bennet boasts of
the fact that, unlike their friend Charlotte, *her* daughters never
have to help in the kitchen. Charlotte herself is described as a
"well-educated young woman of small fortune" and a "daughter,
to whom [her parents] . . . could give little fortune." Even
though Charlotte's "freedom" comes by way of Mr. Collins, her
younger sisters rejoice at her betrothal because it means they can
be introduced to society and begin their own husband-hunt
sooner than anticipated, and her brothers are relieved that she
will not die an old maid. Yet Sir William's death will not make the
same dramatic difference in the material situation of his family as
Mr. Bennet's will. As her brothers marry, a spinster sister might
come to live with one of them, perhaps the one that settles at
Lucas Lodge, and continue with the domestic responsibilities she
has already undertaken. If we consider actual *need,* Charlotte's

position is a great deal less precarious than that of Elizabeth Bennet; in strictly material terms, it is really Elizabeth who should have been grateful to receive Mr. Collins's proposals!

Near the end of *Pride and Prejudice,* when Jane Bennet is happily engaged to Mr. Bingley, but Elizabeth assumes that her family's connection with Wickham, for which he himself supplied the monetary "shotgun," precludes any renewal of Mr. Darcy's offer to herself, the two sisters discuss their prospects. Jane extolls her own betrothed and wishes that an equal joy were possible for her sister. Elizabeth replies that she does not deserve Jane's happiness because she has not her goodness, and concludes, "No, no, let me shift for myself; and perhaps, if I have very good luck, I may meet with another Mr. Collins in time." We know Elizabeth's ironic wit does not spare herself and her own affairs, and surely, although she has renounced Darcy in her mind and Lady Catherine's visit has not yet occurred to inspire fresh hope, she still has her fantasies about Mr. Darcy. Yet there is some bitterness in this self-mockery. Maybe she will, with "very good luck," find herself another Mr. Collins. No one could wish her such fortune. But—outside the realm of her own and Jane Austen's imaginings—what else has she to look forward to?

Elizabeth is still quite young. Pressed by Lady Catherine, during the visit to Rosings, she admits, "I am not one-and-twenty." Charlotte Lucas, more than six years older and without her friend's looks, brains, and character, could tell her something about what lies ahead. For Charlotte knows it is not only penury and need that make an old maid's life so grim that everyone is delighted when even Mr. Collins comes along to take her off the hands of her family. Charlotte is not as bereft of funds as Elizabeth would be should she remain a spinster after Mr. Bennet's death. But there is no social role for her, and Jane Austen makes it quite clear that the material condition of woman involves more than the price tag attached to her dowry and the income that portion, combined with her personal attributes, can win for her.

What Charlotte wants that Mr. Collins can provide is an "establishment."

Jane Austen caustically defines matrimony, "however uncertain of giving happiness" as being the "pleasantest preventive from want" for a young woman in Charlotte's circumstances. It is, further, "the only honourable provision" that can be made for such a woman. Fanny Price in *Mansfield Park* and Jane Fairfax in *Emma* may face something like real want if "honourable provision" is not made for them; Charlotte does not. But she does face a life of superfluity on the margins, presumably, of her brothers' flourishing households. Whatever contribution her efforts might make to such a household (for we know that Charlotte is a competent housekeeper even before she becomes Mrs. Collins) would not be valued at its true worth. And wage labor, even were any available and acceptable, is not the answer it might be for a young woman in our century. For this last point, the conversation in the opening chapter of *Emma* reveals certain crucial semantic differences. When she was employed as the governess at Hartfield, Miss Taylor was a "dependent." Now that she is Mrs. Weston, "settled in a home of her own . . . and secure of a comfortable provision," her marriage is said to have made her "independent." Earning her own living, even were that possible, would be degrading for a woman like Elizabeth or for Charlotte, and in *Emma* Jane Fairfax refers to the "governess trade" and "offices for the sale of human flesh" precisely as one would speak of the slave trade or prostitution. Naturally, working for "fulfillment," an interest, something to do, is no more of a real possibility than doing so for survival. The only way Charlotte can put her skills and energy to work in a recognized, socially useful way is through marriage.

The summary of the betrothed Charlotte's sentiments when urged to set the wedding date is succinct: "The stupidity with which . . . [Mr. Collins] was favoured by nature must guard his courtship from any charm that could make a woman wish for its continuance; and Miss Lucas, who accepted him solely from the pure and disinterested desire of an establishment, cared not how soon that establishment were gained." It is tempting to interpret this notion of "establishment," coming as it does in the same passage with the references to an "honourable provision," in the narrowest material sense. Charlotte's parents are certainly judging it in such terms: "Mr. Collins's present circumstances made it a most eligible match . . . and his prospects of future wealth were exceedingly fair. Lady Lucas began directly to calculate, with more interest than the matter had ever excited before, how many years longer Mr. Bennet was likely to live." Such a calculation is not far different from Mrs. Bennet's assumptions about how the Collinses must spend their time planning for Mr. Bennet's death. It is probable, however, that Charlotte is thinking less about being Mrs. Bennet's successor as eventual mistress of the Longbourn estate than she is of being mistress of the parsonage at Rosings—a prospect that, in itself, constitutes the defined social role she had been missing.

Elizabeth's visit to her newly married friend provides us with glimpses of that establishment, as well as of the Collinses' relationship. The house itself is pleasant; although it may be small by the standards of Jane Austen's gentry, we know it can accommodate three house guests without apparent inconvenience, and it is well to bear these relative categories in mind. Lady Catherine, as patron, remodeled the house when Mr. Collins took over the living, although Elizabeth attributes all the neatness and consistency of decoration to Charlotte's good taste and housewifely touch. Charlotte herself, as mistress of this domain, is an active housekeeper, sewing and mending, superintending domestic work, ordering meals (when offered some refreshment, Lady Catherine notes that Mrs. Collins's joints of meat are too large for her family), tending the cows and poultry about whose care Lady Catherine gives further officious advice, and perhaps still being occasionally "wanted about the mince pies" as she was in the days of her spinsterhood.

But Charlotte has leisure to "sit" in some sense entirely foreign to us, and has chosen for that purpose a room whose limited access to what is happening on the road will not attract Mr. Collins away from his own study. Mrs. Collins supervises the servants who do most of the food preparation and probably all the cleaning, as well as the outdoor work; it is not to be expected that she would perform any of this labor herself. Jane Austen does not tell us Mr. Collins's present income, but a plural number of servants is taken for granted. When Mr. Darcy comes to propose to Elizabeth, she is surprised to hear the doorbell so late in the evening, but she does not have to answer the door herself; the next thing we or the heroine know is that Darcy is in the room. That eternal busybody Lady Catherine urges Charlotte to be sure to send the manservant (she even names him, so minute is her knowledge of the Collinses' home life) to accompany Maria Lucas and Elizabeth on their return trip. Upon learning that Elizabeth's uncle, Mr. Gardiner, is sending someone for them, she seems surprised that his bourgeois establishment supports a manservant. But such an expense is apparently acceptable in a country clergyman's home, though we all know how Lady Catherine feels about both extravagance and low-status people aping their "betters."

This matter of servants is one of the elements that make it difficult to interpret Jane Austen's social universe. The servants are always there, usually unnamed and practically never mentioned, but *there*. No one in Jane Austen's novels is so poor as to have to take personal charge of maintaining food, shelter, and clothing. Not even the Bateses in *Emma*, respectively the widow and the daughter of Highbury's deceased vicar, must do without domestic help. And destitute Mrs. Smith in *Persuasion,* an invalid defrauded of her property, has attendance from her landlady and the services of a nurse well thought of by Bath's visiting gentry. Experiencing full force the "squalor" of her parents' home, the returned Fanny Price turns up her nose at the "slattern" who opens the door to her, then is shocked anew to learn, by seeing an even sloppier maid, that the first one was the "upper servant."

(We are more likely to be shocked that so narrow an income as the Prices' supports two servants.) In *Sense and Sensibility,* when Lucy Steele's engagement to Edward Ferrers is made known, Mrs. Jenkins thinks of placing the sister of her own maid with the young couple; but when it is clear that Edward has been disowned and disinherited and that his household, as the incumbent of Colonel Brandon's parish, will be very meager, she realizes it will not do. A strong young maid of all work is all they will be able to afford.

It gives one pause, all these families living on the tightest of "genteel" incomes, in the shadow of far richer segments of their class, still able to assume that the menial aspects of caring for themselves need not be their own responsibility. One's reaction should not be the basis for a moral judgment, however, but rather for insight into two related phenomena of class society: the status of servants and the cultivation of female leisure as a by-product of capitalist development. For the first of these, *Pride and Prejudice* provides some index of how large a proportion of the British work force, even after the Industrial Revolution, was engaged in domestic service. Indirectly, it also reminds us how very low the wages must have been for those who did such work if no one with any claim to gentility, however "poor," had to forego their services. As Lady Catherine's inquiry about the Gardiners' staff emphasizes, there were considerably more women servants than men. The existence and the role of these women is something that constitutes the underpinnings of the class upon which Jane Austen's novels are focused. From the literary point of view they have a limited function and almost no identity. From the standpoint of social analysis, although the massive historical forces were certainly having an effect on the lives of women servants (for instance, as they came to be paid cash wages for at least part of their earnings), they serve chiefly as a measure of what was happening to the job and the role of housewife. Which, in turn, has a bearing on Mrs. William Collins passing her mornings in a sitting room that faced "backwards."

"For myself," announces Mrs. Bennet at Netherfield, "I always keep servants that can do their own work; *my* daughters are brought up differently." Not long afterward, that lady takes the opportunity to correct Mr. Collins, who, praising the dinner served him at Longbourn, has assumed that one of the Miss Bennets had cooked it. "But here he was set right by Mrs. Bennet, who assured him with some asperity that they were very well able to keep a good cook." Mrs. Bennet, of course, is singularly lacking in that ease of manner, that gracious acceptance of both privilege and responsibility that our literature informs us is the mark of good breeding. She should not have to boast about how her daughters never lift a finger at home. Still, they do not, and they will not have to even if they all remain unmarried and share their mother's home after their father's death.*

This leisure for country gentlewomen was a very new thing, rather inappropriately borrowed from the bourgeoisie and from the members of the landed classes accustomed to spending at least part of the year in London. It had its origin in the particular sex division of labor that characterized early capitalist society, when the cash market and the wage labor system came to mean that most men engaged with that system earned their money in sectors of society removed from the home. The work that women did at home was consequently degraded by its nonproductive nature and its removal from the cash market, and it became evidence of a man's success in that market that his wife and daughters not be absorbed by the traditional women's tasks, since their leisure would demonstrate his ability to purchase domestic services.

---

*This prospect keeps recurring in my argument, I know, although of course Jane Austen does not allow it to materialize. But references to Mr. Bennet's demise and the subsequent arrangements for his widow and orphans help define the material context in which the human story works itself out. The measure of that material context and the class distinctions to which it gives rise is its ability to encompass the entire life cycle and its eventualities. No character in *Pride and Prejudice,* whatever his or her own stake in the event, would have been as squeamish as we are about what will happen when Mr. Bennet dies.

In the country, there were more domestic tasks to be done, since there were fewer institutionalized forms for their accomplishment. There would be a cook, for instance, in almost any gentleman's house, be it an urban or a rural establishment. But the country cook's job, in the absence of a commercial butcher, began with catching the fowl and killing it. (In *Mansfield Park* Miss Crawford laughs at her sister's preoccupation with whether the turkey will keep: "The sweets of housekeeping in a country village! . . . Commend me to the nurseryman and the poulterer." The reply recalls the difference between city and country life for members of the privileged classes: "My dear child, commend Dr. Grant to the deanery of Westminster or St. Paul's, and I should be as glad of your nurseryman and poulterer as you could be. But we have no such people in Mansfield. What would you have me do?") We know that the Collinses keep cows and chickens and that these are Charlotte's responsibility. This means that the household supplies its own eggs, milk, and butter, and probably cheese and poultry for the table as well. Some of the work involved would probably devolve upon Charlotte, although the regular milking or the care of an ailing creature would not. Similarly, many other household products that we think of as readily purchased commodities were objects of domestic manufacture, which means that in Rosings Parsonage Charlotte herself would make them or oversee the endeavor. And of course the more familiar parts of the "job description"—cooking, and the cleaning of clothing, utensils, people, and the house itself—all had to begin with the fetching and heating of water. All of these occupations, those she performs herself and those she supervises, make a direct contribution to the economy of her household, and one whose material value, though declining in an economy where it is Mr. Collins who brings in the income, is still acknowledged and unquestioned.

The Lucases live in much the same way, perhaps because Sir William's retirement from active involvement in his business has created financial strains that it is up to the women in his family to make up for. (Mrs. Bennet's unintended tribute to Lady Lucas is a footnote to her questions about Charlotte's housekeeping abilities: "Charlotte is an excellent manager, I dare say. If she is half as sharp as her mother, she is saving enough. There is nothing extravagant in *their* housekeeping, I dare say.") At Lucas Lodge, we know, there has been enough domestic work to occupy the unmarried eldest daughter—and perhaps her sisters too. But even in an old-fashioned household this work is no longer all-absorbing to a daughter at home and it is not her own. Nor is she in charge at her mother's house. At her brother's, even if her effort remained the same, her credit for it would be even less. There is scope for it *as* productive work only if she marries.

The facts of Charlotte Lucas's marriage to Mr. Collins are a sharp reminder that to Jane Austen the words "marriage" and "family" did not simply represent a system of personal relationships, but also implied the historical institutions within which such relationships evolved and were conducted. Charlotte knows that becoming the mistress of an establishment, with an accepted role in its supervision and maintenance, will require an intimate relationship with a man who will embarrass and perhaps even disgust her. Even before Mr. Collins appears on the scene, she has observed enough of her world to conclude that "happiness in marriage is entirely a matter of chance," and that a couple's having a great deal in common before marriage is no assurance, since people change so much: "They always grow sufficiently unlike afterwards to have their share of vexation; and it is better to know as little as possible of the defects of the person with whom you are to pass your life." She is certainly determined to know as little as possible of Mr. Collins's shortcomings, glaringly evident though they may be, and hastens the courtship along so that she may have the security of wifehood from which to observe the constant spectacle he makes of himself. When Elizabeth goes to stay with the Collinses, Charlotte's strategies of accommodation to her husband's follies are detailed with some admiration. Looking over the house itself, Elizabeth is impressed by what has been accomplished: "When Mr. Collins could be forgotten, there was really a great air of comfort throughout, and by Charlotte's evident enjoyment of it, Elizabeth supposed he must be often forgotten." At the close of her first day, moreover, "Elizabeth, in the solitude of her chamber, had to meditate upon Charlotte's degree of contentment, to understand her address in guiding, and composure in bearing with, her husband, and to acknowledge that it was all done very well."

Nothing could be plainer; a transaction has taken place, and Jane Austen throws an unflinching light on both the object that has been attained and the coin that has been paid for it. Throughout the visit to Rosings, however, and particularly before Mr. Darcy's arrival gives prominence to another theme, a darker underside of the bargain is continually apparent. Mr. Collins's profession is not one that takes him away from home. His Sunday exertions are not overly taxing, and Lady Catherine appears to be the only parishioner on whom he lavishes much social or pastoral energy. Since toadying is not a full-time occupation even for him, he is often about the house, and Charlotte's shifts to avoid too much of his company are a reminder of how insufferable that company must be. Jane Austen makes a great joke of those devices of Charlotte's: her encouragement of his endeavors in the garden, her choice of an unattractive sitting room for herself, her efforts to show Maria and Elizabeth over the parsonage without his assistance. After the first time, it is not very funny, and the deliberate accumulation of such occasions makes it clear that these arrangements are a daily part of Charlotte's married life. That she is unfailingly civil not only to her husband but to the DeBourghs argues for her sense that the bargain was worth making. Living with Mr. Collins may be one long, weary joke with him as its butt, yet sensible Charlotte is wise enough to realize that, in worldly terms, it is he who has conferred a favor in marrying her and he who has the upper hand in the relationship. Moreover, whether Jane Austen wishes to remember it or not, the repulsive Mr. Collins cannot be avoided in bed. The joking strategems must fall short of that, or Charlotte will not be doing her whole duty as a wife, an important part of which involves providing an heir. Indeed, in Mr. Collins's correspondence with his cousin over the premature rumor of Elizabeth's betrothal, proud reference is made to Charlotte's pregnancy. Charlotte herself, who comes on a visit to her family, retains the independence of mind to rejoice at her friend's engagement to Lady Catherine's nephew, but she has not the physical or material independence to avoid carrying a child, fulfilling her husband's fond "expectation of a young olive-branch."

Essentially, Charlotte Lucas married Mr. Collins because it was the only way she could have a *life*—whether or not provision existed for her to subsist in tolerable material comfort as a spinster. Elizabeth Elliott, of *Persuasion,* with a better social position and a defined social role as the lady of Kellynch Hall, is still weary of the meaningless quality of her spinsterhood. In *Emma,* the heroine tells Harriet Smith that it is not so dreadful to be an old maid, but rather to be both unmarried and poor, like Miss Bates. She herself is assured of being a rich old maid, secure in her income, her charities, her cultural interests, and a provincial social life, seeing herself as an affectionate aunt who "would often have a niece" staying with her. The Woodhouses' style of living requires her to do less work and more supervising than someone like Mrs. Collins, but she remains the lady of the house at Hartfield, ministering, as far as she is able, to her father's mental, social, and physical comfort, ordering the meals, and overseeing the smooth running of the entire concern. But, despite Emma's fantasies of a wealthy and cheerfully advancing spinsterhood, and despite her being born to confident prosperity, she has not much more of a social role than the fading Miss Lucas. It may be Mrs. Elton's self-importance that causes her to run on about "young ladies" and "married women," but she hits on part of the truth. Even Emma must marry in order to create an adequate definition of herself.

And if Emma must, how much more so the Miss Bennets, caught between two worlds and likely, in consequence, to get the worst of each. On the one hand, their sex prevents them from inheriting the landed part of their father's estate and he can leave them very little to live on. This continuity of feudal inheritance patterns into a society where even the land is dominated by a cash market means that, as they seek marriage partners, the shabbily-dowered Miss Bennets will be at a disadvantage in competing with young women whose own marriage portions are in inflated cash. Side by side with this set of contradictions is the fact that they are the daughters of a country gentleman, brought up on a productive estate, but they do not know how to manage or maintain such a household themselves because their mother, following the customs and values of the newly rich bourgeoisie, considers their leisure a proper mark of their status as gentlewomen. The result is that the Bennet ladies live in the country, but *off of* the land, rather than on it; they enjoy its income during their father's lifetime, at least, but they have no relation to it. Its significance to them is the same as that of any other investment under capitalism, whether the return be in the form of interest or rent. That their schooling has been haphazard is acknowledged in Elizabeth's first conversation with Lady Catherine, but their education for any useful future role has also been left to chance. As to either the "accomplishments" or the true cultivation of the gentlewoman, Elizabeth points out that "such of us as wished to learn never wanted the means. . . . Those who chose to be idle, certainly might." She and Jane have not been idle; their minds are "improved" and their principles good. In this sense, they may be said to have formed themselves to be suitable brides for the sort of gentlemen they do marry. In a larger and more cynical sense, however, all the Miss Bennets are being trained to marry men of large property. The situation, in its fullest cultural dimensions, is precisely the converse of Charlotte Lucas's, but the conclusion is identical. The clear imperative is to marry.

One evidence of Mrs. Bennet's foolishness and vulgarity is her eagerness to marry off her daughters. The ethical shortcomings of Lydia Bennet and Charlotte Lucas are different, though both are presented through the young ladies' approach to getting a husband. In Jane Austen's other novels, husband-hunting females are portrayed and judged very harshly; a good marriage must be for love and love must not be actively sought. At the end of each of the six completed novels, the heroine is joined to the man she loves and their marriage, like those at the end of a Shakespearean comedy, is normally accompanied by the love-matches of several other couples. Yet marriage, as Jane Austen understands it, is based on and within material institutions. And the material role of women in those institutions was changing in response to the shifting balance of class society. The central contradiction in Jane Austen's work is the tension between the ideal of marriage for love and the social reality of gentry life. Her extraordinary achievement is that she encompasses this contradiction through the consciousness and the ethical decisions of a young woman on the verge of choosing a husband.

NOTES

1. Raymond Williams, *The Country and the City* (New York: Oxford University Press, 1973).

2. My understanding of Jane Austen's more conservative phase and its social origins is informed by discussions with Linda Hunt of the University of Massachusetts, Boston.

3. A useful discussion of the particular noble families whose names Jane Austen appropriates may be found in Donald L. Greene, "Jane Austen and the Peerage," *PMLA* 68 (1953), 1017-31.

On Reading Trash

But history, real solemn history, I cannot be interested in. . . . I read it a little as a duty, but it tells me nothing that does not either vex or weary me. The quarrels of popes and kings, with wars and pestilences in every page; the men all so good for nothing, and hardly any women at all. . . .
—Northanger Abbey

LITERATURE BELONGS to women, history to men. This misapprehension, fostered by our society's attitudes toward aesthetic events and "real" ones, is confirmed in the historical fiction written by women, for women, and with women at their center, a literary genre which makes it abundantly clear that, apart from a few remarkable figures—chiefly queens who reigned in their own right—the principal women in history were the mistresses, wives, mothers, and daughters of famous men. The events these novels chronicle about women's lives—love, marriage, adultery, childbirth—reinforce the idea that female history is essentially sexual, the stuff of literature, in fact, not of "real, solemn history." In the type of fiction I would characterize as the female historical novel, these sexual events take place in the margins of the larger movements of history, which are motivated and enacted by men, those transfers of kingdoms and affairs of nations whose details are state quarrels, wars, and pestilences. Thus the historical novel which, as a form of high art, is supposed to unite the concerns of private and public life, serves in its popular avatar as a means of keeping them separate and of attaching gender labels to the two discrete categories thus created. Because they afford a way of thinking about history and about women's potential as an agent in history, popular historical novels are a fruitful subject for feminist criticism, and a consideration of the genre can provide insights into the way we understand women's role in both history and literature.

For a good many years, I was under the impression that most writers were women. Moreover, my youthful delusion would probably have gone unchallenged if I had remained on the literary trajectory normally marked out for working-class girls who love to read. From children's books to "young adult" novels to the adult fiction directed at a female audience, with mandatory detours through the poetry and prose considered acceptable school reading twenty or twenty-five years ago, the path is defined by women's names and pseudonyms. Not even the classics to which I was first introduced—*Jane Eyre, Wuthering Heights, Pride and Prejudice, The Mill on the Floss*—did much to shake my notion of female predominance in the literary arts. The production, as well as the consumption, of culture seemed to me to be women's proper business.

An elite secondary education began to change all that. Although the girls' school I attended did include Emily Brontë in its standard curriculum, by the last two years, when Advanced Placement courses introduced us to the historical and critical methods then favored by college English departments, we were reading only the Great Authors. Not a woman in the lot, of course. For someone whose tastes and approach were formed by the women's fiction at the lending library, this exposure was a real jolt. But Aeschylus, Pope, Richardson, and Donne were, after all, absorbing fare, so the exposure "took," and by the time

I went away to college not even my leisure hours were beguiled by any female author less demanding (or less demonstrably Major) than Virginia Woolf. Yet I knew the other kind of fiction was there, and eventually I turned back to it for a kind of self-indulgence that is qualitatively different from the satisfactions of high art.

I proceeded to earn bachelor's, master's, and doctoral degrees in literature, taking courses at three major universities. Had I not audited some summer lectures in the French Renaissance, for which we had to read a couple of sonnets by Louise Labé, my entire course of study would have been innocent of female contributions. I realize, of course, that the odds could have been improved—if, for instance, I'd specialized in prose fiction of the nineteenth century—but the point is that it was not only possible but easy for a student to omit all female products from scholarly consideration and to remain unconscious of their absence. I do not intend to repeat the arguments of commentators like Elaine Showalter, whose "Women in the Literary Curriculum" thoroughly documents the gross underrepresentation of female authors and experience in both introductory and specialized courses in English. What is unusual about my own literary education is that I encountered the male literary tradition against a background filled with trashy popular fiction by, for, and about women. The result is a rather different perspective than I am supposed to have on the two parallel traditions of English literature. Most of this essay will be focused on a contrast between the works of Jane Austen and those of Georgette Heyer. The pairing is honestly come by, in my own history, but I believe it has larger implications as well; the concentration on women as they appear in both high and popular fiction makes possible some useful distinctions between the two and forces a reconsideration of such categories as literature, entertainment, and propaganda. Once the absurd incongruity of any connection between the two writers is duly acknowledged and assigned its proper weight, it has much to tell us about female literary experience.

The literary commodity called a paperback comes in two distinct strains nowadays: the "mass market" and the "trade" versions. Once a paperback edition is indicated for a novel, these categories determine its price, packaging, publicity, and distribution. A number of social factors—class, culture, life style, even geography—influence whether one is likely to buy one's reading matter at a pharmacy, an airport, a suburban chain, or a traditional bookshop. But gender cuts across all social categories, so that, although there is no clearly defined "trade" fiction for men only, and almost no all-male preserve among the "mass market" novels (Westerns, where they still exist, being the major exception), there does exist a discrete and distinct market category for women readers. The contemporary (or "drugstore") Gothic, the historical novel, and the contemporary "romance" are the important, sometimes overlapping subtypes within the general phenomenon of "women's fiction."

Even these labels for use in the marketing of the new literary types are somewhat inexact: they are borrowed from scholarship devoted to high culture, where they have quite different meanings. A case can be made, certainly, for the drugstore Gothic's legitimate descent via *Jane Eyre* from the eighteenth century fiction to which the term Gothic was first applied, and particularly from that by female authors.* But when I speak of the contemporary "Gothic" I refer to a genre that represents a separate and self-conscious form, one conventionally entailing, among other elements, an isolated heroine, a house, a withdrawn man, and a mystery.

Similarly, historical fiction for the female audience has little in common with the work of Stendahl or Tolstoy, but centers on the lives of historical women (or invented female characters) whose role in history was determined by their husbands, fathers, brothers, or lovers. Although struggles for social power and

*Katherine Ellis, in her work in progress on *Paradise Lost* and the Gothic novel, points out important distinctions between "masculine" and "feminine" development of the genre.

preeminence often have an important place in such fiction, it tends to emphasize the emotional and sexual lives of key figures in history, normally attributing to them an ideology about love and an experience of it that is at least an anachronism. (The novels of Anya Seton—*Katherine, The Winthrop Woman, My Theodosia,* and so on—are exceptionally fine examples of female historical fiction. Margaret Mitchell's *Gone with the Wind* and Kathleen Winsor's *Forever Amber* represent another important strain within the general type.)

Another—and, to my mind, more interesting because more characteristically "feminine"—subgroup is made up of novels that take place in the past (more often than not in Regency England), but that use the great events of the time as a more or less distant backdrop to a love story enacted in a context of carefully described dresses and scenes of elegant high life. The novels of Georgette Heyer and Barbara Cartland, in their different ways, epitomize this strain of "historical" writing, characterized by retailers as "historical romances" or "Regency romances."

Quite different are the novels I would place under the simple heading "romances," which have in common a contemporary setting, often an exotic geographical or class locale, and a straightforward focus on a stylized heterosexual love story; Harlequin Books takes such fiction for its stock in trade.*

Study of these four fictional modes is an essential element in the sociology of women's literature because it provides access to

---

*A new subgenre has recently attained enormous popularity: soft-core pornography, frequently with an historical setting, some actual historical personages as characters, and a title involving both love and illicit wildness (*Wicked, Loving Lies* and *Sweet Savage Love,* for two). I am indebted to Linda Phillips-Palo and Diane Yawney for the term "rape and plunder novels" as a description of this brand of fiction. Although I feel unqualified to comment at length on the type, being neither specialist nor addict, much of what I have to say about the milder historical romances also—ironically—applies here, for these books serve to sexualize history and the female experience of it in a sense that is fully genital in its definition of sexuality. Fiction of the Heyer-Cartland sort also sexualizes female history, but in the less direct, more allusive, and culturally more complex fashion analyzed in this essay.

all facets of the phenomenon of literature: the female author as an historical development; the characters, situations, and themes she typically creates in the various popular modes; the female audience in its relation to the experience of reading; and the production, packaging, and distribution of the book as commodity. Traditional critical methods, whether they stress the work of literature as an individual monument or consider it in its purely literary history, do not often consider this range of issues with reference to "good" or "serious" literature. In a sense, it is precisely because novels written for women are less aesthetically compelling than serious fiction that the contextual and sociological questions arise: What is the fascination of these books for their audience? What are those readers typically looking for when they read? What do they find? And how do they (or we, since I've made my own confession) use it?

As with any form of culture addressed to a mass audience, these issues contribute an essential complement both to intrinsic criticism, which such literature rarely inspires, and to ideological criticism, which it patently invites. It is insufficient and ultimately misdirected to read Georgette Heyer or the Harlequin Romances and simply analyze what they are trying to tell women. To attack the reactionary image of women and the ideology about our nature and roles that such novels present—as, for example, Germaine Greer has done—is to mistake the thing on the page for the experience itself. A fully feminist reading of women's books must look at *women* as well as at books, and try to understand how this literature actually functions in society. As a literary person who remains frankly addicted to trashy fiction, I make no claim that this approach will reveal an underground and unexpected feminist literature. Rather, though no less ambitiously, I think it can tell us something about the materials women use to make their lives in our society.

All too many commentators have been tempted to assess the influence of the modern Gothic and the contemporary romance in

strictly psychological terms. In the case of the former genre, it is
the pervasive impact of certain repeated symbols and motifs—
first and foremost, the house itself; the woman's helplessness; the
secrets; the servants; the child—that is explored. In the case of
the latter genre, the sexual fantasy, its narrative complexities and
exotic setting, is the starting point. Both of these modes make
their appeal as explicit escape reading.*

Once the psychological aspect of both content and influence
has been understood, however, a feminist reading demands that
these categories themselves be placed in their history. Why, for
instance, should the image of a house become such a potent one
for women at the time of the Industrial Revolution? How and in
response to what social forces has the popular Gothic civilized
and transformed the notion of the house? How has the symbol of
the house as inherited property—possibly even the heroine's own
property—assumed new meanings in our common imaginative
life? What are the mechanisms by which escape is sold to women,
and what are the real or ostensible reasons for pushing it? In all of
these questions, however, it is historical method, not historical
content, that is primary.

By contrast, the very nature of the popular historical novel
forces the reader into some definition, whether considered or
superficial, of history and historical process. The image it presents of social forces, their effect on large historical developments, and the influence of both on the lives of actual or imaginary women thus serves to promote a vision of historical
possibilities for the woman reader herself. It should come as no
surprise that those possibilities are limited to aspects of life that
remain the major feminine preoccupations, even as professional

---

*Harlequin pioneered book advertising on television (so successfully that other
publishers are beginning to follow suit) with commercials that are sensuous,
though not directly sexual in tone. The woman to whom they are directed is
assumed to have a busy life of her own—perhaps even a paid job in addition to
housewifery—but the commercials seduce her, in so many words, into yet another
life, the "world" of Harlequin Romances.

and political opportunities for women have increased in our own times; in this sense, they provide affirmation of present experience rather than the vicarious experience they are often dismissed for offering. Moreover, since historical fiction almost invariably takes the position that progress is desirable and that which in character, taste, or judgment most resembles present Western civilization is best of all, the context is created for a melioristic approach to historical process. At the same time, human personality tends to be portrayed as static, in that the most admirable and heroic characters have a modern view of themselves and what happens to them. The general impression one comes away with is that things used to be different (harder) for women way back then (whenever), but that women themselves were precisely the same. Not only were they the same in what they needed, asked, or found in life, but the same in belonging, by and large, to the periphery of history, and in being unable, except through the exercise of their sexuality, to exert any influence on more central historical events. There is evidently a large ready-made audience for literature written from this ideological perspective and, equally clearly, a certain political benefit to be obtained from inculcating such a view of history and of women's potential to act upon it.

If the drugstore Gothic can trace its origin back through modern revivals of the Brontës to the romantic fiction that flourished in eighteenth-century circulating libraries, its counterpart among historical romances claims a similarly elevated lineage. Around 1966 Georgette Heyer's novels were issued in paperback for what I believe was their first mass distribution in the American market. The cover of each novel proclaimed it—and Heyer's Regency fiction generally—to be in the tradition of Jane Austen. Subsequent novelists who treat the Regency period have been described by their publishers as following in the romantic tradition of *Georgette Heyer*. Like the Gothics, then, these novels are products whose peddlers stress their resemblance to others of the kind, by the same author or by other established specialists in the genre, rather than emphasize the innovative uniqueness of each product. The appeal is to familiarity and success, assured by reference to places, customs, and ideas well known from earlier productions of the same type. Georgette Heyer is the acknowledged Queen of the Regency romance (later paperback editions make some such peculiar claim), and it is a clear selling point to say that the book you are touting is just like "a" Georgette Heyer, has the same Regency background, and affords (therefore) the same "delight." But for Heyer herself there can be only one predecessor sufficiently glamorous and sufficiently connected in the public mind with the Regency period and that is Jane Austen herself, whose heroines, her own contemporaries, did, unquestionably, live out their personal dramas during the years that the future George IV reigned in the place of his mad father.

As a selling point the comparison can only prove disappointing, for Heyer's novels concentrate on precisely those minutiae of dress and décor that Austen takes for granted. Not even in *Northanger Abbey,* where Mrs. Allen is satirized as a woman obsessed with her own gowns and trimmings and, for a secondary interest, those of her young charge, Catherine Morland, does Jane Austen bow to the necessity of describing a single garment in any of her novels. A bit of dialogue about fashions may serve to delineate character—as when Mrs. Elton simultaneously fishes for praise of her gown, deprecates the necessity of being so ornately dressed, and plans aloud to add some more trimming to another dress—but they are of scant interest in themselves. Heyer (and, with even less skill, her sister Regency buffs) tells us about colors, cut, fabric, and trimming, about half-boots, pelisses, and cloaks, not only because the acquisition and display of clothing are more central to the existence of Heyer's heroines than they are to Austen's, but in order to invest the novels with that meretricious quality Henry James would have called "the tone of time."

Similarly, in Jane Austen's novels, the varieties of carriages are used as a social marker (Mr. Collins drives a gig, the Bennets keep a closed carriage but have to use farm horses to pull it when they want to pay a call, and so on). Elsewhere, conversation about horses and vehicles reflects the personality and temperament of various characters (John Thorpe mistreats his horse and gig and boasts about his trading in these matters; Mrs. Elton can never forbear to mention that her rich brother-in-law, Mr. Suckling, keeps two carriages, including a barouche-landaulet). In Georgette Heyer's novels, however, the niceties of phaeton and perch-phaeton, of driving to an inch, and of membership (in appropriate and fully described costume) in the Four Horse Club are built directly into the texture of events as they make up the narrative.

Perhaps because she was writing for contemporaries who knew what the world of the Regency period looked like, but more likely because these facts inform her historical sense in a deeper and more thoroughgoing fashion, Austen is able to make a more complex use than her imitators of the aesthetic culture of her own time. The mourning Captain Benwick in *Persuasion* has been reading so much Scott and Byron that Anne Elliott recommends a therapeutic dose of prose; Byronism has affected *Sanditon's* Sir Edward Denham less innocently, as he plots a cut-rate abduction; Fanny Price knows Cowper; and, of course, the young ladies in *Northanger Abbey* read all the "horrid" novels they can get their hands on.

But drawing, music, literature, even amateur theatricals tend to be an organic part of life to the people Jane Austen writes about. Everyone in Bath goes to the theater and the concerts. Catherine Morland's recital of her week's schedule (the Upper Rooms Monday, the theater Tuesday, the concert Wednesday) to an amused Mr. Tilney is no less true because it can be so mechanically evoked. And the musical evenings attract social climbers like Sir Walter Elliott and his eldest daughter quite as naturally as they do someone like Anne, an able musician herself who can translate Italian songs at sight. Highbury, remote though it may be, shelters not only Jane Fairfax, who is an accomplished pianist, Emma Woodhouse, who would play better if she applied herself, and Mrs. Elton, who is determined to signal her entry into the married state by abandoning her music, but amateur critics like Harriet Smith, who knows she is supposed to throw around terms like "taste" and "execution" although she is unsure just how to recognize these qualities when she is exposed to them. Appreciation of cultural productions, opinions and attitudes about them, thus becomes another attribute of character.

The only remotely comparable cultural attribute in the works of Georgette Heyer is a taste for the fiction of Jane Austen herself. Thus, in *Regency Buck* Judith Taverner is delighted by an ironic passage in the copy of *Sense and Sensibility* she comes upon at a circulating library. Jenny, in *A Civil Contract,* prefers the same Jane Austen novel to the Byronic effusions her friend Julia adores; *Sense and Sensibility,* she believes, is down to earth, deals with real people—precisely the qualities that make Julia feel it is flat and prosaic. After her marriage Jenny tries to read her husband's agricultural manuals, sweetening the task by alternating it with chapters from the newly published *Mansfield Park.* Those of Heyer's heroines who read Jane Austen share some small part of that author's ironic social vision, but once we understand that a taste for those novels signifies humor and good sense—personal traits that Heyer always values—there are no further subtleties to be revealed by her heroines' choice of reading matter.

However superficial this use of taste to illuminate character, it remains the only reference to contemporary culture that serves any purpose beyond historical decoration. When Lady Serena, in *Bath Tangle,* reads Lady Caroline Lamb's *Glenarvon* and delights in identifying the models for that *roman à clef,* the incident serves simply to " place" her and her mismatched fiancé in their respective social and moral spheres. Reading Byron becomes the mode in several novels, but it really is a fashion like those concerning dress and has rather less influence over what actually happens than the vogue for a certain shade of blue or the choice of a gentleman's tailor. Literature, which is pressed into service rather frequently as the source of historical color, and the theater and fine arts, which are referred to somewhat less often, furnish detail rather than depth, and a kind of detail, moreover, that tends to support the general picture of women's lives that emerges from these novels.

The niceties of social behavior, like the references to artistic production, serve quite different purposes in the historical romance than they do in the novel of manners. Jane Austen could assume that her readers knew the rules of polite social intercourse. When an impromptu dance is held at Mansfield Park, Maria Bertram knows it would be incorrect to dance only with her foolish betrothed, Mr. Rushworth, and uses that knowledge to claim her share of Henry Crawford's attentions. Mrs. Norris and Mrs. Rushworth chat about the proprieties of the matter, but the real tension subsists in the rivalry of the two Miss Bertrams, in Maria's impatience with Rushworth and her hopes of Crawford, and in Fanny Price's feelings as she watches the action. Who dances with whom—at Mansfield, Netherfield, Highbury, or Bath—is always of greater significance than the way a Regency gentleman craves the honor of a dance or the fact that partners are invariably paired off for two dances at a time.

Not only are such regulations and breaches thereof more central to the action in Georgette Heyer's novels, but there are more *of* them. The reader of Heyer and of her Regency sisters rapidly learns that the coveted vouchers to Almacks could be obtained only from one of the aristocratic patronesses (and she learns those ladies' identities, habits, and crotchets); and also that, once accepted, gentlemen must wear knee breeches, not pantaloons, there; that alcoholic beverages are not served; and that a young lady may not waltz until her doing so has been approved by one of the patronesses. All this comes under the heading of what I would characterize as pseudoinformation not because it is untrue (repetition, at least, would suggest that what these books have taught me about Almacks is accurate) but because, ultimately, it reveals nothing about the society that fostered an institution like Almacks as its elite marriage market. Yet the pages of Georgette Heyer's works are full of passages in which character is defined through young men's boredom at a club where the card room stakes are so low and the refreshments so mild, and entire plots turn on their being refused admission for being improperly dressed or arriving after 11:00 p.m.*

One result of this passion for the specific fact without concern for its significance occurs in the matter of sexual morality, precisely the area of life that the social proprieties are intended to regulate and define. Georgette Heyer's high life is a great deal higher than Jane Austen's, embracing those segments of aristocracy and fashion that in fact represented an extravagant and dissolute threat to the sort of country families with whom Jane Austen is most at home. Gentlemen in Heyer's universe are expected to have experience with loose women at various levels of society, but however daring her ladies may be, they never actually breach the double standard. Indeed, in their innocence, they have the rare gift—albeit commonplace in women's fiction—of being able to captivate and hold on to the most experienced and worldly males. Her gentlemen are considered morally acceptable because they are candid and generous with their mistresses. The heroines who eventually enchant them are daring in their wit and, some-

---

*Unlike the true historical novelist (even one writing for women), the Regency *romancière* does little research. (Some of the hastier books seem, indeed, to have been based on reading exclusively in other novels about the period.) Even Heyer, the best of the lot, relies on a fixed repertoire of historical facts and characters on which she rings (eventually predictable) changes. Thus, when Beau Brummell appears—as he does extensively in *Regency Buck,* for instance—all conversation that is not directed to one of the fictional characters comes directly from the four or five best-known anecdotes about the man, precisely the ones retailed in Virginia Woolf's brief essay on him.

times, in their knowledge of the existence of sexual misbehavior. But they kiss passionately only at the end of the book when love has terminated in betrothal, and they are revolted by sexual advances made on the mistaken assumption that they are of the class that is assumed to be universally available to gentlemen.

Jane Austen's people do not giggle over "crim. con." stories; their world is superficially a great deal more straitlaced. In her fiction, however, the facts of life—the real ones, free of rakes who can be instantly reformed by refreshing virgins and of the knowing virgins themselves—are never far below the surface. Seduction, elopement, illegitimacy, divorce, living in sin are not alluded to in every chapter of a Jane Austen novel. Nonetheless, *Northanger Abbey,* which began, after all, as a youthful burlesque, is the only one of her books that does not include a major incident or character touched by one of these breaches of the sexual code. Sexual misconduct, moreover, is not limited to the unknown "bits of muslin" or the discarded aristocratic mistresses who populate Georgette Heyer's pages, but involves people— although never heroines, of course—whom the reader has come to know as characters. One does not *like* Maria Bertram, Lydia Bennet, or Mrs. Clay, but all are fully developed persons, not symbols, and their motives and emotions are no less complex than those of any of the other women Jane Austen depicts. Not even Mrs. Clay, who is announced as "designing" before she makes her first appearance in *Persuasion,* is reduced to the purely sexual component of her misdeeds. The social distance between a sexually virtuous woman and one who has "fallen" is much more palpable in the novels of Jane Austen than any twentieth-century novelist writing about Austen's period can adequately imagine. The gulf, however, the difference between one kind of person and another, is a great deal easier to bridge when we are reading the real thing than in any modern imitation.

In Georgette Heyer's fiction, the public events of the day— economic, political, or military—are very much to the fore, although Heyer necessarily betrays a far more shallow sense of their significance than does Jane Austen, who barely mentions them. Thus, for example, Viscount Linton, the hero of Heyer's *A Civil Contract*, an aristocratic ex-officer with heavily mortgaged ancestral acres, turns to scientific farming. Against the advice of his bourgeois father-in-law, he adds to his shares in government bonds at the moment when it looks as if Wellington may have lost at Waterloo. He thus lays the foundation for a renewed family fortune based on the old values (loyalty to his country, his party, and his former commander), shoring up the new (the land is still mortgaged and its owner is introducing modern agricultural methods, with their attendant destruction of a way of life and a livelihood for the rural population). Some historical "color" is provided by references to Tull's drill, Coke of Norfolk and his experiments in farming, the effect on the stock market of defeatist military rumors, and the Corn Law riots. Similarly, the plot of *The Toll Gate* revolves around the theft of some cases of newly minted (and not yet circulated) gold sovereigns; the characters in several novels (*The Unknown Ajax, The Talisman Ring,* and *The Reluctant Widow* come immediately to mind) have dealings with French brandy smugglers; and the Bow Street Runners, the new national police, figure in these four novels, as well as in several others. But in all this there is no hint of how deeply the events reflected by the specific details influenced and altered the entire fabric of the society in which they occurred.

In Jane Austen's novels, the details are always basic to our understanding of characters or plot, for she is aware that new social forces do encroach on the way of life—prosperous, decorous, and cultivated—that is the common heritage of Mansfield, Pemberly, Hartfield, Kellynch, Norland, and Northanger. These places and the style of living they simultaneously shelter and reflect are menaced by political-economic developments external to the English country house and its usual surroundings. Sir Thomas Bertram, for instance, must see to his Caribbean property (who works his plantations, what do they produce, and just what *was* he saying about the slave trade that interested Fanny Price far more than it did his own daughters?). John Dashwood's first action at Norland, after dispensing with his stepmother and half-sisters, is to apply capitalist values and methods to his inheritance, enclosing Norland Common and adding to his holdings by engrossment. At Kellynch, it is Sir Walter Elliott's own extravagance, which might be interpreted as an inability to make the rents from an inherited estate cover all the temptations of modern life, that necessitates the family's removal to Bath and their rental of the house to a retired admiral made prosperous by England's naval wars. Questions of taste and manners, which are, at the deepest level, questions of class, are always dependent, in Jane Austen's works, on the material situation created when the gentry are placed in relation—and very often in confrontation—with the conditions of insurgent capitalism.

Jane Austen, like Heyer, focuses on getting her heroines married for love to suitors whose fortune and character are both adequate. The historical context in which the eventual marriages are achieved, however, has a far more profound significance for her than it ever could for Heyer. Heyer's characters may marry for money, as in the case of Adam Linton; or marry for love and find great wealth as well, as with the majority of her heroines; or marry, as happens in *April Lady, The Convenient Marriage,* and *Friday's Child,* for immediate material motives and find love through the marriage; or be frankly pursued for their own fortunes, as in *Regency Buck* or *The Quiet Gentleman*; but any understanding of why some groups are poor or rich—even when they are newly so—has no place in her kind of fiction. By contrast, Austen's novels are rooted in an understanding of the fact that cataclysmic social changes were affecting not only relative wealth and poverty, but also class definitions and class relations, sources and amounts of income, and the cultural life informed by these forces. Austen could hardly share the modern reader's knowledge about the eventual direction and meaning of these changes, but she has and communicates a far more vivid sense than we can attain to of the daily reality that the new conditions demanded.

After Sir Walter Elliott's financial difficulties necessitate his renting the family estate to a retired admiral, we are privileged to overhear the baronet's fatuous strictures on a profession that enables men who merely have uncommon abilities—rather than gentle birth—to rise above "their betters." Sir Walter's porings over the Baronetage are far less rewarding in human qualities than the roster of naval officers that Jane Austen brings to our attention. But although the author does not join her character in deploring the fact that England should have fallen into the hands of men of intelligence, courage, good will, and enterprise, she is nonetheless aware of the larger social and economic changes behind this shift. Her doubts about the new culture are embodied in the Miss Musgroves, the refined descendants of honest country squires. She sees the generations of the Musgrove family, in fact, as representatives of the old England and the new, reflecting that the ancestors whose portraits hang in the parlor must be surprised to witness the goings-on of the young generation. The chief difference is that the two Miss Musgroves have been away to school and learned accomplishments. Those accomplishments sit lightly on them, to be sure, but the result is, in fact, that they can live "to be fashionable, happy, and merry." They have leisure, whereas the older generations of Musgrove ladies, gentlewomen though they were, were also mistresses of their rural households, with real work to do.

The fine articulations of class society are important to both authors, although this concern reflects quite different views of what a social order is and what purposes it serves. Georgette Heyer's preferred milieu is what her characters would call "the first circles" of English society (and, in the novels with eighteenth-century settings, of French society as well). All of her heroes belong to this class; most of them are earls, although there is at least one baron, one viscount, and one marquis among them, as well as several dukes, some baronets, and a few younger sons of the nobility. The heroines are not quite so uniformly placed: if they are from equally aristocratic backgrounds—or even the country gentry—their families are poor; if heiresses, they are not usually from the very highest levels of society. In almost no case is the Cinderella theme entirely absent, and it is frequently the central device of Georgette Heyer's plots.

The emphasis on "the first circles" implies, of course, the existence of other circles. Heyer concerns herself principally with those just beneath the tier occupied by her main characters. Thus, in addition to Almacks, there is the Pantheon Ballroom, an inferior and unexclusive establishment more often referred to—as a kind of negative social touchstone—than visited. When a heroine takes part in a masked ball there, as at least two do, she is stared at and accosted by rude, vulgar "cits," the same fate, indeed, that attends a wellborn lady in Heyer's works whenever she is in a situation where she may meet men of the middle classes.

Men of the bourgeoisie and below are usually unmistakable in their crudity even when they are not drunkenly pawing the heroine. When Heyer portrays characters who lack polite manners and an elite education she can never resist making them stupid as well. Thus, Jenny's father in *A Civil Contract,* who we are supposed to believe is a brilliant and shrewd financier, one of the new self-made capitalists, is by turns short-tempered, irascible, babyish, foolish, and awkwardly falling all over himself with whatever emotion is dominant at the moment. Middle-class women are either unshakably practical, of-the-earth earthy, or deficient in judgment, their poor grammar being only the outward sign of an inward vacuity that not infrequently fades off into viciousness.

These careful distinctions among the first, the second, and the third ranks and among the overlapping layers in the first are really

where the action is. The poor are people, of course, but no sense
is conveyed of what their poverty means or how it interlocks with
the lives of the very rich as this fiction depicts them. A few
characters, to be sure—Arabella in the novel named for her, Sir
Waldo Hawkridge, the Nonesuch for whom another novel is
titled—engage in philanthropic ventures, but a hero or heroine
need not spare a thought for the sufferings of the masses in order
to be considered wholly admirable. There are chimney sweeps
and children working in mines and factories, but such matters are
alluded to only if an aristocrat, in the course of advancing the real
plot, rescues one or two of them from that fate. There are also
country folk, innkeepers, and, of course, servants by the score,
because they are required for the support of a lavish style of life,
and there are a few lumpen characters who live in alleys and swill
gin, but they have neither identity nor brains. Low status
(whether the possessor is a Bow Street Runner or Leaky Peg, a
kindhearted backstreet girl), is invariably accompanied by low
intelligence.

Georgette Heyer introduces us to characters who speak of fashions and fashionables as being "of the first stare" or "highly
select" and she can bring in figures who are indeed at the very
peak of the social order. In *Regency Buck,* Judith Taverner re-
ceives the marriage proposals of the Duke of Clarence; Heyer's
fictional creation thus has the opportunity to become the mor-
ganatic Queen of England. As long as she does not tamper with
history to the extent of bringing about such a marriage, the
twentieth-century novelist can place an actual historical figure in
the picture, put all manner of foolish speeches into his mouth, and
have him rejected by Miss Taverner. Jane Austen could hardly
take the same liberties with a royal duke who was her
contemporary—not simply because decorum forbade them, but
because her sense of both fictional and social order would have
made it inconceivable *and unnecessary* to do so.

Yet the same issues that are so important to Georgette
Heyer—the size of dowries and the income of estates, the pre-

tensions of the newly rich, and the impact of conflicting class styles on the marriage market—are also important to Jane Austen. The difference resides not only in the less elevated social and economic level that Jane Austen's characters occupy, but also in the reasons why social distinctions are so much to the fore. Fundamentally, Jane Austen shows us snobs and social climbers, but she is not one herself. Indeed, no character whom the reader is expected to admire has aspirations to associate with anyone above her own station, and it is a sign of vulgarity to be overly concerned with adding to or demonstrating one's own social importance. Not even the interests of an advantageous marriage can move Jane Austen's heroines to seek company above their own rank and, again, ardent pursuit of an eligible *parti* is one of the chief touchstones of poor breeding and defective character in any young woman.

Heyer's heroines are at once more pragmatic and less realistic. They take part in the London "Season" in full knowledge that it is their *job* as well as their role to find a husband through the process of social mating that is one function of the brilliant assemblies they attend. Her novels are about love, successful, lasting love, but Heyer and her heroines are well aware that, for Regency society in general, love is only incidental to the functions of the institutions of courtship and marriage. With the energy they devote to the social round, however, and the passionate detail with which Heyer describes the events and the costumes that so absorb them, a completely artificial world of balls and parties comes into being. Heyer's novels introduce the modern reader to a Who's Who of Regency high life where fashion is elevated to the position of a major social force. Her heroines want love; some of them even read books and want also the more esoteric pleasures of rational intercourse and virtuous conduct. But in the novels there is no other measure of success for an individual, a party, or a custom, than to be accepted by those who are identified as leading, making, or following the mode.

The problem is that Heyer realizes how important this sort of success is for the kind of heroine she chooses and almost mass-produces. Yet on some essential level she does not know what to do with that understanding, because she does not know what a society is. Thus, she shows a society articulated by class and one in which class feeling, especially snobbery and ambition, runs high, without conveying any sense that class is something other and more than style. Jane Austen's world is less fashionable, though by no means less class-conscious, than that of the Regency romance; there is no possibility, however, of her readers' confusing class itself with its most superficial expressions, because the novels make it clear that everything they are about—ethics, manners, attitudes, sentiments, distinctions—has its basis in class. Understood in this way, class in Jane Austen's novels becomes, as it is in actual human history, the defining and motivating force of society itself.

I can imagine no greater waste of energy than an elaborate demonstration that Jane Austen is a better writer than Georgette Heyer. In drawing so extensive a comparison between the two, my intention has not been to belabor the obvious points about what makes a great writer great, but rather to approach the question of women's light reading from a perspective that avoids the pat formulas about "escape" and "vicarious experience." That there is some overlap between the present-day audience for both kinds of work is reflected not only in the early advertising of Heyer's books but also in the marketing of Jane Austen's works. Two unfinished Austen novels, *Sanditon* and *The Watsons*, have been completed by twentieth-century authors and are now available in mass-market paperbacks, with cover illustrations and (grossly exaggerated) plot descriptions that seek to render them indistinguishable from their presumed pop-fiction successors. And they are displayed side by side with romances by Heyer and her imitators. I wonder that happens to a reader who picks up one of these books—both, admittedly, containing a rather denatured product—instead of one of its shelf-mates? (Say, the novel called something like *Bath Cotillion* by one of the Heyer epigones that I bought at the Indianapolis Airport and, having finished, left on the plane and that made so slight an imprint on my consciousness that less than two weeks later, I almost bought it again at Hengerers department store in Buffalo.) Does the reader who relished *Bath Cotillion* find that the issues and problems Jane Austen raises stand in the way of her story? Does the more elegant style interfere as well? Or do the superfluous elements of superior character, incident, and analysis simply go unnoticed? If this last is the case, as it must be for one segment of Jane Austen's modern readers, then it becomes somewhat more challenging to examine both the Regency romance itself and the sources of its appeal.*

If it is possible to read Jane Austen for the same reasons one reads Georgette Heyer, then coming to understand what makes it possible suggests some conclusions about what women read and why. In both its high and its popular avatars, this sort of novel centers on the private concerns of women, domestic, marital, and personal. For Heyer, these concerns must be bolstered by a mass of sartorial and decorative detail that Austen readily dispenses with in order to underscore the true ethical context in which the action unfolds. Both novelists, however, are saying that the personal *matters,* and those twentieth-century novelists who choose an historical period when great public events were in the making seem to be saying it with particular force. Historical incidents become the backdrop for that message, and exalted social position serves to enhance the argument itself.

At the same time, the import of historical fiction for women is to reinforce the notion that the public world, however much its vicissitudes may influence women's lives, is always at one remove from women. And, conversely, women remain at one re-

*The problem is becoming acute, moreover. I recently saw a vending machine called a Convenience Center in the lobby of a Holiday Inn. It dispensed such items as body lotion, hair spray, tampons, deodorant, and copies of *Price and Prejudice*!

move from it. Larger political considerations may affect what happens to a woman, but her participation in history, as chambermaid, queen, or the Cinderella who is transformed from one to the other, consists in being a female, dressed—always—in appropriate period costume. It is not so much that this kind of fiction "tells" or "teaches" women something about their nature, role, and sphere. Rather, it repeats what direct experience and dominant ideology have already succeeded in communicating. In this sense, it would appear that female readers do not seek out trashy novels in order to escape or to experience life vicariously, but rather to receive confirmation, and, eventually, affirmation, that love really is what motivates and justifies a woman's life. At best, it is much too slight a compensation for the weight of stiff velvet and the chill insubstantiality of sprig-muslin into which our historical imaginations have been laced.

Working/Women/Writing

WHO SPEAKS for women—and is it literature? The first half of this admittedly ambiguous question should present few problems for a critical perspective informed by the insights and analysis of feminism. Women speak for women—for our experience and the viewpoint it shapes, if not necessarily in our common interests. The historical experiences of the two sexes are sufficiently different that no man, however sincerely our partisan, is able to speak with our authority about the lives, the feelings, or the consciousness of women. Feminist criticism can add a vital element to the understanding of male authors and of the literary tradition in which they participate, a contribution that is vital in both senses of the word, at once urgent and alive. But, in addition to this essential work of reinterpretation, we—critics and scholars, but also the women's movement and women in general—have been listening with increasing attention and growing commitment to the voices of women.

It is the second part of my question that provokes controversy. Do the words of women come together to make what we would be

223

justified in calling and treating as literature? The writing of
women is unquestionably expression, but is it art as well? There
are four possible answers: Yes, No, Sometimes, and Who Cares?
For a long time I inclined to the last of these positions. If a piece
of writing fulfilled its functions as a statement, what possible
purpose could be served by fussing about whether it also met
some arbitrary aesthetic criteria? Recently, however, I have
come to see the real significance of the question, for an
affirmative response to it, one whose tendency is most inclusive,
signals a radical redefinition of literature itself. In its fullest implications, it means not simply a shifting of the boundaries, but a
total upheaval in the bourgeois understanding of art that is our
common intellectual heritage. This revolutionary task, properly
understood and applied, is the chief responsibility of feminist
criticism.

Exploration of female writers and their work began with the
recognized figures, those women whose achievements—however
undervalued, imperfectly apprehended, or misperceived—have
nonetheless earned them a place in literary history. A feminist
approach to such writers was and remains necessary in order to
correct the partial or distorted readings to which even the major
authors have historically been subject. At the same time, many
critics have pursued the parallel course of rediscovering or
reevaluating the production of women writers whose sex, literary
subjects, style, or audience had consigned them to obscurity.
Thus, in addition to reawakening interest in artists whose sensibility has been defined as esoteric because its expression is characteristically female (Dorothy Richardson comes to mind), this
effort has also involved critical examination of domestic,
sentimental, and popular fiction. And it, in turn, has entailed
critical evaluation of the kind of standards that judge certain writing about and for women as being intrinsically unworthy of serious attention. Women's private writings—diaries, journals, and
letters—have also assumed a public character as literature; and

that literature, particularly poetry, whose source and impetus is the women's movement itself comprises another element in the rich new canon that continues to come into being. I don't mean to denigrate either these various aspects of women's literature or criticism devoted to them. I am convinced, however, that the most thoroughgoing challenge feminist criticism can issue to either literature or society focuses on writing that encompasses and gives form to the experiences of the majority of women, writing that emphasizes commonality over uniqueness, collectivity over idiosyncrasy, and the truths of history over those of fiction. In order to clarify this assertion and give it substance, it is necessary to examine certain theoretical assumptions of feminist criticism—both as feminism and as criticism—and also to consider some examples of the kind of women's writing for which I am claiming the status of literature.

Those of us who practice feminist criticism are accustomed to attacks from positions to the right of us. Given the political assumptions—indeed, the bias—inherent in the word "feminist," how can what we do be considered criticism? Ironically enough, this challenge has tended to strengthen the feminist enterprise by forcing us to confront biases behind the objective façade of traditional criticism. At the same time, much of my own work has embodied a commitment to keep feminist criticism honest in the opposite direction: that is, to assure that its conceptual categories and interpretive methods reflected *and served* the concerns of the women's liberation movement. To my mind, this involved understanding sex as an historical, not merely a biological or psychological, category and exploring how that category works with the forces of class and race. But, despite my continuing concern with elaborating a feminist criticism that would in fact be feminist, I don't think it occurred to me until quite recently that there might really be a contradiction between the two terms. From the beginning, I have been saying that to tack the labels "feminist" or "and women" onto the fundamentally bankrupt methods of traditional criticism is not enough. And I have attempted to suggest analytic modes that would take our work beyond such methods. What I would now suggest, however, is that to demonstrate, albeit concretely, that compromise is not enough—is not enough. It is possible, by avoiding certain compromises, to take a more explicitly feminist stand, but there is no assurance that such a stand will be productive of a vision of art or of social relations that is of the slightest use to the masses of women, or even one that acknowledges the existence and the struggle of such women.

It is a fundamental precept of bourgeois aesthetics that good art, although probably adhering and contributing to a tradition, is art that celebrates what is unique and even eccentric in human experience or human personality. Individual achievement and subjective isolation are the norm, whether the achievement and the isolation be that of the artist or the character. It seems to me that this is a far from universal way for people to be or to be perceived, but one that is intimately connected to relationships and values perpetuated by capitalism. For this reason, I would seriously question any aesthetic that not only fails to call that individualism into question, but does so intentionally, in the name of feminism.

A good example of this tendency, and one that helped me to identify it as an aesthetic, may be found in Honor Moore's review (*Ms.*, December 1976), of some recent anthologies of poems by American women. The review evaluates three collections: *Amazon Poetry* (compiled by Elly Bulkin and Joan Larkin), *We Become New* (compiled by Lucille Iverson and Kathryn Ruby), and *I Hear My Sisters Saying* (compiled by Carol Konek and Dorothy Walters). Moore's clear preference is for the assumptions, the format, and the contents of the first two volumes.[1] I hope it is not just my own contrary taste for *I Hear My Sisters Saying* that inspires my remarks, for the issues that Honor Moore's review forced me to examine go well beyond the confines of all three exciting books. Moore likes the way *Amazon Poetry* and *We Become New* are arranged, describing the sequence of poems as "intuitive," since it is not chronological, biographical, or thematic. Such an arrangement constrains the reader to take the book seriously as a created whole, which clearly adds to the power of the endeavor. But a grouping by themes, which is how Konek and Walters put their collection together, has another kind of strength, in that it directs our attention to the subject matter of the poems and hence to the content of the lives that underlie them.

If the thematic division itself does not correspond to Moore's sense of what she needs and seeks in a compendium of women's poetry, she is even more distressed at the specific choice of categories. She acknowledges and, I think, applauds the inclusion of a section of poems about the making of poetry and the special conditions of women making poetry. But that preoccupation does not inform the other categories, and Moore remarks on its absence, deploring the (sexist) limitations of the segment on childbirth and motherhood. For this section, she complains, the compilers have selected poems about women giving birth to babies, but none about women giving birth to art or to themselves. This book, in short, which is supposed to be feminist in its inspiration and intention, gives its implicit sanction to the same old female roles, rather than suggesting or celebrating new ones.

I think it is significant that the sentence about "only" giving birth to babies and not to a work of art or a new self is the one that *Ms.* picked out to print in large, bold type across the top of the review's continuation page. But the editors of *Ms.* can hardly be considered suitable adversaries, nor is my quarrel directly with Honor Moore, since it is clear from her poetry and from this very review that she and I share a thirst that is at once nourished and sustained by the writings of women. The review did serve, however, to define my sense of aesthetic polarities. No one would seriously deny that the demand for a vision of new possibilities is feminist, much less that the creation of such visions is a noble and proper function of literature. I do believe, though, that the kind of feminism that is impatient with poems about motherhood when we *should* all be busy building, being, and depicting the New Feminist Woman is ultimately an incomplete feminism. The vision it reflects may be radical on some level, but because it is utopian, it is eventually less thoroughgoing in its challenge to the dominant view of human personality and its cultural expression than one centered in material history.

Women have babies. Some feminists locate our oppression in the reproductive capacity itself, some in the social institution of the family, some in power relations intrinsic to heterosexuality, some in the narrowing of life options attendant on sexist assumptions about pregnancy and motherhood. None of us denies the physiological fact, its social consequences, or its global implications. The question is whether the best feminist literature concentrates on the historical experience or goes "beyond" it to experiences that touch only a small fraction of womankind. I am not proposing a crude quantitative game. Childbirth and motherhood are mass experiences of women not primarily because they happen to a great many of us but because they are intimately bound up with our oppression. Thus, I would consider lesbianism to be such an experience, even though most women remain heterosexual, since it puts women into direct confrontation with the historical forces that define a sexist society. And work—both paid participation in the labor force and unpaid labor in the home—is critical to an understanding of the life lived by women in capitalist society, providing, in fact, the context within which our sexual relations and our experience of reproduction are defined.

Those same social forces are responsible for the exclusion of most women from the creation of art that is recognized as such within the dominant community and its culture. Such creation is not only a privileged experience but also an aspect of human existence that tends to be unavailable to women because of dominant social definitions of art as well as dominant definitions of women. As for giving birth to oneself, I am not entirely sure what it means: it may connote simply the cumulative process of becoming that is part of all our histories, but, with more self-consciousness, it can mean the personal dimension of revolution, or an experience of self-realization, or a strengthening of an individual's sense of wholeness and integrity. As a deliberate act, these latter versions of fulfillment are, to utter an understatement, outside the life histories and even the consciousness of most of the women in the world, not necessarily because we are deprived, but because our sources of strength and of consciousness are different. For many of us, moreover, our history has created a situation in which the "self" to which we give birth is a social, even a collective, entity rather than a strictly personal one.

The issue is not whether some women should be "permitted" the privilege of experiencing and trying to communicate aspects of life that are marginal to the female condition as the majority of women on this planet know it. I do not even question the value, for women in general, of isolated attempts to change individually and to act on the change. So the problem does not reduce to whether it is better to have babies or to make poems, much less whether it is preferable to make one's poems about having babies or about making poems. It is, rather, whether the best role for the arts and for criticism is to celebrate that which is basic or that which is marginal, what is common or what is exceptional. In industrial society, the arts have historically been the province of the person who is different. The writer is separate from other people—separated, indeed, by the very sensibility that defines him as a writer. (I think, for this analysis, it has to be "him.") And the characters—heroes and antiheroes alike—are special people, set off from others. For both artist and audience, cultural expression serves as a refuge for one's uniqueness against the brutality, the uniformity, and the conformity of life under capitalism. But this retreat is not necessarily the place most conducive to revolutionary changes in our condition. It is not role models we need so much as a mass movement, not celebration of individual struggle, however lonely and painful, so much as recognition that we are all heroes. Only from an understanding of the mass experience that forces us to *become* heroes can we build a movement to make fundamental changes in social institutions or our own lives.

Literature, therefore, should help us learn about the way things are, in as much depth and fullness as possible and by any means necessary. It is essential for women in the struggle for liberation to learn to hear what our sisters have to say about bearing children, for instance, in any tone that is true to the things that happen to them. And labels like "sentimental" or "brutal" that might characterize the tone of what they write ought not to be applied as a way of forestalling or limiting expression. Any diction, moreover, be it figurative or clinical, that can convey some essential of the experience is appropriate to the task. I do not mean by this to call for a spiritualized glorification of our past or our potential as matriarchs, for I think that such an approach also falsifies the way social forces actually function in women's lives. In fact, I am not speaking of the creation of myth at all, but of the expression of fact, and of the usefulness of literature as a way of helping to distinguish, through the facts, between those that are basic and those that are not.

But what about art? What about my Who Cares answer? To identify the experiences available to the mass of women as the subject for women's literature certainly challenges some traditional assumptions both about what themes are "universal" and about the primacy of special cases. But to do so is not to demonstrate that the narration of mass experience—in whatever form— is therefore something called literature. Indeed, our whole understanding of art concerns making something, which in turn entails notions of intention, craft or technique, separation between subject and object. It also involves some sense of standards, a code within the culture according to whose stipulations it is possible to determine whether something is art at all and then whether it is good art. There are other radical artists and critics, I know, who are able to accept this distinction between personal expression and real art.[2] They tend to locate the difference in that quality of making, of working at the thing, which implies sufficient detachment to enable one to see it *as* a thing. Of course, one identifies with a work of art one has made, and often has a great deal of ego-involvement in it, but, according to the prevailing view of the process, one is still supposed to act as if it were an *it*.

Such a set of definitions reinforces the separation between the artist and other people, since it tends to enhance the notion of art as a restricted profession to which only a limited number of us can aspire and which even fewer of us can master. Art, from this perspective, is supposed to require something like a "gift," "talent," "genius," and also the application of labor to something outside the self. In this complex of issues, the fundamental separation on which all the others depend is the one between the producer—the artist—and the product.

It seems to me that, although certain writings by women who are acknowledged "official" writers do partake of the impulse towards wholeness that characterizes the movement itself, this quality is likelier to be found in the efforts of women who were not only unrecognized, but who did not live in such a way as to give the label "writer" any meaningful application to them. For such women, the act of expression is not a discrete phenomenon. The expression cannot be arbitrarily divided from the feelings that give rise to it, nor either of these from the lived reality at the base. It is writing that gives voice to a real integrity of being, and thus attains even more completely than "made" literature to an aesthetic and political norm that might be called connectedness. Refusing the alienation that is supposed to be built into the process of creation, the writings of women who do not know they are writers manage to assert implicitly that the person, the personality, and the expressions of personality are one.*

Some useful examples of the principles I have been attempting to establish here may be found in the writings of rank and file factory workers who studied at the Associated Schools for Workers in the 1920s and '30s. These summer institutes—the Bryn Mawr Summer School for Working Women, the University of Wisconsin's School for Workers in Industry, and New York State's Vineyard Shore Workers School—trained potential trade union leadership, offering courses in economics, history, and public speaking as well as in English. The women whose personal histories were collected in the scrapbook *I Am a Woman Worker* were encouraged to write about themselves, their jobs, their experiences with bosses and with unions.[3] They wrote about their lives in order to develop their potential as part of their class and its struggle—a commitment that they did not separate from self-actualization. The idea of oppressed people's writing as a means of establishing identity is intriguing. But I am even more impressed by the notion that doing so may be understood as a process that integrates one into one's community and helps to create and unite the community itself, instead of underscoring the purportedly inherent conflict between the individual and the group. I

*For this reason, I respond rather differently than Honor Moore to the parochial element in *I Hear My Sisters Saying.* Moore complains, on the one hand, that the compilers of this collection have not done the fullest justice to the range of contemporary women's poetry and, on the other, observes critically that too many of the poets previously unfamiliar to her come from the editors' home city or state. As an avid reader of contributors' notes, I had observed this fact, myself, with a mild pleasure that was certainly not intended as endorsement of literary nepotism. Rather, I felt it reflected a new sort of respect for what women write, and therefore the application of a fresh critical standard. Although it is doubtless true that the writings of one's friends and students may be susceptible to a partiality that causes one to suspend normal criteria of judgment, there is reason to believe that, in the case of *I Hear My Sisters Saying,* such a new criterion had come into being. At any rate, the inclusion of poets with no professional identity or aspirations and the most strictly local reputation was one of the elements that helped me to redefine what I was listening *for* in the writing of women.

chose to focus on a book about the mass experience of work rather than, say, that of childbirth because work is the aspect of our lives from which official literature, writing by writers, is the most alienated. Thus, the subject, as well as the form, of this writing challenges established ideas about the literary endeavor.

The selections included in *I Am a Woman Worker* are normally very brief. Most take only a page or two of single-spaced typewriting and, probably on the advice of the instructors, tend to be devoted to one incident: being hired and trained, a typical day, an altercation with the foreman, an arrest for organizing. Only the accounts of strikes—where the single event is defined by stages that create a clear beginning, middle, and end to the narrative—grow to the length of conventional short stories. Because the pieces are defined and categorized by their subject and because the subject, in turn, is defined by one incident—sometimes, indeed, by one conversation—little artistry is displayed by most of the authors in constructing a tale that builds the reader's interest to a climax. The end, after all, is structured into most of these stories through the close of the work day, a clear victory of defeat for the organizing effort, or the remark that ends a quarrel over piecework rates. If the story has a conclusion beyond that natural end point, it is likely to be in the form of political morality: what the narrator has learned from the incident, what she wants for the future, or what she hopes other workers will gain from reading about it.

For this reason, the piece unambiguously entitled "We Won!" (p. 96) is worth reproducing in its entirety, since it is the only selection, other than the descriptions of lengthy strikes, where construction and even the creation of suspense have been taken into account by the anonymous author. This is the complete story:

> "So you went and made a complaint to the Union! Well, I'll fix you, you little rat!" yelled the boss at R.

R. blanched, but stood her ground. The other girls cowered and kept very still. The anger of the boss was terrible to see. They looked at each other and wondered what R. would do.

"I've a right to complain to the Union," she said quietly.

This seemed to anger the boss, for he yelled louder than ever, "You little skunk, you're fired! Get out! Get out!"

All work had ceased in the shop. Everybody was watching the scene. Now what would happen?

"You have no right to fire me. You've got to make a complaint to the Union and give a specific reason why," answered R. as calmly as she could. She turned back and continued her work.

The boss glared and sputtered, got red in the face, and looked as if he was ready to murder the calmly working girl. He finally turned and ran to the phone, grabbed it with such a jerk that he knocked it off the table. He yelled into the speaker for the Union office. Finally getting it, he started pouring out a torrent of words to the manager and threatening to lock out all the workers. The manager told him to calm down and he would come over and see what the trouble was. As the boss turned from the phone, everybody started to work furiously, striving not to get in his way. He went around swearing and growling and calling all the girls skunks and rats and little louses who just ate their way into the boss's bones.

The manager finally arrived with the bosses' association representative. They called R. and went into the office. The girls whispered among themselves, "If he gets R. out, he'll do the same to all of us. I hope she wins."

Moments passed; the girls became fidgety and more worried. Finally R. came out beaming, walked to her table, and started to work.

The workers had won that time!

I do not mean to maintain that "We Won!" is anything more than an anecdote, but the incident it describes is far from trivial in the lives of the narrator and her fellow workers. The anxiety they feel is not effectively communicated: we are *told* that they became "fidgety and more worried," rather than being *shown* what they go through while the case is being argued out by the representatives of labor and management. What makes the retelling come alive for us is the behavior of the boss, for his anger and agitation come across most vividly, whether he is excoriating the worker who stands up for her rights, knocking the telephone off its stand, or hurling imprecations at his employees, those "little louses who just ate their way into the boss's bones." The boss, in fact, is close to being a true character, in the literary sense, and his ire is the true subject of the anecdote, for we never learn what conditions R. had complained to the Union about or whether these matters or simply R.'s right to her job are the subject of the negotiations in the back office. What we see, instead, is the boss, the small manufacturer, at the moment of learning that the arbitrary power underlying his temper has been officially curbed. He can continue to exploit his operators, but he can no longer fire them at will or prevent their enjoyment of the concessions they have already attained. The workers in the shop feel their victory, but we never find out what they have won, other than a mediated relief from the irascible demands of the boss's personality.

Although the boss is the only character in "We Won!" (there is not even a first-person narrator, just R. and a collective group of coworkers), the piece is more than a character sketch, because its purpose is not to illuminate the particulars of an individual—even an erratic individual who exercises his full prerogative to make life miserable for his subordinates. Another story, however, tersely entitled "The Boss," (pp. 27-28), lacks even the plot motivation provided by an occurrence like the dismissal of R. Instead, the boss's entrance is the beginning, his departure is the end, and his actions while in the shop are the only events in between:

> He enters the factory bringing with him an atmosphere of untiring activity. His worst victim is the shipping clerk.
> "Louie! What are you doing?"
> "I'm—eh, I'm—eh—!"
> "All right—get through with it!"
> "The next minute he's at the blockers. "Who made this hat?"
> The forelady approaches. "Is there anything wrong with it?"

"Isn't there? Does it look perfect?"

Forelady: "It looks all right to me."

"Is it just like the sample? Get the sample, get the sample."
Impatiently—"Now listen! If the girl can't make it right give it to
someone else."

"I don't see anything wrong with the hat; it looks all right to
me."

"Now listen, I'm running this business. Do you want me to stay
in business? If the hats will keep on coming out this way, I'm going
to stop making hats altogether." As usual he has the last word.

"Louie! Get away from the girls. Look how you handle the hats.
Watch out, you big dope!"

A spry little man about 5 feet 4 inches tall, always doing something, even too busy to take off his hat and jacket on the warmest
days.

"Miss Bee, trim up those brim hats right away." The next minute he's discussing business with his partner.

Now he's near the cutter. "Did you get the material? Is it all
right? Order fifty more yards."

Now he's pressing. The chairlady is asking him to settle prices.
"Just a minute, just a minute."

"When will you come in?" she insists.

"In a minute. Wait—in a minute. Louie, did you ship Baer's
order?"

"I'm packing it now."

"Hurry up. Don't get lost."

"Mr. T. . . ," the chairlady calls impatiently.

"All right—I'm coming. Louie, come here. Press those crowns
and don't watch the girls."

In and out, here and there, sometimes the eye is too slow to
follow his movement. Sh! The boss is out, disappeared as fast as he
appeared, and the hurry and bustle disappears with him.

Nothing happens in "The Boss," or, rather, the many things
that happen in it are illustrations of character and in no way come
together to make a plot. But we are not merely being treated to a
portrait of this bustling, nervous, self-important little man. Once
more, as the title underlines and as his own actions make abundantly clear, we are seeing a demonstration of something about

the nature of power as it is expressed on the job—not, to be sure, in its most brutal or degrading manifestations, but as personified in ill temper and the casual mistreatment of those who are unable to fight back. The atmosphere conveyed is one of chaos and irrationality, which nonetheless have the power to break into the normal rhythms of the work day and disrupt them.

Another worker makes this point more explicitly in her description of one day in a garment factory. Here, things have been operating far from serenely: the foreman barks at the narrator for arriving late, although other workers come later still, two girls fight over the easier work and the short-tempered foreman has to arbitrate, the repairman yells at the operators whose machines are broken. After lunch, "the afternoon wears on with the usual quarreling, singing, and the hum of voices above the drone of the machinery." Yet here, too, the arrival of the boss makes a dramatic difference:

> Suddenly all is quiet. The smell of cigar smoke is strong upon the air. This smell is a warning that the owner of the shop is near. You can always smell him before you see him. Presently he enters, a tall well-built man with slightly graying hair. He walks up and down past the girls, who are working swiftly now. No one talks except when spoken to by the boss.
>
> He picks up garments, inspecting each one separately and closely, looking for bad work. Everyone holds her breath for fear it is her work he is looking at. If he finds work that is poor, his temper explodes, and we have an exciting half hour. Then he stalks out swearing to shut up the place immediately. When you can no longer see or smell him, the atmosphere changes. Voices again buzz excitedly all over, and keep on until 5:30, when the bell rings and the girls slowly and wearily depart, calling good night to each other. ("My Clothing Shop," pp. 30-31)

The heavy-handed irony in the term "exciting half hour" does not alter the facts; the boss's menace of shutting the place down may have no more substance than one girl's threats to tear the other's eyes out, but it is his actual ability to put them out of work that permeates the atmosphere of the story, just as his cigar stinks up the shop.

It is this power that makes it important for working people to be able to write about their bosses and for other workers to read what they write. The three-paragraph piece called "The Banana Argument" (p. 95) thus comes alive only in the middle section, where the manager makes a speech to the workers about the union's "excessive" demands. The workers are indignant that management has offered only $4.50 for a piecework job they believe should be priced at $6. Then the manager enters, expounding the logic of his breed:

> "It is the duty and to the interest of the workers to see that the employer does good business; otherwise how will you be employed? If you demand such high prices, how can your employer sell his merchandise and compete with other firms?" And, pointing to me, he said: "This woman evidently wants to live on Riverside Drive and go to Broadway shows, so she tries to get high wages. We ought to know better than to live above our means. We are workers, and we have to live where rent is cheap and food is cheap. Of course, where our boss lives, one banana costs a nickel, but where I live I get two bananas for a nickel. I am sure that on First Avenue, where most of you live, you can get beautiful fresh bananas four for a nickel, and that goes for everything else we need."

The workers are convinced by this circular argument and, for the moment at least, the narrator, their union "chairlady," has lost her influence. It is this fact that really matters to the author, not the vividness or even the humor with which she presents the manager and his specious reasoning.

Similarly, one of the articles in the section on company unions talks about a plant with an early and apparently fraudulent profit-sharing plan and a paternalistic welfare policy. Here, the boss to watch out for is not the owner, but the duplicitous Miss Anna:

The largest clothing factory in Ohio is the R—— Brothers' Shop. They had no children of their own so they adopted their employees. Miss Anna when very young had been a household employee in the home of the parents of the R—— brothers. The oldest boy had her educated so she could work in the office. And now she is a boss. Once during the first five years I worked in the old department, the manager had a disagreement with Miss Anna. So he had to go. The Superintendent also had a disagreement with Miss Anna, and he had to go. Miss Anna is strongly built, plain looking and plainly dressed, a woman without a heart or soul! Cold penetrating eyes! But she could be very sweet when she needed a girl. ("The 'One Big Family' Shop," p. 59)

An explanatory note introducing the recent reprint of *I Am a Woman Worker* refers to the contributors' characteristic prose style as "unadorned." To a student of literature, however, there is all too much tired ornamentation in the description of Miss Anna as a woman "without a heart or soul" and in the exclamation over her "cold penetrating eyes." Yet the richness of expository detail contained in these opening sentences suggests narrative possibilities that are far from hackneyed. In the hands of a realistic novelist a character like Miss Anna, the faithful household retainer elevated from domestic to office manager, her childless employers who are sure they know what is best for their employees, her rivals for administrative power, constitute a potentially intriguing human situation. The anonymous narrator who introduces the situation to us has no interest, however, in rising to the dramatic challenge. It is more important, from her perspective, that Miss Anna tells lies, gets workers in trouble, makes them go on working when their industrial injuries are unhealed, and does it all—the hypocrite—in the name of the company's "one big family" slogan. The narrator admits she was taken in by the mystique, the lunch-hour dances, the free chicken dinners before holidays, but she does not write about her disillusionment for confessional release. Rather, her description of Miss Anna and her role in the company's functioning connects human personality and social relations to institutional policy. She has a penetrating analysis of why a capitalist enterprise cannot afford genuine concern for its employees' well being, and why the model of the benevolent, paternalistic family, so assiduously cultivated by the employers and maintained by the curious figure of Miss Anna, cannot serve the real needs of those who are supposed to be the grateful "children" in such a setup. My hypothetical novel based on this situation, if it were a work of mainstream American fiction, would derive its interest and its point from the interconnection and conflict of personalities; whatever the reader knew about the history of American industrial practices in the years following World War I would help to illuminate the situation and the characters who were involved in the novel. Individual personality is by no means irrelevant in the story as we actually have it—the difference between working under a fair-minded foreman and a mean one is vividly illustrated, for example, in two contrasting paragraphs—but it operates to describe the origins and context of personality itself. It is always at the service of history.

The selection ends on a personal note:

> Another devil came [to be our foreman]. The last two months I cried every day. I never saw so many girls cry in my seventeen years of factory experience. At last I broke down. I was five weeks sick at home. When I reported to work again I was told by Miss Anna that my job was taken. I said to her, "But you know, Miss Anna, that I can do all the operations in this place, and you are hiring over thirty girls today."
>
> "I sent for those girls so I must give them work. I'll send for you in a week. There'll be something in your line."
>
> I knew she never would. And here I was one of the children. I belonged to the big Family, and was a stock holder of the company too. I thought I had a life job. (p. 61)

If the narrator's own disappointment were her principal theme, this conclusion would be an anticlimax at the very least. The irony works because she is not concentrating on her feelings alone, but on the system that made her have them. She does not deny her own individuality and her own pain, nor does she offer them up on the altar of abstract ideology; nonetheless, her motives for telling her story—and hence the things she chooses to recount and the manner in which she does so—have only incidentally to do with the expression of that individuality or that pain, centering more directly on the attempt to understand and communicate something about the *common* condition of working people within which her private experience takes its particular form.

Throughout the scrapbook, there are narrators whose individual personalities force their way through the anonymity in which they are presented. In each such instance, however, the function and the effect of this individuality are not those that cultural tradition would lead us to expect. There is, for example, the woman whose English prose is still tinged with Yiddish syntax and whose idea of high fashion gets her into difficulties:

> The leather jacket that came with the Revolution, was to me a symbol both of Revolution and elegance. My admiration for the jacket I brought with me to America, and made sure to get one as soon as possible.
>
> But my desired leather jacket brought me a lot of trouble after I had lost my first job and was looking for another one. ("The Symbolic Jacket," p. 22)

At shop after shop, she is questioned suspiciously and then rejected on slender grounds, before she is told to her face at one place that "these leather jackets and bushy hair" are political symbols and "we don't like Bolsheviks." Later, having been hired at a men's clothing factory, she repels the sexual advances of her boss with some spirit: "For that he got the coat in his face and I quit the job. The reason for such behavior was again the leather jacket which made him think I was a Communist." After another year of rejections, the narrator has to take more drastic action:

> I got sick and tired of it, and decided to get rid of my Jacket. I dressed myself in the latest fashion, with lipstick in addition, although it was so hard for me to use at first that I blushed, felt foolish, and thought myself vulgar. But I got a job.
>
> This occurred some years ago. Now, however there is no more danger in wearing a jacket. It does not signify radicalism, because the American student took to wearing it. (p. 23)

This woman, with her gutsiness and her modesty, stands out as a person, highlighting a conclusion that is even more ironic to us than it was to her; I am sure she would draw the right political conclusions if she knew how hard it is today to get a factory job if one looks like a student and how young working women who are identified as "hippies" or students are subjected to sexual abuses based on the same sort of false generalizations she encountered.

In another piece, the claim made by several authors that their work made them intolerably "nervous" is substantiated in such a way as to make the woman herself clear as a character. The narrator in this case works in a radio factory, performing a delicate process clipping copper wires, that eventually "got on everyone's nerves":

> Everything was fine and dandy for a while. I got along all right, until I began to find when I left the shop at nights I was awfully nervous. I would get into arguments with the girls at work over nothing at all. One day, while I was working, very peacefully, indeed, I suddenly began to feel very shaky. I felt as though I were going to scream. I laid down my razor blade and put my hands to my head and to my amazement I was seized with a violent trembling and I seemed to be screaming at the top of my voice. After that things seemed to be rather vague. I remembered feeling cold water dashed in my face. Some one asked, "Did she cut her finger?" Others wanted to know if I were sick. Then I found myself in the dispensary. I had been carried there by some of the men that

worked near me. I lay there very quiet for a while, trying to figure out just what had happened to me. I felt shaky and nervous. I tried to sleep, but it was useless. The nurse had given me some medicine and I felt after a while as though I would be able to go back to my work.

Before I started working, I asked my foreman if I could go home. We were very busy at the time and he said he could not spare me. I went back to my place and tried to work. It was no use; I could not do it. My hand trembled so I could not hold the blade. I just put my head down and cried. I did not know why I was crying; I just could not help it. When the foreman saw this, he told me to go home; he would get some one to take my place. ("The Effect of Employment on One's Health," p. 54)

And there is the young woman whose story I find the most moving. This narrator, like her contribution, is known only by her job title, "A Seamer on Men's Underwear" (pp. 31-32). Her opening is stark, although we do not yet know enough about her to be touched by it in any personal sense:

I am seventeen years old, but look to be fifteen or younger. When I was twelve, I was hurt by an automobile. Because of the injuries I received, I could not go to school. That was a bitter blow, not only to me but also to my parents. They had worked hard in factories so that I could get an education. At the time of the accident, my mother was working in a cotton mill. Being tired and over-worked, the terrible shock of my accident caused her to have a nervous breakdown. She could not work. The few hundred dollars that they had saved, dwindled to nothing. I knew this, and worried.

So, at the age of fourteen, I went to work. The doctor who took care of me said that I was in no condition to work, and if I did I would pay for it in a few years. Because I had no training in any kind of work, I always got jobs that were the most monotonous and the poorest paid. I finally got work in a knitting factory as a seamer.

The seamer takes us through a typical work day, one whose details may strike one as either coloring the overall effect or flattening it out. She describes her walk to the shop, the line of job-seekers she has to pass, the process by which the piecework is recorded and compensated, the health problems that arise, the condition of toilet and water fountain, the spoilage of her lunch, the wait for the final bell of dismissal, and her walk home. For a great many people trained in literature, this matter-of-fact piling on of miseries is just too much: tragedy is acceptable, a "clean" (not to say cathartic) emotion, but pathos and its attendant sentiment are dull and embarrassing. A piece that begins with the narrator's accident, her mother's consequent breakdown, and proceeds—through such horrors as crippling, unpoetic industrial complaints (rupture from carrying piles of finished union suits to the bin has little heroic stature), filthy, unflushable toilets, and a lunch that must be crushed on the work-table to be saved from rats—all this may be redeemed only by style, wit, and plot, or at least some literary "point." But the seamer's style remains intentionally discursive:

> I seam men's heavy underwear. After I finish twelve union suits, I get a check for 6 cents for size fifty, and 4½ cents for the smaller sizes. At the end of the week, I paste my checks in a book and give the book to the boss, who pays according to the number of checks I have. After I finish a dozen union suits, I tie them up and carry them to the bin. The dozens are heavy, and grow heavier as the day goes on. The bin is usually full, and as I throw my dozen up on top it very often comes down on me. Of course I fall. Rupture is quite common from carrying the heavy dozens. (p. 32)

A real personality does come through as the narrator traces the pattern of her day. This woman, looking fifteen or younger, walks three miles to work in the morning, far from resigned to her condition: "I look at the older people and wonder if as the years go by their spirits are deadened." When her mind goes numb with the pressures and tedium of her job, a trip to the washroom serves to "stimulate" her with disgust. All day she has been longing for fresh air, but by quitting time she is so tired that the first gusts refresh her only subconsciously, for ''I only felt my aching bones and my tired eyes.'' Yet the active sensibility we have begun to know is still functioning:

> As I walk home, I see some of the people for whom my class works. The priest rolls by in his big car, and gently nods his head to me. The superintendent's daughter waits in her car for her father. I think of my father who has to stay one more hour in the mill, then trudge home where his daughter will be too tired to greet him.
>
> As I think of these things, there is a terrible rage in my heart, but I do not stop with that. I want to learn what crushes out the lives of the workers, and what takes the children of these people and places them in the stuffy factories, even before they have time to fill their lungs with fresh air. (p. 33)

The ''terrible rage'' and the accompanying need to know why things are this way comes as the result of a carefully constructed catalogue of outrages which are described, however, with the same dispassionate thoroughness as the paragraph about finishing each bundle of twelve union suits. I do not think anyone would deny that the seamer's feelings are intensely personal, but her anger and her search for understanding have a social—in fact, a deliberately class-conscious—dimension. Her two-page sketch reveals a great deal about its author, but, although her voice is clearly her own, she says nothing in it that would prompt us to exclaim over what an unusual, heroic, weird, or wonderful woman she must have been. The strengths of this sort of writing are precisely in its capacity to show what is individual, not as if it were unique, but as a way of illustrating and elaborating on the common condition of what the seamer does not hesitate to call her class. Like the wearer of the Symbolic Jacket and the woman who describes the effect of the radio wiring job on her health, she understands her own responses as part of a larger situation, and her reason for detailing them is to tell more about that larger situation. In the case of the seamer, there is a clear ideological conclusion as well, but it is one that is profoundly rooted in immediate experience.

I Am a Woman Worker is at its strongest, in fact, when the political observations or exhortations are clearly based in the author's own life. Even so, it is not always easy to make it clear that these general statements are as heartfelt as, say, a worker's hatred for the foreman who unfairly sticks her with all the rejected pieces. This is the concluding paragraph of "A Job in a Laundry" (pp. 42-43), a piece describing and contrasting conditions of black and white, old and young women workers:

> My personal experience and those figures from the surveys taken during the prosperity years of 1927-8 have made me realize the vital need for organization in American industry. I hope that in the near future workers will realize that the racial hatred that is being bred by the capitalist class is not to the advantage of the Negro or white worker who should have one common purpose: that of organizing against capitalism.

This woman writes rather stiffly, even when she is describing what happened to her, as when she explains how she got fired:

> I did not last very long at my job in the laundry because I refused to work more than eight hours for the $10 that I was getting. The employer would probably have submitted to my conditions because I did twice as much work as the others, but several of the younger workers had asked me why I was so privileged. I told them that if they would refuse to work until 10:00 at night as I did, the employer would have to get used to the idea of parting with them at 6:00. The employer realized that I stirred up the older workers to leave on time, and he told me that work was getting very slow and that he could not keep me any longer.

Nonetheless, the infelicities of her style cannot entirely hide the liveliness of her replies to her fellow workers and her boss—a liveliness that is notably absent from her conclusion about not allowing racism to divide the working class.

The same point is made far more effectively and more characteristically in the piece entitled "Strike Call" (pp. 109-110), where the narrator anxiously waits for the strike signal she knows will be given at ten o'clock. The boss has no suspicions of the Gentile workers and the narrator comforts the motherly German woman next to her, "Helen, please don't be frightened. He don't know that you belong to the union. He suspects only the Jewish girls!" Yet the narrator is not above such ethnic stereotyping herself. The old fat woman with the blank face offers "No hope!" to the eager striker, and she faces "Opposite, 2 Italian girls who have probably never heard of a union." But the story's denouement, when it comes, eradicates all her preconceptions about who can and cannot be organized, or where the energy for a movement comes from:

> The shop is unusually quiet this morning. It is before a storm, and we wait impatiently for the cloud to burst. At 9:30, a young girl with a red ribbon on her hair runs past me and whispers, "Comrade, get ready for the struggle!"
> The older worker looks up with contempt. "She must think it's a picnic! A fine time they pick to call a strike!"
> "But what have we to lose?" I ask. "Nothing but our misery."
> Will 10:00 never come? Fifteen minutes more! What's that! Like a black cloud the coloured pressers are moving towards us. Fifty-three strong—the first ones to throw their work down! Just as a flame would spread through the shop, shaft after shaft is cleared. No power in the world can stop this moving cloud!

The racism of bosses is a commonplace of these authors' experience, one to be recorded but not usually commented upon. One piece about an employment agency is a masterpiece of understatement. The personnel manager takes a phone call, approaches one of the young women who are waiting and whispers something to her. Then,

> The young woman gets up, goes to the desk, gets a slip of paper from the manager, and walks out, a smile on her face. Everybody's eyes escort her to the door with envy.

> An hour passes. She comes back looking sad and disappointed.
> She goes up to the manager and says something in a whisper.
> " But you don't look Jewish. I thought you'd get by," we hear
> the manager say. ("An Employment Agency," p. 5)

Much more attention is devoted to women workers' efforts to
overcome their own fears and suspicions about fellow workers
from different backgrounds, as well as to their efforts to use the
ties of an ethnic community—the common language and
customs—to build solidarity. Where it fails, we find narrators
who cannot understand why "they," their former shop-mates,
would not permit themselves to "be organized." But, where it
succeeds, the narrators show us how close informal relations developed across and within ethnic boundaries are the basis for
warmth and trust in a strike situation. The narrator of "We Go
out on Strike" (pp. 113-114) retains a rich stock of stereotypes,
but her experience has emphasized the strength to be found in
these images:

> I got work, together with about twenty-five other girls, with a
> firm manufacturing children's dresses. My job was sewing on but-
> tons, making button-holes, trimming and packing dresses, as well
> as giving out work when Mr. K. was too busy to do it. For this I
> was receiving the magnificent sum of $13 a week and a promise of a
> raise "when business picks up."
> Our shop consisted of a long narrow room with three windows
> on each end. The windows at one end were partitioned off for the
> office and cutting table, leaving the rest of the room with the light
> only from the three remaining windows. The rest of our conve-
> niences consisted of a curtained corner with nails and hooks on the
> wall to hold our coats, a tin sink with a mouldy green faucet, and a
> toilet for which we had to stand in line during lunch hour.
> Crowded together in this shop, the twenty-five of us lived like
> one big family. We did not go down for lunch often; it cost too
> much and it was not pleasant to climb four flights up and down
> when one got only three-quarters of an hour for lunch. So we
> worked, talked, ate and sang together for eight hours every day
> and for five and a half days every week.

L., a Spanish girl, managed to keep us laughing by making fun of everything, laughing heartily herself, her white teeth gleaming while speeding along with her work. The two M.'s were the ones who would start a beautiful Italian song in the afternoon when we were all getting tired. We would all join in, or else we would sing spirituals with J. and P. We loved to sing, but we didn't sing often, conditions were too wretched.

"I would sure quit this place if it wasn't that Bob and I are going to be married soon," J. would declare every second day or so.

"I am married, but I will sure have to take up some line to make my carfare and rent; after I pay for the eats there isn't anything left," would come from L.

"You go and tell that to the boss. Just yesterday as I was complaining about the price on style nine he told me 'You can take it or leave it; there are plenty others who would be glad to work.' "

"Don't let him be so snooty, this is positively the last week for me in this dump, look at this work. I won't even make enough to keep me in chewing gum!" exploded P., the flapper.

"What are you bellyaching for? Chewing gum isn't refined. Mr. K. wants you to be a lady." This from L., of course.

"You are always talking of quitting as if that would help. Quit this place and take a job in the sweat shop of Mr. K. Don't you know that sweat shops are like the plague? They spread, and you don't escape them by quitting."

"B. is preaching union again, girls," said one.

"It will take you five unions to get anything out of this dump!" declared another.

"We don't need five unions. Smarter men then our boss have had to pay more when the girls joined the union and struck," spoke up M.

"Strike, and walk up and down the street like a fool, not me! My boy friend wouldn't stand for that," and J. would wrinkle up her pretty nose.

Our conversation would break up. The girls kept scanning the want ad page every day. The bosses continued to set prices to suit themselves.

It was a Thursday morning. The evening before we had received our pay. "I had a lousy pay for last week and it seems I'll never make out any better this week, either, not with this rotten work. I am quitting!" exclaimed one girl, jumping up and throwing her work aside. The girls all stopped work looking at her.

"Girls don't let's quit. Let's strike. Come on to the union! Let's make this damn shop stop sweating everyone." I stand up.

L. follows me. "I've had enough of this too," she says. The girls all jumped up as they saw the boss coming on the run from the other end of the shop.

"What's the matter? You don't like the work? We are cutting another lot of good work, you'll get it next, why—er—you'll get it right away, it is—"

"Oh yeah, we know your good work. We've had enough of it, and we are on strike. Come on girls, we are going to the union." My heart thumped fearfully as I said it. But the girls all followed me, leaving our boss open mouthed.

I have reproduced this selection in its entirety because the dialogue, which sounds quite authentic, is one of the few places where women workers are shown discussing their boyfriends and husbands, how being married affects their role in the labor force, or how the "feminine" image they are supposed to present to their men conflicts with the identity they must develop to survive on the job. Elsewhere, the emphasis is on women's relation to the productive process, to their coworkers, and to supervisors and bosses. Parents and children appear as persons to be supported by the wages of a woman worker; sisters or cousins may be employed at the same shop; and working-class men are almost nonexistent in these pieces. Factory owners are almost invariably male and many supervisors are as well, but most of the women who wrote for the scrapbook worked in industries characterized by almost total sex-segregation. Occasionally, mention will be made of male workers from another department or shop encouraging (and, in at least one case, discouraging) the women's efforts at organization. For the most part, however, the men who appear are in positions of power over the women workers, not primarily because of their sex but because of their position and function in capitalist production. Sexual familiarities are among the abuses that these women have to fight, but there is no evidence that those with female bosses felt themselves to be better off because they had one less indignity to cope with.

Several of the longer pieces about strikes, particularly the two about textile workers' strikes in southern company towns, show the effects upon the family of what happens on the job. The community is depicted in these stories as a source of resistance, one that suffers a common oppression and a shared defeat. In these stories, as in the ones that concentrate on women's workplace experience, there is little that a contemporary feminist would acknowledge as "women's consciousness," and not all of the selections reflect traditional "class consciousness," either. What there is instead is a sense of solidarity that may include these recognized analytic categories, but that often transcends them. These women know who they are, as individuals and as part of a larger whole.

Although all this is very fine, the student of literature may be saying, what about style? Aren't there literary standards, too? Don't your quotations abound in clichés, genteelisms, hackneyed or conventional sentiments, forced humor, disordered arguments, plain bad writing? And don't these tend to increase as one descends the scale of literary awareness and craft? Not to speak of errors in grammar, sentence structure, and diction that can deprive unskilled writing of its capacity to communicate effectively, much less to move the reader? I could hardly deny the presence of such factors or the difficulties they pose. But I call them "difficulties" advisedly, because I believe it is all too easy to exaggerate their significance and thus to disregard what we have to learn from this literature. Most of the stylistic shortcomings originate in the self-consciousness of this writing and the consequent desire to impress *as* writing. The women workers are trying to write well—even elegantly—perhaps at the instigation of their teachers, but just as likely because of socially communicated definitions of what is acceptable, definitions that vary with the educational level and the class of those to whom the message is being communicated. Contrast, for example, the poetry that is read in grade schools, in high school, in community college, and in universities. The stuff that college professors know enough to

despise and that properly bores most high school students is the
only model most kids are likely to encounter for what poetry is.
The message is that poetry is fancy language strung together to
convey irrelevant or dishonest sentiments. In the ninth grade, my
classmates and I had to memorize and recite in chorus the following lines on the same subject addressed by the scrapbook authors:

Work
by Henry Van Dyke

Let me but do my work from day to day,
  In field or forest, at the desk or loom,
  In roaring marketplace or tranquil room;
Let me but find it in my heart to say,
When vagrant wishes beckon me astray,
  "This is my work; my blessing, not my doom,
  "Of all who live, I am the one by whom
  "This work can best be done in the right way."

Then shall I see it not too great, nor small,
  To suit my spirit and to prove my powers,
  Then shall I cheerful greet the labouring hours,
And cheerful turn, when the long shadows fall
At eventide, to play and love and rest,
Because I know for me my work is best.[4]

In offering this reminder of what passes for appropriate style,
theme, attitude in the literary education of most working people, I
do not mean to apologize for the ways in which *I Am a Woman
Worker* deviates from high cultural values. Nor am I attempting to
impose *its* norms on literature with very different origins and
intentions. Rather, I wish to suggest that, whatever we have been
taught, clichés or sentimentality need not be signals of meretricious prose, and that ultimately it is honest writing for which
criticism should be looking. It is essential to recognize literature
that can enhance our understanding of the conditions that define
women's lives, and, in order to gain insight into what women
experience, I do not feel that we have to "relax our standards."

Instead, writing like this can force a reevaluation and a reordering of those standards and turn them on their heads. And this sort of process, this sort of reading, tells us something we urgently need to know about both women and literature.

NOTES

1. All three collections are discussed, along with a number of other feminist anthologies of poetry, in my essay, "The Keen Eye . . . Watching," elsewhere in this volume.

2. I think, for example, of a disagreement I had with Denise Levertov, when she visited my writers' workshop at SUNY/Buffalo in December of 1975. Although she recognized the importance to women of the writing the women's workshop enabled them to do, Levertov insisted on a separation between mere expression and art that I have ceased to believe has any worthwhile meaning.

3. This scrapbook, like the other collections from the Associated Schools, was a mimeographed volume with a paper cover. Fragile copies, sometimes bound, may be found in libraries, and I found it worthwhile to use these, because the form effectively conveys the nature of this particular venture into literature and publication. (I have consulted copies at the Buffalo and Erie County Public Library, the New York Public Library, and the Tamiment Collection, which is housed in the Bobst Library at New York University.) A more enduring reissue of the scrapbook—far more useful for most scholarly purposes—has recently been made available: *I Am a Woman Worker,* ed. Adria Taylor Hourwich and Gladys L. Palmer, Women in America series (New York: Arno Press, 1974). Since the Arno reprint is a reduced photocopy of the original, page-number references are the same for both.

4. In the interests of scholarship, I looked up this poem in the Public Library's collection of Van Dyke's poetry. After twenty-two years, I found I had one word wrong. More interesting, I learned that "Work" is one of three connected sonnets under the rubric "The Three Best Things." (The others are Love and Life).

The Keen Eye . . . Watching: Poetry and the Feminist Movement

That you never question *me,* or my right
to speak up, to explore
what I think.
There is the warmth of sisterhood
And the keen eye of politics,
Watching.

—*Sing a Battle Song*[1]

"THIS POEM is about how I spent my lunch-hour yesterday." As Bonnie distributes the copies, a couple of people remind her that we're not supposed to "preface": read the poem first, then let *us* comment. That far, at least, we're like other writing workshops. But both the reminder not to make introductory apologies and our sly evasions of the rule constitute a running joke. Bonnie's voice, as she reads to us, is without expression, and her face seems pale under the painted blush; I notice her tense hands and her carefully polished nails.

The poem, called "Lady in Waiting," is about an abortion (lunch-hour yesterday? my God, she works in an office downtown), and the controlling metaphor is violence, punishing violence between men and women. Her father used to beat her, and the images in the first half of the poem capture the feelings of a ten-year-old waiting in her room for punishment. Already whipped, helpless and hysterical, the little girl is offered a glass of soothing cognac. She throws it in her father's face. In the later stanzas, it is the lover who punishes, who makes her wait for what's coming to her, who makes her get rid of the child. She has done so, the abortion is over (yesterday, on her lunch-hour), but the climax is angry, not numbed or bitter. She imagines a glass in her hand and, once more, she throws it at the man: "Here's cognac in your eye."

It takes us a while to sort out what is "happening" in this poem. Who are the two men? What is their power over this woman's body? Why does she feel impotent? What has been done to her? There are too many "he's," some confusion—what's intentional, what's inept?—between the father and the lover. The irony in the title and the last two lines seems forced, unconvincing, and the anger gets out of control, knocking the poem off balance. We say all these things, slowly deciphering what is indirect or ambiguous, trying to put together how this poem is made, how it operates, whether and how it "works." But, through our analysis, there is still Bonnie, who took a long lunch-hour (Wednesday, just yesterday) to have an abortion.

"The second time is worse than the first." In the poem, it is clear that this means the violence the lover does and the pain he causes are worse than the punishment inflicted by the father. But all of us in this room have heard Bonnie's personal history two or three months ago, and recall that this is also her second abortion. That other time she was twelve, and she'd waited so long, an eighth-grader with no idea about where to go for help, that she'd had to have a saline injection, which means you go through labor to expel the fetus. It took her an exceptionally long time, surrounded by older women who believed she was the age she'd been forced to claim. Now she's an "older woman" herself, nineteen, and, securing the abortion earlier on in the pregnancy, she can have the vacuum-aspirator procedure—much simpler, and she can go back to her office that afternoon.

In the workshop we talk about why the second abortion, with its mental anguish, was "worse" for her than the fruitless labor

pains the other time. We talk about her fury at her child's father
and at her own. We are twelve or fourteen women and I am the
only one over thirty. One is a lesbian, one identifies herself as
bisexual. All of us in the room have faced the question of
whether, when, and how to have children. Half of us have had
abortions. None of us has borne a child. We talk about that
anomaly, but more about what caused it: about the irony of slo-
gans declaiming a woman's right to control her own body, about
the pain of denial and the contradictions of motherhood. No one
is allowed easy generalizations about what you can and cannot do
"in this society." We try to specify what we mean by that phrase,
how the forces of class and race intersect with our womanhood
and further define what we believe to be our choices. And we
discuss how, short of revolution, a new generation can be raised.
We also talk about how strange and alienated it is for us to be
talking about it at all.

The class runs an hour over time, from seven to eleven on a Thursday night in spring. At the end of it, I feel exhausted by the imme-
diacy of our discussion, but I leave feeling that I have learned
a great deal, that we have explored some new intellectual and political territory, that the problems have been defined and codified in
a fresh way. I also feel that we have discussed Bonnie's poem.

So my reflex defenses are slow, at the beginning of summer
school, when a new poet, an English major, says she's unsure
about signing up. "It sounds like all you do is confessional
poetry." I am silent, having forgotten, temporarily, that such
categories exist. She takes my silence for resistance, not stupidity, and elaborates her point: "I mean, don't you ever talk about
the *craft* of poetry, about the poem itself? I'm interested in
poetry, not in all these digressions." When I begin to speak about
the subject as the poem (even the poem "itself"), she interrupts
eagerly, to show me how well she knows the lingo, and goes on
about "form" and "content." (Look, I am hard on her because I
once *was* her.) I explain that there is an historical tension in the
workshop between women who thought that discussing those as-

pects of our lives and our world suggested by our poetry constituted something (illegitimate) called a "digression" and women
who thought those "digressions" were the whole point. By now I
am getting defensive, a fact I attempt to mask by coldly observing
that it's a matter of aesthetics—which, in turn, is a matter of
politics. "But *do* you work only in the confessional mode?" she
persists. "Because I'm rather tired of that, and I'd like to try
something more objective."

What I want to do is explain what I have learned from
participating—as "student" and "teacher"—in the Women Writers' Workshop, as well as from reading the poems that have come
from our movement. The critical theory underlying my own academic training took Literature as a given, a material phenomenon
whose primacy and "interest" were axiomatic. Yet at the same
time the creative process, in its objectivity and its exclusivity,
was something of an unnatural act, even a cherished aberration.
Departments of English existed to identify and cultivate the per-
version. My own experience as poet, critic, and teacher suggests
that this state of affairs is itself a cultural artifact, with its basis in
the historical forces that define our society. The isolation, specialization, and differentiation of the artist and the autonomy of
the aesthetic product are both concomitant parts of the dominant
myth. Feminist poetry, the poetry of our movement, serves to
revive the notion that life and letters need not remain discrete and
that writing can be a genuine, natural, and fully human act.

"Poetry of our movement"—the phrase evokes at once more
and less than I mean it to. Many of the writers in the Women's
Workshop would not consider themselves Poets in any sense of
the word that seeks to distinguish the writer from the mass of
womankind. This is not just ideological tenacity; it also means a
lack of confidence, and a continued belief in the existence, somewhere, of "real" writers who *are* different from other people.
Their own impulse toward poetry—the sense that they had something to say and language in which to do it—came with the experience that has come to be almost codified as the "raised con-

sciousness." Despite a distinctly literary sort of precocity in my background, I belong to this group myself. But I do not claim that those who would not be poets were it not for the women's movement are the only feminist poets. For there are recognized poets, "real" writers, whose lives and work have been transformed by the movement and who have found their true audience in it. And there are women writers whose own understanding of the world and of their situation could not be defined as feminist, but whose work nonetheless has something important to give to a movement trying to analyze and to change the lives of women.[2] Although I believe that a feminist reading of this last sort of material is valuable and significant for both the sociology of literature and the interpretation of female experience, there are important distinctions to be made between it and work that is more directly connected to the movement for women's liberation.

To speak, as I do, of feminist poetry as belonging to and coming out of a movement implies the existence of a culture that is not yet in being. It assumes a movement whose artistic expression is organic to its total form. It presupposes a community that is at once the source of such expression and the audience for it. And it takes for granted a feminist aesthetic in cases where I would suggest that such a standard has not yet been articulated. The movement for the liberation of women has a mass character and potential that no other movement of white Americans has attained. It has the demonstrated capacity to effect extraordinary changes in individual consciousness and to work some influence on the structures of society itself. But its revolutionary capacity, in theory or practice, its ability to make an essential difference to the forces that operate on us and to alter fundamental power relations, remains unrealized.

For this reason, the poetry that is "of" our movement sometimes lags behind it, sometimes spends itself in exhortation, and sometimes constitutes itself a rhetorical vanguard that can reduce the struggle to a series of metaphors about blood. It is at least as far from its full development as the movement itself. Yet it is beginning to put the pieces together. The function it serves is both cognitive and analytical, tending, first of all, to examine or report on those facets of human experience that belong to women alone or on which women have a special perspective. It works, as well, to celebrate the emergence of a new consciousness and new possibilities for women.

Nine books are spread before me as I write. These are the anthologies; smaller books, containing the work of a single poet, are in a pile on the chair. Taken together, the titles of these collections are intriguing: *Woman to Woman, I Hear My Sisters Saying, No More Masks!, Rising Tides, Mountain Moving Day, Amazon Poetry, Sing a Battle Song, The World Split Open, We Become New.*[3] It makes a found poem in itself, the sense of action and energy warring with, seeming to belie, the staid, discursive subtitles to the right of the colon: *A Book of Poems and Drawings by Women, Poems by Twentieth Century Women, Twentieth Century American Women Poets, An Anthology of Poems by Women, Poems by Women, Poems by Women in the Weather Underground Organization, Four Centuries of Women Poets in England and America, Poems by Contemporary American Women.* The compilers are using images of cosmic and natural convulsion, earth, mountains, seas, all surging uncontrolled, to convey the significance of women speaking face to face and to one another in their own voices. Something very dramatic is supposed to be happening here, in and through the poems themselves.

On the most immediate level, the language of cataclysm is accompanied by a new fierceness of tone and by the repetition of the word "woman" with a new frequency and intensity. Although much of what is most valuable in the works of poets like Edna St. Vincent Millay or Elinor Wylie derives from their sexual identity, and they have poems that capitalize on that identity, they do not declaim that they are women as if the fact had a *self-evident* significance. The very words "woman," "women" are neither talisman nor banner to them. Indeed, I learned a very different lesson from reading the accepted women poets of the twentieth century—those included, say, in the Oscar Williams *Little Trea-*

sury I have owned since I was ten years old. When I say that "I
learned," I do not mean to imply that I used their works as
repositories of history or social theory. There was, however,
something that their poems had to teach about women that was
intrinsic to the act and the art of poetry itself, for it has, on the
one hand, to do with the permissible role-definitions, the sexual
stance of the female poet and, on the other, with the complex
texture and connotations of words. From this point of view, the
major thing I learned from what these poets had to say about
female sexuality was that a certain coy daring in how one "told
all" was both titillating and licit; even celebrations of a woman's
heterosexual experience from a male-defined perspective were
allowed. But for the rest, for the direct implications of the word
that names us, it was Louise Bogan and no male poet who taught
me that

> Women have no wilderness in them,
> they are provident instead
> content in the tight hot cell of their hearts
> To eat dusty bread.

It is a judgment that makes it clear what we are to understand by
the word when Eliot's J. Alfred Prufrock complains about the
way those women come and go, speaking of Michelangelo.

Something different is surely happening when Judy Grahn can
tell us, in successive poems, that the common woman is as common as the common crow, as a rattlesnake, as a nail, as a thun-
derstorm, as the reddest wine, as solemn as a monkey or the new
moon, concluding the sequence

> the common woman is as common
> as good bread
> as common as when you couldn't go on
> but did.
> For all the world we didnt know we held in common
> all along

the common woman was common as the best of bread
and will rise
and will become strong—I swear it to you
I swear it to you on my own head
I swear it to you on my common
woman's
head.

                    (*The Common Woman*)

Similarly, a new sense of our sexuality is emerging when Alta can
point out

if you come in me
a child is likely to
come back out.
my name is Alta.
I am a woman.
   ("Bitter Herbs")

The word "woman" is employed in anger and celebration:

i, woman, i
can no longer claim
        a mother of flesh
        a father of marrow
I, woman, must be
        the child of myself.

And when the mood is one of resignation, that is still not contentment, but rebellion deferred, for

Time locks a woman's brood
of wish into the drawer of some
other day.
                ("To A Sister")[4]

For, "A Chant for My Sisters" assures us, "it's all right to be
woman."

In her preface to *The World Split Open,* Muriel Rukeyser quotes a male publisher's remarks about poems by women: "If they are any good they can stand up in an anthology with men." The contributors' notes in the women's anthologies range from matter-of-fact self-descriptions to explicitly feminist declarations to the clearly articulated hope on the part of some poets that their work has not been selected and will not be read "merely" because of their sex. The assumption of this last group, like that of the competition-minded publisher cited by Rukeyser, is that poetry has no gender. There are poems by women, of course, and the ones that are "any good" can make it to fighting weight in any man's ring, but there is no "women's poetry."

It is certainly true that if you examine any standard anthology containing work by poets of both sexes, the work of the women who are represented there will not force you to alter whatever generalizations are suggested by the rest of the collection. It is possible, for instance, to draw certain conclusions about the characteristic forms, styles, and subjects of twentieth-century poetry—or even poetry of the last couple of decades—that are by no means violated by consideration of the work of those women who make it into such compendia. But the sheer concentration afforded by the women's anthologies, some of whose contributors also appear in collections with male poets, makes it possible to discern that there is a new voice, a new set of concerns and preoccupations in this poetry, a subject matter entirely outside whatever descriptions might serve for the poetry of our time in general.

In fact, this last point has two connected aspects, for not only does a different subject matter characterize poetry coming out of the women's movement, but so does the very primacy of subject matter. And the aesthetic governing the choice and arrangement of poems is as firmly grounded in the concrete subject as the poems themselves. These are good poems, the various introductions tell us, because they are *true,* true to the experience, the responses, and the voices of women. If I were to add that I find the language equally "honest," equally "clean" and "precise," that would not remove us from considerations of content, but rather present a series of critical euphemisms for them. Insistence on the separation becomes both inappropriate and tendentious.

The anthologies tend to be arranged with all selections from the same woman clustered together, often accompanied by a biographical or aesthetic statement from the poet herself. Only *I Hear My Sisters Saying* divides its contents thematically, with epigraphs and categories reflecting the life-cycle of the female sensibility. In volumes devoted to the work of a single poet a conscious connecting thread is usually observable, but the poems are rarely clustered by "topic" in any obvious way. Nonetheless, certain preoccupations appear that "everyone knows" are not those of contemporary literature in English: the relation between parents, especially mothers, and their daughters; pregnancy, childbirth, and abortion; the female body as locus and identity; relations between women; lesbianism, marriage, motherhood, and housewifery; the power of women and the shape of revolution. At the same time, there is far less about heterosexual love, less about men in general, than familiarity with the traditions of either poetry or politics might suggest.

The poems about inhabiting a female body, with all the definitions and limits that nature and culture have placed on our identity, afford perhaps the clearest demonstration that poetry of the women's movement is not simply a new point of view on a familiar subject. The poetry that men write tells us a great deal about the specifics, both physical and psychological, of masculine sexual experience but very little about the life of the body beyond that localized situation. It is not simply that the human has been understood as the male, with the female representing a departure from the norm, but rather that the full life of the body—in all its functions and discomforts—has not been apprehended in men's poetry at all.

It is not, of course, "the body" in some abstract sense that is the subject for women, either, but the female body. Nor is the tone usually one of self-praise, be it narcissistic or spiritualized. Anne Sexton's "In Celebration of My Uterus" cries out to the

> Sweet weight,
> in celebration of the woman I am

but even Sexton does not mystify the female sexual capacity *as such,* seeing it rather as the creative instrument that ties her to a chain of sisters. "My women," she exults, "are singing together of this." And she lists them:

> one is in a shoe factory cursing the machine,
> one is at the aquarium tending a seal,
> one is dull at the wheel of her Ford,
> one is at the toll gate collecting,
> one is tying the cord of a calf in Arizona,
> one is straddling a cello in Russia,
> one is shifting pots on the stove in Egypt,
> one is painting her bedroom walls moon color,
> one is dying but remembering a breakfast,
> one is stretching on her mat in Thailand,
> one is wiping the ass of her child,
> one is staring out the window of a train
> in the middle of Wyoming. . . .

If anything, it is sisterhood that Sexton's celebration mystifies, not the uterus itself. For women, the sense of sweetness and universality can never be restricted to the body, for we cannot make an alienated symbol, much less a myth, about our own most daily realities. Feminists understand that exaggerated worship of the woman's body is another expression of contempt, not only for our sex, but for the continuing processes of life. Muriel Rukeyser expresses both sides of this tension:

> Whoever despises the clitoris despises the penis
> Whoever despises the penis despises the cunt
> Whoever despises the cunt despises the life of the child.
> ("The Speed of Darkness")

The same contradiction runs through the work of women a full generation younger, sometimes with the same sense of universality, but often substituting for the more cosmic declaration a concentration on the normally excluded minutiae of physical and even gynecological experience. For Alta, living in a woman's body means that an otherwise untitled poem can begin with the line:

> euch, are you having your period?

One called "First Pregnancy" can summarize her relationships this way:

> lonely and big
> a couple of times i cried
> hearing you
> beating off under covers.

Printed between these two short poems in *No More Masks!* is another one by Alta that seems at first to make its point and derive its strength from the same approach to the body and its parts:

> penus envy they call it
> think how handy to have a thing
> that poked out; you could just shove
> it in any body, whang whang and come,
> wouldn't have to give a shit
> . . . .
> penus envy, they call it.
> the man is sick in his heart.
> that's what I call it.

Denise Levertov explores some of the same physical and social realities in a poem about

> Those groans men use
> passing a woman on the street
> or on the steps of the subway

Without the bitter detachment Alta uses to define male sexuality, Levertov can express compassion for the men. The groan is

> a word
>
> in grief language . . .
> language stricken, sectioned, cast down.

Yet the woman has to live with what it means to be the object of desire to the less than human. Even if, like Levertov, she recognizes it as a tribute (which most contemporary feminists would not), still

> she wants to
>
> throw the tribute away, dis-
> gusted, and can't,
>
> it goes on buzzing in her ear,
> it changes the pace of her walk
>
>   ("The Mutes")

Levertov's woman, mature, has assimilated, if not resolved, the confusions experienced by the black teenager in Yvonne's poem about the men in the street, "dead in what your mother calls their low-class desire." She asks,

> Who are men? who seem always white
> with coal ash
> who seem always black
> as thick turtle skin
> never anywhere.
> They do not seem
> like your brothers who guard
> your hours more than any husband
> or mother. Who are men? They stare
> less awkward than your father.
>
>   ("Rachel at Thirteen")

It is the sentiment of shame that all women learn and with which we continue to identify, so we can declaim with Rochelle Owens:

> I am the meat that dances
> American style!
> > ("All Owners of Meat are Hospitable and Speak
> > German Albanian French & Colorado Springs")

The body is imposed as an identity, but, in and of itself, it is not only the source of shame but of a sense of inadequacy and self-hatred. The obsession with parts of the body, seeing ourselves as fragmented and literally alienated, reflects this feeling, as does the parallel obsession with detailing the rituals and conventions of self-adornment. In "The Evening Gown," Karen Swenson describes living in

> a vision of myself
> developed from the doubling negatives
> of fashion magazines and movies

The strapless gown she coveted as an adolescent was denied her, and, the poet says, the dream of it remains, as the dream of a denied and better identity:

> But still it is there, a resonance in the mirror.
> That is why your face is never enough
> only a bare sketch
> and you, with mascara and lipstick, paint in
> all the women forbidden and never filled.

Yvonne sets one of the poems about Rachel's growing up in Miss Booker's beauty shop for black women, focusing attention on the sensual concretion of the scene:

> Your young long soft wool hair,
> sweet lime
> and yellow liquids mingle
> and foam.

> Lu Anna's hands are cold, brisk
> her palms grown dark.
> Years of spattered perfumed grease
> on hot comb handles
>   ("Rachel and the Truth, c. 1945")

Only consciousness of being defined, measured, and judged by
our bodies, achieving or failing to the degree to which they could
be made to approximate an ideal, could eventuate in something
like Kathleen Fraser's "Poem in Which My Legs Are Accepted."
For here Fraser acknowledges her own failure to conform to
sexist standards of beauty and the self-hatred her shortcomings
engender. They also generate contempt for the strength that is
represented in those legs. The final acceptance is real, but it remains contingent on the acceptance of a man and of full heterosexual identity:

> Legs, you are a pillow,
> white and plentiful with feathers for his wild head.
> You are endless scenery
> behind the tense sinewy elegance of his two dark legs.
> You welcome him joyfully
> and dance.
> And you will be the locks in a new canal between
>   continents
>   The ship of life will push out of you
>   and rejoice
>   in the whiteness,
>   in the first floating and rising of water.

But the problem and hence the subject of our own poetry is not
simply trying to come to terms with the parts of our own bodies,
their appearance, and their functions. Our social universe is not
restricted to the relation between our real selves and whoever we
see reflected in the mirror. Instead, the most common and destructive form it assumes is an almost reflex sense of competition
with other women. Alta's prose-poem (I *think* that's what you'd

call it), "Pretty," catalogues the things we do to make ourselves look good—which means different from what we are—bringing out the desperation behind the search for "prettiness" and the oppressive social forces motivating the search. The judging eye of some man, of men in general, is present, she says, in all relations between women:

> [we] could have been friends all that awful lonely year but i was afraid to be around her & have him look at my lousy skin & big nose & bitten nails next to her perfect complexion & little nose & nice nails. how could he possibly want me more than her? everything becomes a handicap: every time i take a pill i think jesus no man loves a sick wife (to quote mother). men don't make passes at girls who wear glasses. blondes have more fun. fat ass. big boobs. clear skin. sheeit . . . then it got so i could count on being the second prettiest woman in any situation. . . .

Nor does the existence of the feminist movement work by itself or by magic to eliminate this competition. Alta speaks of assessing her coworkers on a feminist newspaper and observes

> my lover used to say how i was prettier than other women in women's lib & i would feel better while feeling worse.

I suppose this is a "confessional" poem. It is certainly not a traditionally "feminine" one, though, because the feelings it admits to are far from attractive; they reveal something very ugly that has been trained into most women in our society. And the poem does not seem to regard the revelation as an end in itself, like the literary striptease Simone de Beauvoir says is behind the planned and limited confessions of narcissistic female writers. Alta isn't any prouder of that automatic self-comparison than I am, even though she has had the guts to write about it. Rather, putting the feelings into a poem becomes part of the collective process of changing ourselves that is a goal of the women's movement. It is essential, however, not to confuse the process with the goal.

Acknowledging the rivalry can mean acknowledging the connections with other women, as well. In an extraordinary piece called "My Mother's Moustache" Honor Moore makes a poem out of the removal of female facial hair, an unpleasantly intimate little topic hitherto confined to the greasy prose of depilatory ads. Moore describes the waxing ritual, learned from her mother, in detail. Then she speaks of trying to learn to live with the moustache, claiming to be proud of it while covering it inadequately with pink powder. Next a new set of products, creams, that smell bad or make her skin break out. When the summer sun bleaches her hairs, she realizes she can do this herself in winter, and yet another unattractive feminine process is described. The final coming to terms is still far from an acceptance of the body as it is, but does accept the new process and the female inheritance that has made it necessary:

> I spread the paste around my lips,
> let it dry twelve minutes (no cooking, no pain, no mess) while
> it surreptitiously softens and whitens, lightens
> even brightens the surfacing
> memory, my mother's moustache.

Our mothers themselves are as much at the center of feminist poetry as they were absent from the poetry of male poets and the women who shared their subjects. The sense of an ancient and ambiguous bond penetrates this poetry. As Mary Patten's poem, "Mother," expresses it,

> her signature
> is all over my bed

Helen Chasin begins her evocation of women in their relations to each other and to men with a reference to her personal past:

> Mother, I am something more
> than your girl; still our old quarrel
> brings me up.

> ("Looking Out")

Poems about the mother are often poems about destruction.
Usually the daughter perceives herself as the victim, but sometimes she sees that the process is mutual. And Frankie Hucklen-
broich, with a rare gallows humor, gives voice to the complementary (and creative) fantasy:

> After having been acquitted by a hung jury
> of the charge of murdering my mother
> I wrote three novels, seven poems, and
> an essay on the subject, thus vastly
> improving my wardrobe and the chances
> for the Equal Rights Amendment

At the end, her tone graver, she tells her woman lover:

> We'll do just fine together
> and you can help me bury my mother's hands
> almost nightly.
>   ("Due Process")

The quarrel with the mother that happens in these poems is
rooted in the sense of sameness, of blood descent occurring in an
historical situation that makes the daughters different from the
women their mothers were. Some poems emphasize the natural
bond as one of resistance, like Audre Lorde's "Black Mother
Woman":

> . . I have peeled away your anger
> down to its core of love
> and look mother
> I am
> a dark temple where your true spirit rises
> beautiful and tough as a chestnut
> stanchion against your nightmares of weakness
> and if my eyes conceal
> a squadron of conflicting rebellions
> I learned from you
> to define myself
> through your denials.

But the tie begins with the body. Anne Sexton's "Christmas Eve" is spent beneath the portrait of her mother, "sharp diamond," that presides over the family reunion, over

> your aging daughters, each one a wife,
> each one talking to the family cook
> each one avoiding the portrait
> each one aping your life.

Later, alone, the woman of thirty-five contemplates her mother as she was, outside the serene picture, and the theme of love and hatred is sealed through the identity of the two women's bodies:

> You who led me by the nose,
> I saw you as you were.
> Then I thought of your body
> as one thinks of murder . . .
>
> Then I said Mary—
> Mary, Mary, forgive me
> and then I touched a present for the child,
> the last I bred before your death;
> and then I touched my breast
> and then I touched the floor
> and then my breast again as if,
> somehow, it were one of yours.

The identity is stronger and the conflict less in Ruthe Canter's poem about "The Resemblance," where the image of the breast takes on a different significance. She addresses her mother:

> I am sad, I am singing,
> my breasts become like
> yours, my hands with
> the same lines, I am
> singing for the mother
> whose sorrows I am.

There is physical recognition, first of all, when Robin Morgan writes of a meeting between estranged mother and daughter:

> my theories rearrange themselves
> like sand before this woman whose flaccid breasts
> sway with her stumblings, whose diamonds
> still thaw pity from my eyes.
> You're older than I thought. But so am I

And the resolution remains contradictory. She perceives her mother as if from exile

> unsure of me at last
> who sought a birthright elsewhere,
> beyond the oasis of your curse,
> even beyond that last mirage, your blessing.
> Mother, in ways neither of us can ever understand,
> I have come home.
>
> ("Matrilineal Descent")

The power of the bond and the sense of alienation that coexists with it are frequently communicated by feminist poets through a metaphor about communication, about the speech or attempts at speech between mother and daughter. The shame and self-hatred built into female identity can assume the outward form of rejecting the mother's femaleness in one's own. For Judith Kerman, estrangement from the mother and contempt for one's own womanhood are expressed, as they are for Morgan, in the image of the exile, and the language one speaks is a part of that experience:

> Among men, I stopped
> speaking your language, afraid
> someone would hear my accent.
> When they cut me open
> words spilled out into the street.
>
> ("Exmatriate")

These women do "speak the same language," and that catch phrase is invested with fresh significance by the insistence on verbal power as a means of survival. Margie Fine writes of how her mother taught her that words were a woman's only weapon, "money and muscles having been appropriated by men." Mother and daughter may clash, but fundamentally, through the "fine art of verbal attack," they are on the same side:

> Her words the whetting stone
> My words the sword
> Her words
> became my words
> became one.

The estrangement, too, is expressed as a matter of words. As Muriel Rukeyser explains,

> I cannot fully
> have language with my mother.
> ("The Question")

It is important to recognize, however, that the tension to which these poems refer is not an archetypal conflict that arises naturally and necessarily out of the relation between mother and daughter. The differentness from the mother or the lingering shame in sharing her biological qualities both have an historical dimension. Our lives are different because we are consciously making them different and in so doing rejecting what our mothers were forced to stand for. But the process came into being and continues its evolution because the forces that operate in the lives of women have made different demands on us and fostered different expectations. In a poem written in 1942, well before the present phase of the feminist movement, Margaret Walker raises that differentness as a question, but points to the answer in the conditions within which different generations of women—in this case, black women—have to survive. This is the entire poem, called, "Lineage":

> My grandmothers were strong.
> They followed plows and bent to toil.
> They moved through fields sowing seed.
> They touched earth and grain grew.
> They were full of sturdiness and singing.
> My grandmothers were strong.

My grandmothers are full of memories
Smelling of soap and onions and wet clay
With veins rolling over quick hands
They have many clean words to say.
My grandmothers were strong.
Why am I not as they?

Rejection of the mother's way of life and her way of being a woman is not necessarily depicted, in feminist poems, as constituting rejection of the mother as a person. It is rather a rejection of the conditions that worked, in their different ways, to oppress both mother and daughter. Kathryn Ruby's "Portrait of a Woman" (it is never, when a woman draws it, the picture of a Lady), is actually a double portrait, mother and daughter:

Vassar, class of ——
A later-day Edith Wharton woman,
she married a beefy jew from Colorado
—an orphan, with a booming voice.
Her people thought she was crazy
but found him a job in insurance,
just for appearances.
They bought an old mansion in Roslyn Heights.
She collected first editions,
headed the U.J.A.,
used napkin rings,
died at the age of thirty-two.
That messy story about the abortion
was buried with her, just as she would have
wanted it to be.
No one visits her tomb.
But last week her daughter was busted
for throwing a stink-bomb
at the Miss America pageant.

This time it is a unity of resistance, but, in a daughter's conflict with society, she may well see her mother as an exponent, rather than a victim, of the female condition, willingly policing the borders of women's role and trying to coerce her daughter into those limits. Jan Clausen writes "A Christmas Letter" from the laundromat:

> and your letters
> mother
> come at me
> airmail
> like missiles out of the west
> saying
> when are you coming
> home
> home
> home
>
> and last night i nearly cried
> in a doctor's office
> reading a badly written story
> in some women's magazine
> about a family
> reunited for christmas
> the prodigal daughter
> finally married
> pregnant
> yes cried through my anger
> at mothers
> the systems that back them
> the systems they back
> and all those years
> i believed your
> ladies' home journals.

This differentness, this appetite for resistance, is represented in Anita Barrows's poem about "The Mutant" by a physical appetite of mythical proportions. The woman child eats her parents literally out of house and home:

> Was this the daughter you bargained for,
> a daughter with teeth for an eye?
> . . . .

> The rabbis
> you brought her to lowered their heads:
> she siphoned their beards like licorice
> . . . .
> And what an embarrassment she was!
> If you brought her to a lake,
> she drank it.

Both parents are apostrophized here, but it remains a poem about a daughter who cannot, will not be what her mother is.

There are a few other feminist poems in which the parents are perceived and addressed as a single unit, but the theme of the mother is more frequent and more richly varied in its applications. By contrast, the issues associated with the father not only are less commonly brought into play, but have not been fundamentally transformed by the insights of the feminist movement. The father is still the representative of power in the family, the lover his poet-daughter at once seeks and abhors. The poetry of Sylvia Plath, written before and clearly outside the perimeters of the movement, could stand as an emblem for this set of motifs. The power and control with which Plath conveys a sense of emotions entirely *out* of control are unique, but the drastic sentiment is not:

> Daddy, I have had to kill you.
> You died before I had time
> > ("Daddy")

And the pervasive themes of this poem—the father as Nazi, as vampire, as archetypal lover—have not been resolved in later work. Plath's valedictory has also remained with us, since poems to the father are an attempt to *get rid of* the theme and the conflicts that inform it, much as the poems about the mother, however hostile, are attempts at reconciliation.

There is a simultaneous fear of the father and contempt for the act of paternity—a sort of contempt that is never expressed for motherhood, as such, however distorted the relations between mothers and daughters may become in the social world after birth. One difference the women's movement has made is that we no longer believe we are *borrowing* metaphors from the world of government, law, courts, and newspapers to say something about the politics of the family. For there is no way we can encompass the "Oedipal" situation without perceiving that the contradictions it fosters are intrinsically political. Ann Darr, recognizing that repetition is the essence of comedy and that the father-daughter theme has been enacted over and over, realizes nonetheless that her laughter is forced. As a child, the complications of sexual feeling still unacknowledged, she would roll around him, "weak with laughter." Now, her weakness is displayed in explicit contrast to masculine strength:

> Weak with being your
> child, weak with being
> woman whom you couldn't have.
> Papa, worship is a word
> saved for heavenly bents.
> But you were unearthly to the child
> who ran in my body through the high
> grass, searching for you
> all the nights of my life.
>
> ("Dear Oedipus")

To Elizabeth Lynn Schneider, it is a Texan stepfather whose image haunts both mind and body, forcing her to flee the temptation, though not the need it served:

> When I had grown so that the moon covered me just
> in shreds of light, my breasts like wild plums,
> I sensed the danger in the house still more.
> I left, tossing like a frightened mare.
> Tossing. Tossing. I could not shake him off,
> not after miles or years, not after death.
> Spurs in my side he is still king of the cowboys.
>
> ("Elegy")

Sukey Durham's poem for her father is significantly entitled "The Crossing," and uses similar metaphors about physical detours and barriers. Yet, she says,

> Your image clings to me like wet sand.
> I am climbing, always,
> out of your grave
> away from your death,
> your voice sticking in my throat
> like fear.
> Through your eyes even the sky is opaque.

The more consciously feminist a poem is, the more explicit its identification of the father's sexual and political power. Judith Kerman dreams of marrying her father ("That dream, at last") and her acknowledgement of self-destructive impulse is ironic, intentionally funny:

> In the dream, I married you
> the white dress
> pirate scarf sword
> made of Erector Set
> the proud Papa
> delighted
> you took me over
> I forgot who I am
> . . . .
> I followed you around
> waiting to be made whole.

As is perhaps to be expected, the father, in these poems, is often dead. Indeed, the desperation of our attempts to resolve the issue has its origin in that fact. But a dead mother leaves her mark on her daughter's entire identity, not only on her sexuality, and resolution entails a more global kind of change. Summer Brenner's untitled poem recalls her mother's death, repeating the lines,

> Mother do you want some water?
> Mother, do you want some light?

And the maternal comfort she finds is as illusory as her recurrent nightmares of the death scene itself:

> Mother, there is an old photograph
> of a farmhouse
> two story on the Plains
> One of the windows upstairs is open
> I slipped in and found you here
> It was good to be by you
> Mother, they say you were beautiful

More often, the maternal spirit is embodied in domestic objects and the tasks associated with them—hence with the daughter's sense of herself in the woman's role. Adrienne Rich addresses the dead mother:

> What rises in our throats
> like food you prodded in?
> Nothing could be enough.
> You breathe upon us now
> through solid assertions
> of yourself: teaspoons, goblets,
> seas of carpet, a forest
> of old plants to be watered,
> an old man in an adjoining
> room to be touched and fed.
> And all this universe
> dares us to lay a finger
> anywhere, save exactly
> as you would wish it done.
> ("A Woman Mourned by Daughters")

All women are daughters. Most feminists have contemplated what that means and the results of the analysis tell us something about women, not women in general, but women in this time and place. Contemplation of one's own motherhood—actual or potential—can lead to a similar historical and political sense of our experience as women. An earlier generation of women poets tended to mythologize, even to spiritualize, the phenomena of pregnancy and motherhood. Genevieve Taggard was a political activist whose poems often reflected her understanding of oppressive social reality and the people who were trying to change it. Yet there is a classic and conservative quality to the way she understood her pregnancy:

> Now I am slow and placid, fond of sun,
> Like a sleek beast, or a worn one:
> No slim and languid girl—not glad
> with the windy trip I once had,
> But velvet-footed, musing of my own,
> Torpid, mellow, stupid as a stone.
>
> ("With Child")

I would not wish the reservations in the way I characterized this attitude to be interpreted as a self-righteous condemnation of Taggard. There is, God knows, no correct or incorrect line on one's own pregnancy or the feelings it evokes. And the sloweddown sense of participating in an animal process is something that a great many women share. But it is also important to recognize that even "natural" processes change with historical conditions, and that cultural forces shape our individual responses to them. It is not that Genevieve Taggard should have felt or said something other than what she did, but rather that there are other possible reactions to pregnancy—reactions that might have coexisted with or entirely replaced the one she expresses—to which women poets of that epoch were, by and large, precluded from giving voice.

In two of Kathleen Fraser's poems about pregnancy, for example, there remains the passivity of the mother being fed off. Fraser is explicit in her ambivalence to this position, however, and is also capable of turning the thing around to show herself actively joining the child in the definition of what is going on. Her "Poem Wondering If I'm Pregnant" speaks to the child who may be feeding within her:

> Is it you? Are you there,
> thief I can't see,
>> drinking,
>> leaving me at the edge
>> of breathing?

It is not resentment one senses from this poem, however, but a feeling that a relationship suffused with living, that is, with social, as well as physical aspects, has already begun, so that the poem, despite its biological imagery, is fresh and vital as it concludes by asking,

> is it you, penny face?
> Is it you?

Fraser's "Poem for the New" is informed by the sense of physical relation to the child's growth within her that Taggard speaks of. For Fraser, however, a union and a transformation occur:

> I am
> nothing superfluous,
> but all—
> bones, bark of him, root of him take . . .
> My belly has tracks on it—
>> hands and feet
> are moving
> under this taut skin.
> In snow, in light,
> we are about to become!

Childbirth itself can be transformed into something the woman does, rather than something that happens to her. But the surrounding conditions do not make that so easy, and the woman in labor is more likely to be alienated from the process and her own role in it. Linda Pastan uses the metaphors of capitalist contractual arrangements to describe what birth feels like for women in our society:

> Strapped down,
> Victim in an old comic book,
> I have been here before,
>   . . .
> Bear down a doctor says,
> foreman to sweating laborer,
> but this work, this forcing
> of one life from another
> is something that I signed for
> at a moment when I would have signed anything.
>   ("Notes From the Delivery Room")

Once more, the emphasis on material reality and on the facts of the body leads to a demystification that also stands as an affirmation. She rejects even medical language that appears to mystify the experience:

> She's crowning, someone says,
> but there is no one royal here,
> just me, quite barefoot
> greeting my barefoot child.

Being a mother, once the child is born, is similarly stripped of sentimentality through an emphasis on physical absolutes, the fact that motherhood is work involving filth, exhaustion, irritation, and boredom as well as joy. The "spiritual" dimension of the experience thus acquires roots in women's reality and women's history. It is its foundation of pride in the female body that prevents Anne Sexton's enthusiasm in her poem for her daughter from becoming an overlyrical effusion:

> Oh, darling, let your body in,
> let it tie you in,
> in comfort.
> What I want to say, Linda,
> is that women are born twice.
> ("Little Girl, My String Bean, My Lovely Woman")

Beneath and because of the recognition that motherhood is work, work that involves the physical, there is a sisterhood between feminist mother and daughter and among mothers that is still absent in Sexton. Not only the honesty of her language, but the understanding that language conveys about what it means to be a woman in our time, make Madeline Bass's description of the effort and the reward ring true. The child represents work,

> that pig noise
> now nagging off your dear hours

and work of a concrete and menial sort:

> How could I tell you? and how could I
> not have said it, "You will be tired,"
> oh, Caren, I forget
> in my own rituals
> of toast and bathing,
> purchases and eggshells,
> breath and survival (rising above retorts,
> > divorce crackling in the bacon
> > and snores sputtering firelight
> > in the middle evening; working
> > for the juice, for the lung
> > of birth, and more birth,
> > life each day)
> ("To My Former Student on the Occasion of Birth")

The most striking characteristic of these poems about being a mother is that—unlike the poems that men address to either their daughters or their sons—feminists do not have to ignore the fact that children take a toll on women in labor, time, and tedium, in order to be able to acknowledge that living with children can be a joyful revelation of human personality.*

Ironically, feminist poetry has done little to alter our perception of the subject of abortion. The women's movement has argued for the right to control our own bodies and some of us have strengthened that demand to include free abortions conducted under supportive conditions, with our control encompassing, as well, the right to safe, adequate contraception and the freedom from involuntary sterilization. We see forced motherhood and forced sterilization as complementary products of the social conditions under which we live. And, generally speaking, we place the whole question of abortion in a fuller historical perspective: even if safe, free abortion were available on demand to every woman, it would take us no closer to a society in which abortion would be unnecessary and parenthood—particularly motherhood—would not entail destructive personal or social consequences. When feminist poets write about abortion, however, these various levels of consciousness and the movement we have built around the issue tend to be absent. Rita Mae Brown's "Hymn to the 10,000 Who Die Each Year on the Abortionist's Table in Amerika" is one of the few poems that remind us of the political, rather than the strictly private, implications of the experience. The emotional resolution Brown seeks can thus be reflected by the movement itself, as she concludes,

> We must hunt as wounded women
> The balm to heal one another.

More often, women's poems about abortion are poems of personal loss and individual mourning. Whereas motherhood experi-

---

*Alta's book-length prose poem, *Momma,* which I find impossible to excerpt in a useful way, is one of the best statements about motherhood as both effort and learning. Alta writes, as well, about something even more difficult, the changes in herself and her sense of herself wrought by the experience of motherhood. *Momma* offers a blunt reminder that the concept Motherhood involves the person who is the mother, as well as her role with respect to the child.

enced is susceptible of many interpretations by feminist writers, motherhood denied evokes the same sorrow from contemporary feminists as from their female predecessors. Gwendolyn Brooks's 1944 poem, "The Mother," asserts that "abortions will not let you forget." The poem, addressed to the aborted children, is a dignified but helpless apology:

> If I poisoned the beginnings of your breaths,
> Believe that even in my deliberateness I was not deliberate.
> Though why should I whine,
> Whine that the crime was other than mine?

Her conclusion is passionate, all the more so for having no object outside her own emotions:

> You were born, you had body, you died.
> It is just that you never giggled or planned or cried
>
> Believe me, I loved you all
> Believe me, I knew you, though faintly, and I loved,
>   I loved you
> All.

Anne Sexton echoes the same sense of loss, denial, and guilt in a different and more controlled tone. The refrain of "The Abortion":

> Somebody who should have been born
> is gone.

What we are shown is feeling, not solutions. Lucille Iverson's bitter poem, also called "The Abortion," is more direct in its diction, utilizing the unadorned question, "when should she kill the child?" for an effect that does not depend on the value of shock alone. Iverson also makes oblique reference to the reasons why a woman may seek to abort her child:

> Enslaved now and forever by
> Passion—by the
> Child, herself a
> Child
> Trapped in their circumstance
> Not her circumstance and
> Forbid any circumstance as they
> Walk away
> Laughing.

But in "The Lost Baby Poem," Lucille Clifton is more explicit about those "circumstances," the catalogue of reasons why the decision not to bear another child was made. "We could not afford a baby," is a statement with neither character nor proof. Clifton's list spells out what that phrase, which she never uses, means: winter, the disconnected gas, no car. But her list does not tend to self-pity. She is quite as circumstantial about sending the fetus "down to meet the waters under the city." The drama arises from the strength that going through the abortion has imparted to her will and her resolution:

> if i am ever less than a mountain
> for your definite brothers and sisters
> let the rivers pour over my head
> let the sea take me for a spiller
> of seas   let black men call me stranger
> always   for your never named sake.

Abortion poems force us to suspend our knowledge about motherhood, the complex knowledge on which motherhood poems are built, and see it as a natural, essentially one-dimensional process. Thus, Clifton's imagery of mountains and seas, representing the disrupted order of nature, takes us back to a notion of woman as a quantity symbolic of the earth and its ways. In our deprivation, we can express only the realization that the one experience of whose naturalness we can have no doubts has been made impossible for us. The damaged and destroyed possibility means life denied to the mother, as well as the child.

In this sense, Audre Lorde's poem, "To My Daughter the Junkie on a Train," resembles an abortion poem. Seeing a young black heroin addict on the subway, the poet identifies the maternal failure as her own. The opening stanza sets the tone, before the specific incident is introduced:

> Children we have not borne
> bedevil us by becoming
> themselves
> painfully sharp and unavoidable
> like a needle in our flesh.

The lines are strongly reminiscent of the two poems by black women about abortion, Brooks's and Clifton's, in their emphasis on the person an unborn child would have become. As the "girl with a horse in her brain" takes the seat next to her, Lorde makes the identification more personal, and at the same time, more collective. Futilely, she reaches out,

> My corrupt concern will not replace
> what you once needed
> but I am locked into my own addiction
> and offer you my help, one eye
> out
> for my own station.
> Roused and deprived
> your costly dream explodes
> into a terrible technicoloured laughter
> at my failure
> up and down across the aisle
> women avert their eyes
> as the other mothers who became useless
> curse their children who became junk.

The sense of limitation and denial is also the mood of most feminist poems about marriage, houses, and housework. Denise Levertov's exuberant 1962 poem, "About Marriage," begins:

> Don't lock me in wedlock, I want
> marriage, an
> encounter—

and proceeds to a parenthetical description of birds encountered
in the park and lived with for "a half/hour under the enchant-
ment." The digression is not irrelevant, she maintains, for

> I would be
> met
>
> and meet you
> so,
> in a green
>
> airy space, not
> locked in.

But, as Anne Sexton reminds us, to be a wife is not to meet a man
as one might meet the birds in the park. More often, it means
becoming a housewife, for "some women marry houses," and, if
the house is thus personified in the process, the person cannot
help becoming more of an object. The fetishistic exchange is
complete in Susan Fromberg Schaeffer's "Housewife," which
begins by asking:

> What can be wrong
> That some days I hug this house
> About me like a shawl, and feel
> Each window like a tatter in its skin
> Or worse, bright eyes I must not look through?

It is neither the work itself nor the role itself that engages
women's poetic energies, but the cumulative containment and
definition that is their joint result. The sex division of labor and
the distorted character of time spent doing unpaid domestic work
within a wage system dominate many of our poems. Jane
Mayhall's "Tracing Back" stresses the dailiness of the routine

and the dourness of the household enterprise by making laundry
her central image:

> My mother took care of my father's shirts;
> he did not take care of her cotton dresses.
> I think he would have been ashamed,
> not of the labor, but of a peculiar
> sense of squalor, a man wasting his time.

Yet the relationship, like the atmosphere Mayhall describes, is
"drooped and dull." The injustice is "aboriginal" and does not
flare up into anger or resentment between the two, for it hardly
matters whether or not they love each other; the situation in
which they are caught is permanent and unchangeable.

By contrast, Lucille Iverson employs the first person, and her
tone is as direct and immediate as her fury. She cries out against
both the work she is forced to do and the love that traps her into
it:

> It is not so much
> Cooking
> But being cooked
> That gets me;
>
>   . . . . .
>
> Love
> Is that which detains;
> That magic of detention which you
> Need from me,
> But which tears a
> Woman.

Iverson also brings into play the idea of a woman's domestic work
as the force that maintains life. In her vision, that force breaks
free of nurturing attendance on the needs of others:

> The power of Life is the
> Integration of Life is the
> Integration of Energy and
> If you disintegrate,   I
> will not help you

Her act of defiance consists in taking control of the unmeasured, unwaged time that makes up her working day:

> I
> Raise my fist beside the
> Door of My Dreams and I
> Take Time,
> All of it
> In my Hands.

As its title, "Outrage," makes clear, Iverson's poem is not primarily about housework. The description of roasting a chicken serves as a metaphor for the female life as she lives it. At least as often, however, the notion of sustenance deriving from the woman's work becomes the figurative equivalent of those practical labors. My poem "Political Economy" is an attempt to explain the material and experiential differences between "man's work," wage labor, and "women's work," unpaid and in the home; her domestic work is the same, of course, even if the woman is also part of the labor force. The first part of the poem is about the man's work in a factory, working six machines. (I pictured screw machines, but did not want to intrude the complications brought in with so suggestive a name.) The chief image here is about time, counted off and quantified as it is for the worker under capitalism, and I connect the hours and minutes of human labor-time to the concept of down-time as it applies to his machines. The woman's work day is the subject of the second half of the poem, and here the language is less metaphorical, as I describe work that I have done myself, rather than work that I have heard a man describe. The working day of a housewife is more open-ended, for it certainly isn't over at the end of the poem when she calls her family in to supper:

> Wash your hands, she tells the kids
> and put out the light in there
> (What do you think: We got stocks
> in Edison?)

Her time is somewhat more flexible than his (she watches *Love of Life* while she breaks for lunch), but for that very reason the catalogue of her day's activities is kept drier, more schematic. The repeated controlling metaphor of the poem defines the woman's work in sustaining and reproducing labor power in contrast to the wage–labor system:

> He says, I'm making a living.
> She says, I'm making life.

The cotton dresses and the kind of labor referred to in "Tracing Back" suggest a rural background—and not an affluent one. "Political Economy" has a clearly urban working-class setting: the man's job, the amount of his take-home pay, the family's food purchases and style of life are all explicitly described. In both poems, there is a traditional division of labor by sex, but the *particulars* of that division and what it makes of the woman's experience are dictated by their class identity. In neither poem is the sexual relationship itself at issue, but both convey a sense of working people—men and women in their different ways—caught in a trap that is not of their making.

Genevieve Taggard's "Everyday Alchemy" is about the kinds of human relations that evolve in these conditions and the way that women serve to maintain the family emotionally, as well as materially. She calls this support or sustenance "peace," and admits that women's lives deprive them of it, although their love is a motive force for the creation of that peace for others; peace, she says, is

> poured by poor women
> Out of their hearts' poverty, for worn men.

The contemporary feminist movement, by contrast, has not been content to mystify the love that is supposed to animate and justify women's work in the family. And it has raised the question: "If the woman's role is to meet everyone's needs, whose job is it to meet her needs?"[5] Poetry rooted in the women's movement has tended, by and large, to ignore the way that class functions in individual lives or in history, so that its effect has been to enhance the impression that the sole conflict, in society or in private experience, is between men and women. While abandoning the sentimentality with which Taggard approaches her doubly oppressed women, we have found no adequate replacements in our own poetry for her very real sensitivity to the impact of class relations on private life, on the relations between men and women, and on women's consciousness.

For much the same reasons, feminist poetry is less successful in its treatment of women's work outside the home than it is in its handling of housework. About half of the feminist poems about work with which I am familiar are by women I know personally, and many have not been published. Those that I have found in the anthologies or in single volumes by a particular poet tend to be less immediate than those by working women of my acquaintance or than the published poets' own poems about subjects like sexual experience or motherhood. The first-person power that has made it impossible, throughout this essay, to refer to the "I" in these poems as some alienated being known as "the speaker" is replaced here by a third-person narrator, compassionate but removed. Thus, *Sing a Battle Song* includes a warm poem addressed to a weary woman going home from the job to what the speaker (for now she exists) hopes is not an immediate second job of unpaid domestic labor. She hopes someone has prepared dinner so that the unknown woman in the train can relax

> take a minute or 2
> without rushing
> in the bathroom,
> and then
> slump down in the chair
> in front of your table
>   never mind time-clocks
>   never mind rush-orders
>   never mind good manners

Ready to eat?
Eat good
enjoy it
and make a feast of it
and have fun
while you do it
because

you sure look tired now.
("Riding the Subways")

Marge Piercy's "The Morning Half-Life Blues" focuses, similarly, away from the work process and onto the women themselves, hurrying to their offices. These women have needs that
cannot be met for each one individually and that are neither
envisaged nor accommodated in capitalist society, which uses
them, instead, as replaceable labor and as programmed consumers. They are taught, she claims, to desire products that they
expect to fill the void created by jobs they must do in order to be
able to buy things. Piercy envisions a better world, one in which
the work women do is meaningful and organic to human life. But,
for all her good will, she seems to believe that the office workers
will be progressively deprived of their energy and imagination.
She implies that a system meant to dehumanize actually succeeds
in dehumanizing. Thus, the office workers themselves seem to
have no role in dreaming, fighting for, or building that fair city
where their labor will be unalienated. Piercy assumes that it is for
her, not for them, to give a voice and a shape to their true
aspirations—to have their dream for them.

I realize that my paraphrase reflects too literal a reading of what
are, after all, literary devices. It also fails to take account of
Piercy's subsequent development away from a view in which the
consciously "political" people control how *people* are going to
get control of their own lives. The point is rather that this poem,
which was published in the late sixties, quite accurately measures
the distance between the world of poetry and the world of work.
The poet is not expected to have first-hand experience of clerical
work, or, if she does, to write about her work and what it means

to her. She is allowed—indeed, in a feminist context, almost
expected—to be a sexual being, a daughter, perhaps a mother and
housewife, but the persona of the poet-as-woman tends to be
bound to a definition of "woman" that emphasizes biological or
cultural roles, not specific experience of class and sex. The inherited limits of literature have extended to gynecological confessions, while remaining, by and large, impervious to work as a
component of daily life.

Although Olga Cabral's poem about office work, "Life and
Death Among the Xerox People," does employ the first person, it
is not clear to what extent the work described is the real subject
and to what extent it is a metaphor for something else. The details
of the work women do in relation to the paraphernalia and machinery typical of the offices of advanced capitalism are gro-
tesquely juxtaposed with images of life and death:

> they switched on the current
>   the machine said: Marry Me
>
> I had forgotten my numbers
>   they said it could be serious
> they showed me the paper cutter
>   it sliced like a guillotine
> my head fell bloodlessly
>   into the waste basket

The poem concludes at the point of greatest confusion between
the symbolic elements and the things or experiences they represent:

> They handed me a skin
> and said: Wear This
> it was somebody else's life
>   it didn't quite fit
> so I left it lying there . . .
>   that was quite a cemetery.

What I have noticed about poems dealing with office work, the
most common kind of job for women employed outside the home,
also holds true for waitressing, nursing, cleaning offices or other

women's houses, washing and setting hair, assembling electronic components, or clerking in a department store: the experience of these jobs is rarely described and, when it is, even more rarely as a valid subject in itself. In compiling a collection of literature by and about working women, Theresa Epstein and I found that the modern literary tradition is remote from the meanings of work in human life, and that poetry is particularly alienated from it. The best poems we could find about the work process came, as I have said, from women we know, most of whom have no secure identity as poets, but for whom work, life, and literature are not discrete or even distinguishable.

Jennie Jones's title, "American Standard," is double-edged. It "happens" to be the name of the conglomerate in whose plant she works, but, at the same time, it denominates the quality of life this factory affords her. The poem operates by means of contrasting stanzas that alternately depict the noise of labor measured by the time clock and the rhythms of the natural year, the cries of migrating autumnal birds giving way to the heavy silence of snow. The earth outside the plant waits for the coming of the warm seasons that will bring back green things and the years that must elapse before land defoliated by capitalist industry is once again alive with vegetation. But, inside the factory, the machines wait for the striking worker to return,

> patient in the knowledge
> I must sell my time to live.

In the poem's conclusion, a fantasy of resistance brings the natural world and the exploited world together in a deliberately sensuous explosion:

> (Summer coming by surprise
> to fill the clearing,
> make me drunk on color
> and the smell of wild strawberries,
> the flavor of the sun)

     to throw a bomb
     the factory a sudden bloom of fire
      (in my mouth the taste
      of wild strawberries)

    The cab driver in Judith Kerman's poem also draws her imagery from the defining fact of working life, the sale of the worker's time in exchange for the cash needed to subsist. And, as a matter of fact, she observes,

     the price of money
     keeps going up.

Like the production worker, the cabbie is sustained by fantasies, although hers turn inward, away from the ugly streets, the harassing passengers, and the dispatcher's voice on the radio. In her isolation, she is even more remote from the realities of nature, and her resistance consists in seizing the action or fantasy of action. These themes come together in the concluding lines:

     it's my yoga: sit in the sun
     at the cabstand, enjoy the day
     forget you're losing money
     a practice of love
     with a knocking engine and no seatbelts
     to stop resenting
     a buck-fifty fare with no tip
     I forget
     how long I have been
     moving, looking for the street
     the number, the street,
     check the sheet: 5 minutes
     gluing the corners of the town together
     "You're number 5 at the loop, 41."
     The price of nothing, my time
             ("Driving for Yellow Cab")

    Many women's jobs outside the home require them to replicate the nurturing role imposed on women within the family, and their poems reflect an ironic awareness of the pattern. Beth Moscato, a nurse, calls her poem "Neediness," but speaks of a lifetime of meeting the needs of others. Her job is taking care:

> A woman's role is care-taker—
>> care-taker of John, the house, the dogs and
>> family garden.
> A nurse's role is care-taker—
>> care-taker of the sick, the retarded, the old,
>> the young, the men.

Moscato understands that it is no one's job to meet her needs and, moreover, she has been taught that her own principal need is to be needed. Otherwise,

> who will care for this care-taker?

Laurie Zoloth is a hospital worker whose job is in the delivery room and in the nursery for newborns. With the infants, her work involves socializing them to the world, weighing, measuring, and listing their vital statistics, cleaning and dressing them, and she sees that what she does anticipates the mother's work. Those first moments in the nursery, she reports,

> Before we number them, they are ours,
> This, baby, is a hand, my hand
and this, clothing, water
We comb their reluctant hair with toothbrushes, a true fact
> . . . . .
Crowds of relations fill the window of the nursery
after the babies are born.
>
> They look at our babies, in our arms.
> The women who work in the nursery: we
>> who introduce the babies, explain laughter
>> and the work of women.
>>> ("Women's Work: Nursing, the Cheery Aspect")

The work place, for Zoloth, as for many other feminist poets, is
characterized by an obsession with numbers, and the imagery of
these poems often makes use of quantification and counting.
Zoloth's "Labor" contains a hyperbolic estimate informed by the
numbers that precede it:

> Twelve women in labor. Can you imagine?
> We ran between them, counting, muttering
> 'ten minutes, five minutes apart'
> If I had run straight on out of there
> I would be downtown by now
> That's how much I ran.

Whereas Moscato's piece and Zoloth's other poem are centered
on the way the job resembles women's function in the home, this
one makes a point that is the converse: women's unpaid efforts in
and for the family are real work. The Labor Room is all too well
named to admit any argument about that, harboring as it does

> Women at work
> and women in labor
> waiting inside with each other.

In tone, style, and diction, these poems about work are clearly
part of the emerging "school" of women's poetry. It is equally
clear, however, that their subject matter places them outside the
mainstream of feminist poetry. It is possible to compile an
entirely representative anthology of poems from the women's
movement without including a single poem about the experience
of work outside the home. Feminist poetry, which has forcefully
challenged contemporary norms about the subjects and attitudes
appropriate to poetry, shares traditional literary assumptions
about personal life as the central poetic reality. Adrienne Rich's
poems about women at work tend to underscore this observation.
The problem is not so much that the professions she attributes to
them (landscape architect and astronomer, for example), are un-

usual and highly privileged. It is rather that Rich, particularly where she employs the first person, identifies the work as essentially creative, concerned with making something, as are her own efforts as a poet; in this sense, the poems become poems about poetry and, by the same token, statements about the quest for self-definition and individual identity:

> I am not
> a body, I am no body, I am I
> a pair of hands, ending in fingers
> that think like a brain.
> . . . . .
> I touch stylus, T-square, pens
> of immeasurable fineness,
> the hard-edge. I am I,
> this India ink my rain
> which can irrigate gardens, terraces
> dissolve or project horizons
> flowing like lava from the volcano of the inkpot
> at the stirring of my mind.
> ("The Fourth Month of the Landscape Architect")

Rich's poem uses images of pregnancy to convey something about work in and upon the world outside the body. It makes use of the convention by which creative men have made pregnancy and birth into a metaphor, yet, at the same time, it is a concrete reminder that a woman can engage—unmetaphorically—in both sorts of creativity:

> In my body
> Spaces fold in. I'm caught
> in the enclosure of the crib my body
> where every thought I think
> simply loosens to life another life.

It is an important reminder, but its essence is to say something about the self, not about work as such or work in its relation to procreation.

I believe that feminist poetry's emphasis on the inwardness of individuals distorts the movement's basic perception that "the personal is political," with the result that poems specifically *about* the movement create a picture that is at best incomplete and at worst politically futile. It is important, however, to understand what those poems are before deploring what they are not. Women's poems about "politics," about building a movement to revolutionize the way things are for women, are founded on a revelation of the strength of individual women, and hence on assumptions about our collective potential. On this basis, a myth is developed about a movement that is the sum of new connections of sisterhood among women. This vision of new social relations is at once the strength and the weakness of the poetry of and about the feminist movement itself.

Lesbian poetry—whether expressed in love songs or in poems about what the compilers of *Amazon Poetry* call the full "scope and intensity of lesbian experience"—is at the heart of the new feminist poetry, in that it concentrates on transformed personal relations as the model for revolution. It is poetry that embodies throughout the line Rita Mae Brown revives from the Greeks in "Sappho's Reply":

An army of lovers shall not fail.

Until the present wave of feminism, lesbian literature led an essentially underground existence, while it was possible for a heterosexual poet like Anne Sexton to get away with a vicious retelling of the "Rapunzel" story, with the witch as an old dyke and love between women reduced to an infantile game she calls "Mother-me-do." The repeated motif of the poem is that

A woman
who loves a woman
is forever young.

When Rapunzel marries the prince, the witch falls into decrepit age, her heart shrinking to the size of a pin, since her beloved can no longer keep her young. Rapunzel, by contrast, has "matured," outgrown her childish pastime, and Sexton does not remind us, does not even seem to see, that she has condemned her heroine to the same eventual and grotesque old age.

   In women's poetry, as in the feminist movement itself, a better understanding of lesbian reality and lesbian politics was a long time coming. For this reason, Rita Mae Brown's "Dancing the Shout to the True Gospel," a lovely poem more truly Sapphic in feeling than her "Sappho's Reply," is appropriately subtitled, "Or: the Song My Movement Sisters Won't Let Me Sing." In a somewhat similar vein, Robin Morgan dedicates her "Lesbian Poem" to "those who turned immediately from the contents page to this poem." The poem itself, which is about Joan of Arc as lesbian and true witch, is transformed by this self-conscious dedication from a rather forced and ahistorical resurrection of history into an organizing chant. For a poem to refer to its readers in the dedication is a breach of traditional decorum that assumes a new use to which that reader is going to put the poem she reads. This sense of the poem as functional to the movement is also expressed in Morgan's conclusion. Of Joan and her women lover, she says:

> Such bones as theirs
> rattle with delight
> whenever women love or lie together
> on the night before
> we go to war.

It is nearly impossible, in a poem like this, to distinguish metaphor from declaration and so understand what Morgan really means by "war." (Morgan writes a great deal about a "women's revolution," surely meaning by this a real social upheaval involving armed struggle. I find it hard, however, to take seriously the conceptual leap required when someone says, as Morgan does in her essay, "Goodbye to All That," that women need not fear bloodshed in that revolution because we hemorrhage once a

month.) Yet battle is one of the motifs that recur most insistently
in feminist poems about feminism, and it would be nice to know
what sort of battle they mean.

The enrichment of sisterhood is the other constant theme. In
"Coming Out," Jacqueline Lapidus ties that experience to lesbianism, which she sees as a resolution of the love she once felt
for her mother. Now, she concludes:

> Mother, I would like to help you
> swim back against the foaming river
> to the source of our
> incestuous fears
> but you're so tired
> out beyond the breakers
> and I am upstream among my sisters
> spawning.

The creative energy that inheres in belonging to the community
of women affects straight women with a different kind of power,
for they can contrast their present feelings with the time when
they believed that real life could be lived only with men. Marge
Piercy writes about the male "intellectual conversation" she has
abandoned for the solidarity of what women know and are:

> Now I get coarse when the abstract nouns start flashing.
> I go out to the kitchen to talk cabbages and habits.
> I try hard to remember to watch what people do.
> Yes, keep your eyes on the hands, let the voice go buzzing.
> Economy is the bone, politics is the flesh,
> watch who they beat and who they eat,
> watch who they relieve themselves on, watch who they own.
> The rest, the rest, the rest is decoration.
>   ("In the Men's Room[s]")

Rejecting the doctrine that men define the universe of ideas, issues, or feelings means accepting that the two sexes have different historical experiences, and that the difference is consequent-
ial. Honor Moore writes about an emotional argument with a man
about a sexist mural, concluding,

"If you were a woman, you might feel
differently." "I wouldn't," he says.
("Conversation in the Eighth Street Bookstore")

By contrast, comparatively few poems admit the tensions and struggles that exist within the women's movement, as they exist within any movement that is bringing itself into being. In "The Bumpity Road to Mutual Devotion" Marge Piercy addresses the other woman who was defined as "strong" by their first women's group. The struggle between the two women is a personal one, but, because it takes place in the context of a movement, even the love they now feel can assume a political form:

We will never be lovers; too scared
of losing each other. What tantalizes past flesh
—too mirrored, lush, dark haired and soft in the belly—
is the strange mind rasping, clanging, engaging.
What we fantasize—rising like a bird kite
on the hot afternoon air—is work together
Projects, battles, schemes, manifestoes
are born from the brushing of wills
like small sparks from loose hair,
and will we let them fade, static electricity?

Yet the converse is also true, that in order to get into a poem at all, the intrinsically political conflict and resolution *have* to be reduced in scale to the clashing identities of two individual women. Frequently, moreover, where an individual's own identity encompasses a contradiction, as, for example, someone who is both black and female, the issue does arise of what *kind* of women's movement we are building. Audre Lorde writes about joining a group of (white) feminists before a demonstration. As they discuss their domestic servants and get preferential treatment from the counterman at Nedicks, the poet realizes

There are so many roots to the tree of anger
that sometimes the branches shatter
before they bear

and she wonders ironically, as she sits there,
>which me will survive
>all these liberations.
>("Who Said It was Simple")

The women's liberation movement is taking shape in a society characterized and defined by class struggle and by racism. Sexism assumes certain forms for us because of the way these two historical forces work together. Not all the conflicts that our movement faces in attempting to come to terms with race and class occur because individual women have a race and a class as well as a sex, but the personal aspect is the only dimension of the question that feminist poetry has been able to reach at all. The poetry of the women's movement has failed to challenge a charter assumption of bourgeois literature: the notion that literature in general and poetry in particular exist for the expression of the private, individual, and subjective element in supposedly universal human experience. Recognizing through the movement that our "personal" experiences are in fact shared with other women, we have proudly asserted their authenticity as subjects of poetry. But we also learn through the movement that our shared oppression has a social basis and an eventual social remedy, and that knowledge is also part of how we experience our lives. It is this larger aspect, especially as it affects the internal dynamics of the movement, that feminist poetry has, by and large, been unable to accommodate.

What feminist poets do capture—and that superbly—is the depth and concretion of women's new commitment to women, the conditions and the rage that are at the base of the movement, and the perilous sense, nonetheless, of what it means to take these steps towards revolution. In one poem of this sort, Margery Himel writes of an evolving sense of who "her people" are: her family of origin, her ethnic group, the new family she and her husband create. In each case, there is a shared history, a shared culture of language and reference, that creates a bond she ultimately sees through:

Now I say that women are my people.
I call us mirror-sisters
because when I look inside your words
I see myself.
I call us Awakening Nation
because I think of us as a baby
discovering its body
and the power of its cry.
I call us a people
although we have just begun to move together.
What unites us is not our past
but our future.

("My People")

Yet the history of women does provide models of courage and determination that are essential to integrate into the emerging movement. The consciousness that suffuses Muriel Rukeyser's early poem about labor organizer Ann Burlak has assumed a living reality for the poets of our movement. Rhetorically, at least, the new feminist poetry can endorse Rukeyser's catalogue of

the ten greatest American women:
The anonymous farmer's wife, the anonymous clubbed picket,
the anonymous Negro woman who held off the guns,
the anonymous prisoner, anonymous cotton-picker
trailing her robe of sack in a proud train,
anonymous writer of these and mill-hand, anonymous city-
    walker,
anonymous organizer, anonymous binder of the illegally
    wounded,
anonymous feeder and speaker to anonymous squares.

It is in this spirit that Susan Griffin writes "I Like to Think of Harriet Tubman," using the suffering and the militancy of the former slave as a background to the contemporary situation that forces our movement into action. Harriet Tubman is not a metaphor for the suffering, daring, and militancy we require; rather, Griffin places the black woman's struggle in a longer history, extending it to our time and forward. The contemporary question that Griffin focuses on is a "woman's issue," all right, "the problem of feeding children," and in the attempt to solve it she brings in the concept of law and Harriet Tubman's disdain for a law that made her people slaves. In our day,

> The legal answer
> to the problem of feeding children
> is ten free lunches every month,
> being equal, in the child's real life,
> to eating lunch every other day.
> Monday but not Tuesday.
> I like to think of the President
> eating lunch Monday, but not
> Tuesday.
> And when I think of the President
> and the law, and the problem of
> feeding children, I like to
> think of Harriet Tubman
> and her revolver.

Griffin concludes that it is necessary to think about the revolver so that the men who made the unjust laws will begin to take us seriously:

> I am tired, wanting them to think
> about right and wrong.
> I want them to fear.
> I want them to feel fear now
> as I have felt suffering in the womb, and
> I want them
> to know
> that there is always a time
> there is always a time to make right
> what is wrong,
> there is always a time
> for retribution
> and that time
> is beginning.

At its best, as in this poem of Griffin's, feminist poetry becomes part of the internal life of the movement itself, providing the music to which we march. But ours is a movement that is only half certain where it is marching, and poetry is more often relegated to the "cultural events," the entertainment segment of feminist conferences, rallies, and meetings, the thing we drop into when the real political work is over. It needs to be more than that, and I am convinced that it will be—when there is a movement demanding that this most sensitive instrument be pressed into the service of a more sweeping analysis and a more definite direction than any we have yet devised. Let there be no mistake: I believe that the poetry of the women's liberation movement is the richest and most vital current in American poetry today. I just don't think that's enough.

NOTES

1. The poem from which these lines are taken is called "For L." Like all the contents of *Sing a Battle Song: Poems by Women in the Weather Underground Organization* (Oakland, Calif.: Inkworks, 1975), it is anonymous.

2. Collections like Louise Bernikow's *The World Split Open* (New York: Vintage-Random House, 1974), and Florence Howe and Ellen Bass's *No More Masks!* (Garden City, N.Y.: Doubleday, 1973) contain many poems of this sort. The explicitly feminist act, here, is the criticism and scholarship involved in putting these anthologies together. An unintentional effect of these and other feminist collections is their misidentification of certain poets as "feminist," through taking a few often-reprinted and perhaps atypical poems out of their *oeuvre* and placing them in a new context.

3. *Woman to Woman* (Oakland, Calif.: Women's Press Collective, n.d.), *I Hear My Sisters Saying*, ed. Carol Konek and Dorothy Walters (New York: Crowell, 1976), *Rising Tides*, ed. Laura Chester and Sharon Barba (New York: Washington Square–Simon and Schuster, 1973), *Mountain Moving Day*, ed. Elaine Gill (Trumansberg, N.Y.: The Crossings Press, 1973), *We Become New*, ed. Lucille Iverson and Kathryn Ruby (New York: Bantam, 1975), *Amazon Poetry*, ed. Elly Bulkin and Joan Larkin (New York: Out and Out Books, 1976).

4. All the poems quoted so far are from *Woman to Woman*, a collection that lists all the contributors' names alphabetically at the end. Only if I have read a poem elsewhere or if, like Alta's, it announces the poet's name in its text, have I been able to attribute the quoted lines to their author. One of the cited poems is untitled.

5. I owe this formulation of the question to an as yet unpublished essay by Elizabeth Kennedy and Avra Michelson, "Socialist Feminism: A Critique of Eli Zaretsky's *Capitalism, the Family and Personal Life*."

What's My Line?
Telefiction and
Women's Work

TELEVISION IS the opposite of work. Watching TV belongs to the set of cultural experiences we call "leisure," a category that is explicitly defined in contrast to work and that comes into existence only when work itself is defined, delimited, and measured the way it is under capitalism. Its leisure function provides a reflex excuse for the low quality of what we see on the tube. "Look," runs the defensive argument, "a guy (it's always a guy in these examples) comes home from work, he's tired, he switches on the television, maybe he's got himself a beer, and he wants to relax. He wants entertainment. Not art, not a message—relaxation." Television, according to its own spokesmen, is what we do when we are not working; ideally, in fact, it's what we do when we aren't doing anything.

This essay was written in the summer of 1976, and went to press before the start of the Fall '77 TV season. Any critical study of television that cites concrete examples faces the problem of built-in obsolescence. Programs go off the air and new ones replace them; major characters are added or removed; new emphases are tried; and programming trends shift. Sometimes counter-examples to my observations may emerge or seem to emerge from these seasonal changes. It is my contention, however, that the industry and its product do not experience annual or semiannual revolutions and that fruitful generalizations can still be made.

Certainly television occupies the leisure time of most working people. TV has become one of the ways in which we maintain our own labor power, something—like eating, sleeping, showering— that we do in the intervals between periods of work and that prepares us to go back to work. It is significant, therefore, that television constantly shows us people working or involved in work-related situations. Uniquely among contemporary Western art forms, TV has evolved a series of conventions for the portrayal of the work experience.* It tells us what kinds of jobs there are and what kinds of people do them, what kinds of social relations develop and what attitudes and emotions these evoke.

Now, everyone knows it's just a story. A TV boss is instantly recognizable, not because he's like your boss or mine, but because he's like other TV bosses—in short, a stock character. We come home from work, watch the myths about the job, the routine, the coworkers, the boss, the hostility; we know they're fictions; and we get up in the morning and go to work. Obviously, it isn't TV but necessity that makes us work. But watching television, with its dominant myths about work, helps prepare us for the work day and interprets back to us the experiences we encounter as we live it.

Although these generalizations apply equally to both sexes, I don't believe anyone seriously questions the fact that women and men have different experiences in the labor force. The likelihood of one's being employed at all, the kinds of jobs one does, one's rate of pay and probability of promotion, the meaning of work in one's life and its impact on family relationships, the structure of social relations at work, all are strongly influenced by sex. TV fiction has developed a set of myths specific to women and work elaborating on the themes of whether and why women enter the job market, what occupations they engage in, how they typically

*To test this statement, compare the portrayal of police work in a cop or detective film with the depiction on TV. Whether in a series or on something like *Police Story*, whose main characters change weekly, we are shown TV cops as workers, people doing a job.

perform there, how they interact with the people with and for whom they work.

But not all adult women work outside the home, and the entire phenomenon of "leisure" is quite different for a woman who is a housewife, for her job exists outside the wage system and un- bounded by the restraints or the protection of specified working hours. She may be free to watch television during her work day—either as a break from housework or a partial distraction while that work is going forward—but, in compensation, there are usually no clearly demarcated hours of the twenty-four when she does *not* have work to do. The medium provides an image of *her* job as well, for TV fiction and advertising create a set of myths about what it means to be a housewife, to engage in certain tasks, and to experience the human relations that they tell us come with this particular territory. Like the salaried worker, the housewife knows that her TV counterpart is a myth, and, again like those who work outside the home, she nonetheless makes that myth functional in her own life.

Television's working women, whether they work inside or outside the home and whether or not their efforts are paid for, are not just a special sector of the general category of working people that TV examines. The overriding message it sends out is that their sex is its most important component; her identity as a female informs every aspect of a woman's working life, so that it appears as if she does not so much hold a job as play a role—one of whose facets is expressed through whatever the job happens to be. Al- though television intervenes in the lives of all working people, regardless of sex, its principal function in defining the working woman is to add yet another layer to the myths that define woman herself.

The actual working woman, however, sees herself as a person—both worker and woman—with a job, a boss, a paycheck, and a set of working conditions, not a complex of sex roles involved in a workplace. For this reason, it is important to identify the institutional source of the myths and to try to estimate their influence. Broadcast television is a branch of something called the entertainment industry. The term itself, which is employed by its participants and not (like "culture industry" or "consciousness industry") imposed by critics, is used entirely without self-consciousness. It implies that something is manufactured here, mass-produced by alienated labor for the consumers who constitute its mass audience. The entertainment industry is the form of capitalist enterprise with principal responsibility for what Stanley Aronowitz calls the "colonized leisure" of American working people. But this is not to say that the colonialism of mass culture, the literally domestic imperialism of the tube, does not meet with resistance. The consumers of television and of the myths it communicates are not monolithic in their response, and they are not mere passive recipients. In exploring what television tells us about the work women do, we should remember that whatever TV has to tell, what it has to sell, is not necessarily what we "buy." The myths are intended to operate in our lives, and it is essential to identify what they are and how they are put together. But it is also essential to realize that what is there on the screen is not, in fact, the whole picture and that, in examining one of the factors that *influence* the consciousness of women, we are actually saying nothing as yet about either women or their consciousness.

It is useful to begin by contrasting statistics from the televised labor force with conditions in the actual world of women's work. The former are subject to weekly variation: Kojak may use a female undercover agent one week, encounter only a murdered prostitute the next, while *Medical Center*'s Dr. Gannon becomes entangled with a brilliant but erratic woman surgeon that week and, the following time, treats a teenager whose illness may impede her chances in the Olympics. Even on a series with continuing characters, the exigencies of plot may take Mary Tyler Moore and her "office family" to the tavern downstairs to be served by a male bartender or require the heroine and her escort to dine at a restaurant with a comic waitress. Moreover, although all regular viewers know that Rhoda is a self-employed decorator of store windows and her sister, Brenda, is a bank teller, a particular episode may have to do with their job situations or may preoccupy itself with their family life or their sexuality to the complete, if temporary, exclusion of their work identity. Monitoring a week's programming, therefore, although it helps to dramatize one's points, does not provide a consistent or reliable set of figures. Certain statistical trends are nonetheless discernible within the female work force of TV fiction, and they are very much at variance with trends that can be charted in the actual world of work.

In that world, the numbers of American women who work for wages at least part time and at least part of the year have increased to the point where about half of us are so employed. The vast majority of working women are single, wives of men who make less than $7,000 per year, or heads of families (one out of eight American families is headed by a woman). More than one-third of all U.S. women in the paid labor force, the largest single category, hold clerical jobs; another large percentage have service jobs like waitressing, nonprofessional jobs in the health industry, hairdressing, or clerking in stores; a substantial number are factory workers or domestics. At the more prestigious end of the spectrum, 14.5% of employed women are in fields classified as "professional and technical." Within that deceptive category, however, women tend to cluster in certain fairly sex-specific (and lower-status) positions—teaching, nursing and other health-related technical work, social service jobs, librarianship—and to be grossly underrepresented in the better-paid fields yielding access to power: medicine, law, the upper clergy, diplomacy, military and civil service, science and engineering, university administration, and so on. An employed woman used to be labeled a "girl," with different class connotations depending on whether that noun were qualified by the word "working" or "career." The assumptions behind the use of this term reflect more than mere mechanical sexism. Rather, they stem from the fact that most female workers were thought of as being young and unmarried—a condition that was statistically true and normatively even truer. At present, however, not only are more women working outside the home, but far more of those who do are older, are married, and are mothers. Nearly twenty-seven million American children under eighteen have mothers who work and more than six million of these children are under six.[1]

I summarize these figures here because they will serve to underscore the differences in the demography of TV fiction. The most striking disparity is not even in the area of job distribution; rather it concerns whether TV women are employed at all, their reasons for working, and their preparation for doing so. There is a trend away from family-based situations in both comedy and drama, which necessarily cuts down on the number of housewives whole role is written into the plot. But, despite this pattern, the probability of a TV woman's being employed is about half what it would be for her real-life counterpart. Among married women, particularly those with children, and women over thirty, that probability is reduced still further. Not even childless young wives of the working class or older women whose children are grown are expected to hold a job. Motherhood almost always means leaving the work force, which is not too surprising, but marriage itself tends to have the same result, unless the bride's work can be defined as a Career.

Hence, Dr. Laura Horton, the psychiatrist on *Days of Our Lives,* pursues her therapeutic activities through both her marriages and the widely separated births of her two children. But the town of Salem—as well as her roster of patients—abounds in well-off women whose lives are empty, but who have no professional "excuse" for seeking to fill them with work, while women who *must* work to make a living do so on the fringes of respectability, like ex-prostitute Gerry, the occasional singer at Doug's Place, or her illegitimate daughter, Trish, who takes over that job. On *All in the Family,* Gloria Stivic clerks in a department store to help put her husband through school, but quits work to have a child as soon as he has his degree and a regular job. Her mother, Edith Bunker, a housewife with no marketable skills, seeks an added source of income only when Archie is on strike or laid off. For Ann Romano, the divorcee on *One Day at a Time,* choosing to be free of her marriage means choosing, as well, a series of low-paying, boring, and exhausting jobs. There is some implication that it is also humiliating for this woman of middle-class background to have to work as an Avon Lady, but the "humiliation" is not used to provide insight into the job itself or the kind of life it makes possible for those who do it; instead, it serves as a measure of the marriage she has broken away from and of the limited options available to women making these decisions.* Phyllis Lindstrom, while a doctor's wife on the *Mary Tyler Moore Show,* once earned a real estate license and sold houses as an avocation; when widowed and the central character on her own program, Phyllis conveniently lost this claim to a middle-class status in her own right and had to support herself and her daughter, first with an ill-defined assistant's job in a commercial photography studio, and later with an equally unskilled post working for the Board of Supervisors.

Phyllis's now-forgotten real estate career reflects a tendency for TV wives to seek jobs for "fulfillment" so they won't be bored at home. Maude enters the same field for the same reason, and Louise Jefferson, long accustomed to assisting her husband when his black capitalism was confined to one neighborhood drycleaning establishment, chafes at the restrictions of her home now that he can afford both a nonworking wife and a full-time maid; indeed, she takes a job with one of his competitors in order

---

*In its second season, securely established, this program lost a great deal of its working-class content and its earthiness. As part of the process, Ann Romano was promoted from secretary to executive in an ad agency. At the same time, the semiresident boyfriend left the series, the ex-husband became both more evident and more prosperous, the lecherous superintendent cleaned up his act, and his girlfriend, a tough cocktail waitress, became the sole repository of that particularly female gutsiness that had been part of the show's initial appeal. In the show's third season, the cocktail waitress character was dropped.

to "keep busy." Rhoda was once able, after several months of marriage, to lend her husband money; the profits of her window-decorating business were hers to dispose of and were not called upon for day-to-day expenses, despite the fact that Joe was also supporting his first wife and his child. Before she was widowed, Florida Evans on *Good Times* had an unskilled but always employed husband; this black woman, who seemed to have a job some of the time, is the only example I can call to mind of a married character, much less a mother, whose working was motivated entirely by economic necessity. Mother Partridge, beguiling her widowhood in reruns by joining her children's bubblegum rock act, or the various "Lucys" playing at entering the grown-up labor force, remain far more typical of the motives and experiences of working women on TV—and incidentally tell us something about the level of maturity to be expected from an adult female capable of earning her own living.

By and large, however, TV women are unlikely to work for wages. In the '50s and the early '60s, perhaps 16 percent of them did so.* In the 1970s, the proportion of adult women portrayed as holding jobs has risen to about 25 percent, with weekly variations depending on the factors noted earlier.[2] When I discuss the difference between the kinds of jobs women hold in TV-land and in contemporary U.S. society, therefore, it should be borne in mind that the percentages of TV characters engaged in this or that occupation represent a percentage of an already unrealistically small work force.

---

*One of the recurrent story lines of *I Love Lucy* and *Honeymooners* programs from this period stemmed from this isolation of the woman at home and typically involved the complex machinations that Lucy or Alice would devise to get out of the house and into her husband's world, the real world where things were happening. For Lucy, wife of a nightclub bandleader, this meant breaking into show business—which Ricky was determined to prevent her entering—even if her debut had to be as the rear end of a horse. Ralph Kramden was equally dedicated to the preservation of his all-male space but, as an overworked city bus driver, he lived his real life after hours, in the Raccoons Lodge, with its masculine rituals and fishing expeditions, and it was here that Alice, spending her days in a shabby two-room apartment, wished to penetrate.

The most impressive contrast of this sort is the relative absence of clerical workers on TV, considering the large numbers of real working women who hold clerical positions. Although TV offices, when they are shown, are staffed almost entirely by women, major female characters no longer seem to work as secretaries (much less as file clerks, keypunch operators, or dictaphone typists) or to possess office experience. Brenda is a bank teller; some of the detectives and doctors have a secretary or receptionist; Fay was a legal secretary (described in some postmortems of this short-lived series as a glamour job). In general, though, not only have programs like *Private Secretary* and *Meet Millie* been consigned to the schlockbin of history, but clerical work does not even appear incidentally as the specified, if not depicted, occupation of a woman whose romantic life or physical health is the subject of an episode. In fact, a general absence of skills of any sort characterizes television's female workers.

Until Laverne and Shirley, a pair of bottle-cappers in a Milwaukee brewery, made their appearance early in 1976, female factory hands, another major category of working women, had never been represented on the tube. In large measure, of course, this omission simply mirrors the absence from telefiction of blue-collar people, male or female. But even the few factory jobs depicted simply show us another world that is for men only. If there was a Rosie the Riveter on the wartime *Life of Riley* (and I don't believe there was), she must have shared the fate of many of her sisters in war production, for she did not make the transition to the televised adventures of workers in an airplane factory. *Love Thy Neighbor* was an adaptation of a British sitcom about working-class life that ran as a summer replacement back in 1973. The theme of this program, which appeared to be that class bias is stronger than racism any day, called for scenes in the plant where the white protagonist, a member of his union exec, was a skilled operative and his black neighbor was a time-and-motion study expert. In none of this was there any indication that factories employ both male and female labor. Yet when mechanically-inclined Irene Lorenzo is hired to drive a forklift on Archie Bunker's loading platform, the sexism we are supposed to laugh at is Archie's, not that of the medium where he is entirely and properly at home.

It is revealing that I had to traverse the entire history of television comedy to come up with those examples, and adding dramatic programs would not have appreciably expanded the pool of factory workers. TV characters work in offices—though they no longer seem to do office work in them—or at service jobs that bring them into "interesting" situations. This general falsification of American society and its class nature is the context within which the further exclusion of women from TV's few factories has to be understood. The one also helps explain the other, for the male proletariat is stereotyped as being a great deal closer to animal nature: rougher, cruder, tougher than the insurance salesmen, doctors, and ad men who populate the "normal" world. And their workplace, where it is depicted, is correspondingly brutal, no place for someone—of whatever class—who possesses the stereotyped feminine qualities. All of which is not so much a description of causality as it is a vicious circle.

Now, however, we have Laverne and Shirley. The factory—indeed, the factory of the mid-'50s, when the show takes place—is no longer a stronghold of brutishness and male-bonding. And between them, the title characters purport to cover the range of working-class female possibility. One is crude and direct, apparently satisfied with her class identity, while the other is more reserved, aspiring to a cultivated mobility up the social ladder. For them, more pointedly than for men in parallel situations, class itself is an issue, as the stereotypes of "factory worker" and of "women" directly clash with each another. Thus, in one episode Laverne and Shirley manage a dinner invitation at the home of some (no less stereotyped) Rich People and learn to assert their own class pride when the evening dresses they have acquired under the counter turn out to be stolen from the wardrobes of their dinner companions. Another plot revolves around

Laverne's resentment and revenge against the plant tour guide, a former classmate, who always describes their department as harboring the "unskilled workers." (After all, Laverne insists, she too is a high school graduate!)

But, although the premise of the program involves their class identity, their class consciousness, and the varied responses these evoke when exposed to a televised version of social reality, the subject of class is consistently distorted on this series. The two heroines, first of all, are isolated within their community and their workplace. Indeed, the entire world outside their own volatile but supportive relationship is a hostile one. Most of the time, the sorts of social relations subsisting among working-class people—on or off the job—and the way they may differ from how middle-class people are supposed to interact are completely avoided. Where coworkers, boyfriends, old high school sorority mates, or women with white-collar jobs enter the scene, the result is almost always a heightening of shrillness and conflict. Similarly, *Laverne and Shirley* avoids commenting on class differences in family life via the barely credible device—in a '50s setting—of situating these two women from white "ethnic" backgrounds in their own apartment in the same city where they grew up. Removal from the family also serves, of course, as a further isolating factor for the two heroines. In this context, the class consciousness that Laverne and Shirley display has nothing to do with solidarity, with acting together on their condition, or with any similarly threatening political categories. Nor does it affect and limit their self-concept. Rather, it is reduced to an individual matter of hurt pride and defensive reactions.

The class line—if one can employ so analytic a term for the social mishmash that television tries to sell us—is further blurred by the plot's frequent references to Laverne's family background. Laverne, the more vocal of the two in defense of her "commonness," works in a factory all right, but her background is pettybourgeois; that comic Italo-American father owns and operates an apparently thriving neighborhood pizza parlor-cum-bowling alley. That such small business people are often struggling to get by and tend to have more in common with their working-class customers, both materially and culturally, than with the magnates of big business or even with the managers and professionals who make up the TV norm is beyond question. But that does not make Mr. DeFazio a worker instead of the small-scale employer of labor that he is. Nor does it make his daughter any less a brewery worker than she was before I made this interesting revelation. Rather, it underscores the fact that her touchiness about what seem to be matters of class is actually a defense of ordinary, down-to-earth ethnic people against snobbery and pretension. Her pride does not reflect some protomilitant stance, but the reverse. Whereas Shirley's position is that she doesn't want to remain or look as if she belongs in the working class, Laverne's attitude involves a static satisfaction not only with who and what she is but also with the conditions of her life. Her feistiness is delightful, but gets us nowhere.

If I seem to be placing too much weight on one silly series, my excuse is in the uniqueness of the situation it represents and the classic nature of this last-mentioned theme. For TV—and especially TV comedy— has long cultivated an interpretation of the admirable injunction to "be yourself" that would have us not only stop pretending that we are richer or more cultured than we really are, but also learn to appreciate and be content with our place in the world: an ideology that complements the ethic of consumption as an aspect of identity.

Laverne and Shirley must depend on the existence of certain stereotypes, but their development as characters also serves to enhance those stereotypes. Thus, one quality that Laverne, in particular, has in common with many TV women in proletarian service jobs is a misplaced New York accent. The explanation that actress Penny Marshall comes from the Bronx is, in fact, no explanation at all, since heightening the accent is part of her interpretation of the role; the New Yorkese was by no means so pronounced when Marshall played a Boston architect's wife on

Friends and Lovers as it is in her current part. What was initially regional speech is actually meant as a signal of class, along with the ungrammatical English typically used by waitresses and other (often gum-chewing) service workers on TV. After all, actresses cannot be expected to master the range of regional variations and the class stratifications within them of American speech; enough if they can do a passable southern aristocrat and her poorer down-home neighbor. For the rest, one talks in a "normal" accent to designate middle-class people, and puts on a touch or more of New York to represent the vulgarity of the working class. This has become a convention of the genre, rather like one that decrees that if the secretary (or the nurse, if it's a doctor's office) is smart, the receptionist has to be stupid.

Both the southern and the New York version of working-class accent are in evidence on *Alice,* the first program, to my knowledge, with waitresses as central characters. Flo, the Southerner, lives in a trailer, goes to VFW dances, and talks openly about her sexuality—all stereotyped working-class characteristics. But boss Mel, who looks the part of the hairy-chested proprietor of a roadside diner, has been to college, and the central character, Alice, takes courses at night. Her present life style and personal manner, wholesome and restrained, directly contrast with Flo's. Unlike Shirley, Alice does not have upwardly mobile aspirations; she *is* middle class. Her surroundings, her consciousness, her style of child-rearing, her cultural and ethical standards are all informed by her background as a New Jersey housewife and remain unaffected by her present material circumstances. This is the reason, I think, that *Alice* looks so familiar to us even though the diner milieu and the characters associated with it are not the usual TV settings. As a workplace, moreover, Mel's Diner has a great deal more in common with other TV workplaces than with real greasy spoons, in that the place where she works serves as Alice's personal and social community. The people in the diner participate in one another's private lives, go to parties or on dates together, keep informed and offer advice about each other's sexual or parental problems. In short, they constitute the same sort of family surrogate that Mary Tyler Moore's office family did for her. Within the framework and the plots that develop from it, Alice's life at Mel's Diner is not a job, but a system of relationships in which she plays a certain defined role. In fact, Alice the waitress and Mary Richards the TV producer fill precisely the same roles, serve the same function within their respective circles, just as those "workplace families" do for them. The roles they play rely entirely on stereotyped female characteristics—extended in this case into the sphere of the labor market which comes, thereby, to approximate the old sphere of the home.

Until *Alice*'s first season, in the fall of 1976, waitresses tended to be minor characters, incidental to the action of a particular comic or dramatic plot, and that remains their function on other programs. They may make an apposite or amusing remark to Bob Newhart or Maude Findlay, or provide Ellery Queen or Commissioner MacMillan with necessary information to solve a crime, but they are almost never the center of what is going forward. Prostitutes, however (or women with euphemistic jobs in bars), are frequently victims, accomplices, informants, or perpetrators in police and detective stories. They are sometimes the patients in hospital dramas, and their lives may intersect with the lives of the other characters on soap operas. Occasionally they even appear in situation comedy. Here again, the New York accent and the gum chewing are standard at the lower levels of the profession, along with cigarette-smoking, frequent drinking, and, often, the glazed look of a person hooked on some unspecified soporific. More elegant prostitutes tend to lose the accent and the gum, but acquire a bored, polished hardness of manner and smarter clothes. Although they may be desperate for money, especially if they have become involved in some criminal activity other than their occupation, their work itself is rarely portrayed as a job chosen in contrast to other ways of making a living that might have seemed more demanding or less lucrative. In fact, prostitution is not depicted as a job at all, but rather as a *role,* almost an attribute or facet of a woman's identity—in this case, the specifically sexual aspect of her gender.

TV women, both in offices and outside them, tend to be assigned what I think of as "cutesy jobs," occupations that require human contact and that place the woman in a series of potentially colorful situations. (It's hard to tell exactly how far television exaggerates the numbers of women holding such jobs, because it's impossible to find the corresponding figures in government statistics; these jobs are not grouped as a separate category.) Undercover assignments for policewomen can assume this character. Charlie's Angels, of course, specialize in such jobs. More typically, however, cutesy jobs belong in comedies. *That Girl* and the last of the "Lucy" avatars are archetypal cases, since both characters worked for agencies that afforded a variety of unusual temporary placements. In addition to these protean specialists in the short-term, usually frivolous occupation, though, cutesy jobs are often the ones found for TV wives or for teenagers of either sex who wish to work, as well as for women who are unmarried heads of households. The chief utility of such jobs—which often involve animals, children, silly costumes and other props, or humiliating situations—is to the story line, but they also create a climate of inference about the general silliness of women's reasons for working, women's jobs, and women's characteristic performance at them. Shampooing a huge dog, caring for a spoiled child star, posing seminude in an enormous bowl of goldfish, getting a custard pie thrown at one, handing out movie passes while clad in a stuffy gorilla suit (I think I'm making these particular ones up, but they're the product of a quarter-century's stored memories)—all these are *work* for the woman who does them. That they are normally unproductive and often socially useless is hardly her fault. Nor, obviously, is the fact that most of them pay minimal wages and that those jobs arranged through a temporaries agency create double exploitation. But the frivolous impression remains, and neither hard times nor media feminism has made substantial changes.

One low-status job that TV endows with amusing or dramatic qualities unanticipated by most of its real-life practitioners is that of domestic servant. Here again, TV probably grossly overestimates the proportion of women engaged in such work, but it is impossible to formulate a reliable sense of just how far skewed the picture is, since the Labor Department figures against which the TV world is measured do not include the women who can survive only by working as domestics while receiving some form of public assistance, and whose earnings are consequently not reported to the authorities. This is an extremely common situation, one in which the woman doing the work usually makes some sacrifice of Social Security and other "benefits" in order to hold on to the necessary state subsidy that can make the difference between getting by and failing to make it. And it is one that employers take advantage of by paying lower wages than might otherwise be required. Needless to say, there is no such hanky-panky in televised domestic service, where a bevy of maids clean up after a vast army of model and upright employers.

An uglier and more definite falsification concerns the race of the TV domestics. In the early years of television *Beulah* was a popular transplant from radio, the program taking its name from its chief character, a sensible, respectable black maid whose hustler boyfriend had the good sense, at least, not to take her white employers at their own or at Beulah's valuation. Network sensitivity to accusations of stereotyping preceded any real understanding of racism itself, and *Beulah* was never replaced by another program featuring a black woman engaged in domestic work. (Indeed, the only nonwhite servants I can remember from the '60s were Asian or Asian-American, and that decade also brought us an unreasonable number of *male* house-servants). Only in 1972, when the great liberal, Maude, hired Florida as her housekeeper, was the reverse color bar finally breached. But Florida was soon spun off into a program of her own, where she is no longer a maid; and at present only the black Jeffersons, of all the families on TV, have a black maid. Meanwhile, Maude hired an oft-soused Cockney for a couple of years, the MacMillans retained a white housekeeper who participated in a number of family activities, and a procession of lily-white maids, cooks, housekeepers, and governesses respond to or evade Columbo's interrogations. And, on the daily reruns, the Brady Bunch still have faithful white Alice in the kitchen and the Professor's family hold on to their supernaturally endowed British nanny.

The survival of a substantial white servant population on TV programs that are supposed to be depicting contemporary American life (for *Upstairs, Downstairs* and *Beacon Hill* need not concern us here) reflects how little the networks comprehend or are prepared to act on the complaints of oppressed people. The old stereotypes were not only offensive, but had normative effects: black women work as maids and thus, inferentially, that is the right job for them. With the early successes of the civil rights movement, the grossest stereotypes were eliminated and, with them, any acknowledgment by the medium's characteristic fictions that black people exist at all. In the late '60s, when *Julia* became the first black family sitcom, the knee-jerk response was simply to avoid the old stereotypes that had given offense rather than to find out what black people wanted or needed to see about black reality. The title character of *Julia*, therefore, was a war widow supporting herself and her son by work as a nurse, depicted as living in extraordinary luxury (what *was* the late husband, anyway, a mercenary?). The reasoning went something like this: "You don't want us to show the colored people as poor and shiftless—okay, here's one who's hard-working, a trained professional, and living in style." Even now, with a decade's further consciousness to depend on, we have an only somewhat wider range of black experience represented in situation comedies: one rich family (*The Jeffersons*), one family of working poor (*Good Times*), one "normal" and one zany-lumpen petty-bourgeois household (respectively, the recently cancelled *That's My Mama* and *Sanford and Son*). There are still very few loafers or hustlers; junkies and alcoholics are seen only on cop and doctor programs and aren't usually black, anyway; the people who are struggling to get by *do* get by; and almost no black people have to go to work in white people's houses.

Black or white, domestic servants on TV share certain common characteristics. Unlike waitresses, prostitutes, barmaids, or blue-collar housewives, TV maids do not speak ungrammatically. Nor do they normally exhibit the other traits (gum chewing, showy makeup, smoking) that mark the low-status woman in other occupations. Even Mrs. Naugatuck's drinking is a comic feature, and getting drunk in an establishment where the male head of the house is an acknowledged alcoholic known to slip off the wagon is hardly a sign of servant status. Their correct English and appropriate, though often downright, manners make TV domestics especially suitable adjuncts to the families for whom they work and in whose problems they intervene. Their own problems, particularly those centering on their romantic relationships, are also the stuff of which TV plots are made and, once more, the barrier between employer and servant apparently disappears as everyone pitches in to deal with whatever has gone wrong with the maid's love life or her family situation. The vicious old cliché about a maid's being "like one of the family" achieves a certain grotesque authenticity within the televised myth of family life.

TV's domestic staff share not only the joys and sorrows but also the life style of their employers, since a far larger proportion are full-time, live-in workers than in the real world, where wage-labor, with the maid commuting to the job from home, has become the common mode of domestic service. Many domestics must work for several employers, since a great many middle-class people can afford domestic help only one or two days a week; few contemporary homes posses suitable maid's quarters; and most domestics have lives of their own and often families to provide for, so that paying for the worker's maintenance instead of paying cash simply isn't feasible. On TV, however, domestics do tend to live with their employers, center their lives in that household, and, since rigid class distinctions are not maintained, enjoy a fairly privileged standard of living.

Indeed, a good measure of the collapse of reality into myth (in this case, the myth that the economic crises of capitalism are hardest on the white-collar middle class) lay in a shortlived 1971-72 comedy called *The Good Life,* the *donnée* of which was that an executive and his wife simply could not afford the material comforts they craved on his managerial salary so, in order to live *in,* not just in proximity to, luxury, they hired themselves out as a "couple," maid and butler, to a rich gentleman. Each week's plot revolved around the blunders they made as they gave themselves on-the-job training and their frantic efforts to insure that their employer not find out, through their clumsiness or some twist in the plot, that they were not "really" servants but middle-class people. The implication is that they'd be fired and lose the material paradise they've edged their way into if the deception were discovered. That an entire series could be built on this dimwitted premise is only an extension of TV's characteristic treatment of the housekeeper's lot. Maybe TV is where the clever young couple got the idea in the first place.

A final note on domestic service as TV depicts it: it isn't very hard work. TV maids, unlike housewives, may sometimes be found cooking, vacuuming, or dusting, but their laziness and shirking are mentioned more often than their labor, even by the maids themselves. Creative cookery seems to be the principal vent for the maids' skill, and it is in the kitchen that they are likeliest to be found when a scene involves them and their work. Moreover, in all the thousands of commercials for household products to which I have been exposed, I cannot recall a maid's ever serving as the Expert who explains the merits of a floor wax, detergent, or processed food. Perhaps it is unsafe to remind the housewife–consumer at this sensitive moment that some people get paid for doing the work she does for nothing (and that remains work for her, despite the manufacturers' claims to effect household magic). So much better to think of the TV maid as a

chummy, comic member of the household, and all domestic
work, therefore, as going on where it should, in the heart of the
family, where feelings, not material conditions, are supposed to
determine what happens, and where women do not do jobs but
assume affective roles!

So far, my attention has been directed to that portion of the
female labor force that is engaged in jobs offering relatively low
pay and prestige. But TV shows us professional women as well,
and consideration of what we are told about their jobs is both
rewarding and surprising. The professions or semiprofessions in
which women are actually clustered make a rather poor showing
in the fictional world of television. In real life, for instance, school
teaching has long been dominated—numerically, if not
politically—by women. But on TV in recent seasons, Emily
Hartley, wife of the psychologist who is *The Bob Newhart Show*'s
main character, is the only woman teacher on a comedy program,
while Sara, the frontier schoolmarm, and Jamie, the Bionic
Woman whose classroom work is actually a cover for CIA-type
activities, occupy the dramatic front. Five years ago there was
the chief character on *The Sandy Duncan Show,* and in the '50s
Our Miss Brooks moved from radio to TV. But the black male
teacher cornered most of the wisdom and nearly all the interesting
situations on the old *Room 222.* Nor is there any female competition for the hero on *Welcome Back, Kotter,* who has the field as
much to himself as Lucas Tanner, Mr. Novak, and Mr. Peepers
did in their respective days. As a matter of fact, women teachers,
where they appear, furnish the jumping-off place for amusing and
too often cute plots, but are rarely depicted as being deeply dedicated either to learning as an ideal or to their students' human
needs. It is male teachers, on TV, who take the time to teach in
the fullest sense, and hence to love. This is one extension of
mothering to which—significantly—TV women are not assigned.

Nurses appear with far more frequency, of course, but there is
no prime-time series where a nurse, whether she works in a hospital, an office, or on private duty, acts as anything but the adjunct

to a doctor. Soap operas are a different matter, however, for with hospital settings, illness, and protracted death looming as large as they do in the serials, all medical personnel can be expected to assume significant roles. Actually, the world of the hospital is reduced on the soaps to that of doctors and nurses plus an occasional administrator (forget the aides, housekeepers, dietitians, inhalation therapists, orderlies, ward clerks, and so on; our General Hospital isn't as general as *that*). The nurses on daytime programs are fully developed and often pivotal characters, whose family and love relationships can absorb our attention for months or even years at a stretch. But they do almost no nursing—an observation that is more than a cavil, since their evening counterparts on *Marcus Welby, Medical Center, M.A.S.H.,* or even *Doc* and *The Practice* do play a role in the medical aspect of the medical world, and the soap opera doctors perforce practice a whole lot of medicine. Once again, the job of nurse makes for a credibly feminine character playing in appropriately sex-typed roles, but it is not understood or analyzed as work.

What is unexpected is the statistical overrepresentation on TV of women engaged in the traditionally male and relatively more prestigious professions. There has been no series about a woman doctor, but they appear in the transient *dramatis personae* of the prime-time medical dramas and there is at least one in most of the soap operas. Doctor Gannon has worked with and dated, among others, a career-driven, neurotic surgeon, a lesbian, and an erratic visiting Soviet specialist; and he has supplied avuncular advice to one young medical student whose husband couldn't make the grade in the prestigious senior elective they were both taking and to another who refused to face the medical implications of her fainting fits. Meanwhile, Doctor Welby has assisted an orthopedist who's a reformed alcoholic to rebuild her professional career. As for daytime drama, over the years it has given us medical, emotional, familial, and sexual adventures involving Drs. Laura Horton and Marlena Evans (*Days of Our Lives*), Drs. Maggie Fielding, Althea Davis, Karen Werner, Kate Bartok, and

Ann Larimer (*The Doctors*), Dr. Leslie Williams (*General Hospital*), Dr. Sarah MacIntyre (*The Guiding Light*), Dr. Julie Franklin (*How to Save a Marriage*), and Dr. Dorian Cramer (*One Life to Live;* this last program also featured psychiatric counseling of a character by the real-life Dr. Joyce Brothers).[3]

As my descriptions suggest, it is a dangerous business to be a woman doctor in the prime-time orbit of a Gannon or a Welby. One is subject to a variety of psychological and professional traumas that are connected with being female in a man's world but that also entail some other problem: alcoholism, family conflicts, political pressures, homosexuality.* It is certainly true that the other doctors, the "guest cast," on medical programs with a continuing protagonist tend to be portrayed as screwed-up people—regardless of sex. When do Welby and Gannon simply call someone in for a second opinion or the application of some esoteric medical technique without becoming involved in the visiting doctor's dissolving marriage, failing health, professional impetuosity, or whatever? The doctors whom we know are exceptionally self-contained and competent, even when adversity strikes their own lives. But the colleagues they hang out with are always overeager to try out some half-baked new surgical method or going blind or preparing for their transsexual operation or fighting off a domineering wife or being victimized by an anti-Semite or slowly reestablishing a reputation after some earlier blunder.

There remains, nonetheless, a very real difference in both kind and degree between the problems attributed to women doctors and those of their male counterparts. Far more conflict centers on their initial career choice and their continuation in the profession; they exhibit far sharper tempers and job-related neuroses, far

*For this counts as a "problem" too, in a hospital where Gannon himself has to unlearn his initial disgust at having romanced—even kissed—a dyke. The episode's denouement, occurring after he has come to accept her sexuality as "all right," takes place when the lesbian doctor persuades a suicidal undergraduate not to jump by convincing her that her fears that she, too, might be gay are unfounded. The student, the lesbian doctor declares, is *Normal.*

more emotional turmoil. I can recall no prime-time episode involving a woman doctor where her sex was not somehow related to the plot. (Even Welby's rehabilitated alcoholic has reason to believe that she is experiencing sex discrimination as well as a bias against her drinking problem before she learns that the stern senior physician who has been giving her trouble is actually doing so to make sure *she* realizes that she can now withstand the heaviest professional challenges.) The message that is communicated is that women—lots of women—can be doctors, but that the process certainly takes a heavy toll from the woman herself, her associates, and her patients. Moreover, in a bending over backwards reminiscent of the treatment of black poverty in the '60s, woman doctors are often portrayed as being exceptionally good, indeed brilliant, at their work. But it is their gender and the roles associated with it that define what happens to them in the prime-time plot.

In the soap operas, by contrast, medicine is a sacrosanct profession, and although its practitioners at all levels are immersed in complex and often unsavory sexual adventures they never seem to allow them to affect their medical performance. Mysterious diseases, drawn-out illnesses, sudden deaths, and equally sudden remissions or cures, all the very life blood of serial plots, would appear to underscore the fallibility of bourgeois medicine, but in fact the abilities of soap opera doctors are rarely called into question. It is within this context of unwavering respect for medicine and doctors that the relatively unconflicted professional work of the woman doctors must be understood. For, in distinct contrast to the special neuroses that exercise their female colleagues on evening programs, the daytime women do not experience their lives as doctors very differently from the way men do. Nor are their lives as women, their sexual and family relations, any *more* burdened than those of their soap opera sisters in other occupations. These doctors are characters in programs whose overall female work force incorporates an even smaller percentage of the available women than is the norm, since most soap opera women are not employed at all, yet there is no question in the stories about whether women should be doctors or how, as women, they might handle the contradictions created by their sexuality and a highly demanding career.

Robert LaGuardia, a chronicler of the soaps who maintains, among other inflated claims, that the serials were feminist *avant la lettre* (not to say, *avant* Beauvoir and Friedan), indirectly explains this phenomenon. He argues that female professionals abound in daytime, as contrasted with prime-time, TV fiction because the former is more realistic and "in reality, the professions are filled with women." Although no one who understands either the discrimination or the exploitation that women experience in the work force could take LaGuardia's conclusion seriously, his exaggeration does serve to remind us of the ways in which the soap opera accommodates its predominantly female audience without, needless to say, introducing a feminist perspective or a desire to raise the aspirations of the women who consume the programs and their sponsors' products.

The female doctors and (with the recent exception of Amy Prentiss), the high-ranking police officials who appear on evening dramas devoted to medical and detective work are not regular characters in the series; they are transients written into particular segments, as they also tend to be in comedy series. The continuing characters of prime-time dramatic programs, whose audiences are of both sexes, are almost all male, whereas the problems of women assume central importance in prime-time comedy or in the daytime. For the female audience, the soap opera posits and explores a specific set of propositions about female nature and female relationships. (The "fact," for example, that there is a fairly large category of women whose purpose and mission in life is the destruction of other women's happiness is not only taken for granted but is expressed through a series of artistic conventions as recognizable as the assumption itself.) In the context of her relationship with men and with other women, the serials investigate what a women is and what she can become. That some

women on the serials are professionals and that these professionals experience far less role conflict than their prime-time sisters
neither adds to nor detracts from this analysis. On the soaps, their
professional lives remain entirely incidental to the real questions
of identity that the drama is probing. A moment on *As the World
Turns* some years ago was more germane than may first appear:
shocked to find a child for whom she is responsible lying unconscious at the foot of a jungle-gym, a young physician stands
wringing her hands at least as ineffectually as you and I would.
Her husband has to remind her that she is A Doctor, which helps
her get it together to perform such specialized tasks as fetching
blankets and phoning the ambulance, for, as she wails in response
to his reminder, "How can I think like a doctor at a time like
this?"

As I have tried to show, however, medicine is a somewhat
unusual profession in that the godlike wisdom attributed to most
of its practitioners is not *ultimately* affected by the vicissitudes of
their personalities or their private lives. Other women
professionals—lawyers, judges, scientists, business executives,
sometimes high government officials and diplomats—are also
overrepresented on the tube, with an even greater tendency for
their career to be a source of conflict. Professional women are
often shown choosing (or having chosen at some time in the past)
between career and family life. Even where that option has not
meant an either–or decision, new areas of choice constantly arise
to call the basis of the career back into question. The woman who
achieves is always hardened by the experience and has always
lost something that the rest of us still possess.*

*In comedy, a softened version of this theme may be found in what has been
labeled the "office family," a phenomenon most evident on and functional to the
MTM productions. On *The Mary Tyler Moore Show,* although Mary Richards, a
television news producer in her mid-thirties, conducts her love life with men
encountered away from her workplace, these men—along with every other aspect
of what would normally constitute "home" or "social" life—are rapidly brought
into relation with the permanent essential fixtures of her existence, the people
with whom she puts on the Six O'Clock News. This diminution of the distinction

The woman professional in prime time is equally and dramatically unfeminine whether she wins international recognition as a physicist or as a movie sex-symbol. But she is there, larger than life size and in far greater numbers than the real world, in which most of us still work as typists, waitresses, and saleswomen, would admit. As a warning, this overrepresentation and the drastic fates encountered by the professional women seem superfluous or at least premature, except insofar as they contribute to three interconnected myths: that women enjoy a higher status than we feminists claim; that this status has been and may be achieved without fundamental social upheaval; and that having a career nonetheless poses a very real threat to female nature, to individual women's stability, and to institutions like the family that are built on these twin foundations. It is a threat that is in no way vitiated by the fact that TV's professional women are—archetypally—women first, professionals second.

All these definitions, distinctions, and judgments about the women in the various segments of the TV wage-labor force represent a minority of the adult women characters. Although the picture is changing, this modification is taking place several decades later and considerably more slowly than in the actual U.S. labor market. Thus, a large number of women are depicted as housewives, and television presumably has something to tell those of us who do that job, as well as those of us who work outside the home.

The most remarkable fact about telefiction housework is that it is not work. Aside from a certain (minimal) amount of cooking, the housewife does not have very much to do. No one is ever seen

---

between work and private life characterizes a great deal of TV comedy; the boss seems always to be *there*, in the house, in the bosom of one's family. But it is single people like Mary and Alice and the unattached characters played by Doris Day and Lucille Ball before them, or by James Coco in *Colucci's Department*, whose life choice is *fully* represented and delimited by the constitution within the office of a network of relationships that is the moral equivalent of the family. And most of the single people who reconstruct the family in this way are women.

scrubbing a floor or a tub, shampooing a rug, changing bed linen, taking out garbage, ironing clothes, scouring pots, shoveling snow, diapering a baby, wiping up after the dog vomited, changing the cat litter, or any of the other repetitive, often daily, tasks that make up the job of a housewife. Cooking itself rarely seems to take much labor: no one has much reason to get tired preparing a family meal or even an elaborate company dinner. (Not even Ma Ingalls of *Little House on the Prairie* or Mother Walton herself, both of them without convenience foods, labor-saving devices, even hot running water, is depicted as engaged in backbreaking effort in the home, although they do at least look tired at the end of a day's work.) In the contemporary working-class household, Edith Bunker and Florida Evans stir things around in pots a great deal and spend a lot of time at home and in their kitchens, but do not do any more other work than their middle-class suburban counterparts.

In the '50s and the early '60s, when the housewife–mother reached the apogee of her unquestioned glory, much was often made of the baking skill of the lady of the house. Cakes, pies, and cookies were the specialities. Not even Donna Reed, Harriet Nelson, or Margaret Anderson of *Father Knows Best* went so far as to bake bread; those families were clearly nurtured on the packaged white stuff.* What this baking of sweets suggests, and what the perpetual coffee-making of soap opera women serves to underline, is that cooking, the only part of her regular job that we see the housewife doing, is not a job at all, but, once more, the representation of the nurturant role. More evidence for this may be found in the fact that when a role *reversal* is at issue, the husband doesn't just prepare a meatloaf or macaroni and cheese,

---

*For a class unit on situation comedy in the spring of 1976, a dozen of my students independently noted a *Leave It to Beaver* rerun where Mrs. Cleaver's "liberation" from her role as family cookie-baker was the episode's chief subject. Frustrated at having to make up four batches because her husband and sons like different permutations of raisins and nuts, Mother boldly declares her independence by fixing only one batch, with both nuts and raisins, the way *she* likes it.

but must, like *All in the Family's* Frank Lorenzo, be a certified gourmet cook. The more usual scene, with the mother cooking and serving meals or treats and the soap opera heroine offering the temporary sustenance of coffee, shows us the female maintaining and supporting the members of her family: nursing and nourishing.

As for the heavier cleaning, although I cannot rule out having seen an occasional wet floor play its part in the plot or at least the dialogue of a family situation comedy, floors and toilets do not loom large in these versions of domesticity. In fact, on dramatic programs, an "unattractive" woman dressed for heavy housework and talking about the labors that have been interrupted by this visit from the police is a stock character. Her function in different plots may vary, but essentially the one housewife who is actually involved in her housework is emblematic of an intrinsically female stupidity, for she cannot extricate herself from the narrow confines of her home chores long enough to understand that her neighbor has been murdered virtually under her nose or that her son is being sought by police in three states. For a woman to work at anything but housework may be dangerous, but to *be* a housewife, if that description implies involvement in labor, is also not without its perils.

The home is the setting, but human relationships are the source of family comedy and drama, and relations between parents and children are, of course, central to the action. Certainly, if a reason had to be sought for the fact that married women on TV so rarely work outside the home, it would stress their responsibilities as mothers. It is interesting to observe, therefore, that those responsibilities also tend to be interpreted in the least concrete fashion. Young girls who grew up in the '60s with working mothers envied the children on *The Donna Reed Show,* whose mother was always right there to dispense wise and loving advice about their problems (from women's spontaneous evidence in their personal histories, it appears that this program was exceptionally seductive in its presentation of the myth).

In the more realistic vein of the mid-'70s, Ann Romano, the hysterically vivacious divorcee on *One Day at a Time,* has to perform the same basic functions on a part-time basis. Although she works to support herself and her daughters, her true role within the family is to provide emotional support, not a material background for their adolescent traumas.

Parenthood is an absorbing preoccupation of the soap operas: pregnancy, miscarriages, illegitimacy, kidnapping, abortion, misattributed paternity, fanatically devoted or unnaturally callous maternity have all been the subjects of innumerable daytime dramas. Having a baby is an all-important theme. But the actual baby, once delivered, assigned some father or other, safely unkidnapped and unhospitalized, makes only ceremonial appearances on screen. Nor do we see much more of it once it reaches the age of reason or at least of the ability to memorize lines. For the child, too, is a theme and part of a role for someone else, not a character. Nor is it, by and large, a source of work for the mother or anyone else. Soap opera babies occasionally get sick enough to require hospitalization, sometimes they even die of mysterious diseases or accidents, but normally they cry only to take a character off-stage, they never need to be fed, changed, toilet-trained, cleaned off, or given both custodial and active attention. So people talk a lot about love and especially about the love and dedication inspired by a child, but, whatever dramatically sacrificial form these may sometimes take, they have nothing to do with spending time with it.

Yet all TV-watchers know that "you get a lot of dirt with children," and that there is an enormous difference in the fit and absorbency of different brands of paper diapers. We also know that the biggest problem a caucus of black and white housewives can find to discuss with one another is "grease—oily dirt," that the stuff gets "ground in," thus requiring that you "pretreat or presoak," and that "ring around the collar" is a disease of which American wives are the asymptomatic but guilty carriers. And that's only what we know about heavy laundry. We also know that housewives are concerned about how to clean their "delicate washables," their own and their families' bodies, everyone's teeth, the kitchen floor, the rugs and carpets, windows, porcelain bathroom and kitchen fixtures, the euphemistically-labeled "bathroom bowl," dishes done by hand or machine, walls, woodwork, and so on. And then to deodorize their underarms, their feet, their private parts and public rooms, their breath, their closets, and their toilets. We know all this from the one sector of televised life where housewives really do work, the commercials.

Two genres of home-product commercials appear these days: the traditional ones in which actresses portray housewives in brief scenes extolling the virtues of whatever is being sold, and a newer type featuring real housewives who are "interviewed" in supermarkets or testing labs, comparing their usual choice to some new brand. Both are degrading to women. The traditional genre portrays women as deriving profound satisfaction, bordering on sexual gratification, from the discovery of a product that makes their wash white or their floors shine. It establishes an exaggerated and unattainably high standard of cleanliness. It implies that reaching that standard is not only possible, but achievable (with the product's help) through magic, not labor. It reinforces the idea that, whoever may be doing them right now, these household jobs are the *natural* function of womankind. And it creates a vicious hierarchy of household expertise: in person or in voice-overs, male experts know better than woman and all professional experts are male—even the animated yachtsman who lives in a toilet and is therefore presumably made of *shit* can tell women what to do—but women know better than their own inept menfolks, and those men, as well as all young women, know better than their mothers.

Now, however, a form of *cinema-verité* alternates with these good old-fashioned put-downs. Real housewives are given the opportunity to compare the advertised product with the one they would normally buy, or they compete with users of the new kind, or see if they can taste the difference—and they all come out even dumber than those ladies who have an orgasm over finding the right detergent. This is not because most housewives are really giggly fools who cannot resist squeezing the toilet paper and who were actually being *flattered* all those years by the image of slender, attractive, dedicated housewives. Rather, unprepared women, unaccustomed to public speaking and more particularly to camera work, are exposed to rapid product "tests" that do not prove anything, and those responses that best suit the by-now-secure convention (they all look and sound alike, after all) are screened. Not only don't we see anyone who prefers her old brand, but we never even see a woman who assigns the product only its proper priority as a minor domestic aid or who notices that the demonstration meant to convince her is not in fact a test.

The contrast between what housework is done in the programs themselves and in their commercial intervals is most apparent in daytime television, because the soaps harbor an even larger population of apparently unoccupied housewife–characters than evening comic or dramatic shows, and also because by day there is a greater concentration of advertising for household products. (At night, when men will be watching too, we see ads representing larger products, about whose purchase men tend to make the decision, things like automobiles and cameras, in addition to toothpaste and detergent.) On daytime drama, there are not only more housewives, but they seem to have still less work to do than housewives on evening programs. They dress up in woolen afternoon dresses, stockings, high-heeled shoes and discreet jewelry—clothing no one could work in—for an afternoon at home and, of course, they are free to spend a great deal of time advancing the story line outside their homes. The soaps also include an unprecedented number of wealthy women—wives, daughters, widows, and divorcees—who work at no paid jobs but are not housewives either, and who really do have nothing to do. Some of them make trouble, others just *have* trouble and complicate the plot. Thus, when a woman takes some time off from her housework to watch an episode of her favorite serial or keeps the

TV on as she works at her household chores, stopping from time to time to absorb the action on something she does not feel as close to as the one she calls "my story," she is being told a great many things about real womanhood, its characteristic forms, needs, expressions, and limitations. One of the facts that are marketed is that being a housewife is the normal lot of women and that being one involves a set of human interactions, not a set of practical tasks. Yet the story conveying this is constantly interrupted by a series of short vignettes, sometimes with musical accompaniment, in which the direct selling of soap joins the selling of ideas that only indirectly keep on selling soap. And here the practical work assumes center stage.

It should be noted, finally, that not even the idle housewives on daytime TV are so unoccupied as to watch television, and the only characters on prime time who admit to watching the soaps are those whose intelligence or mental stability has already been called into question. In 1971, when Rhoda was still a *Mary Tyler Moore* character, she was fired from her job and took three weeks to find another. The sign of her psychological degeneration during this period, when she was actually looking quite assiduously for work, was that she watched daytime TV. Five years later, on *Rhoda,* sister Brenda also lost her job, and also went rapidly to the dogs, the equivalent of soap operas for her being long philosophical discussions with Carlton, the drunken doorman. From the viewpoint of nighttime television, those "addicted" to watching daytime programs are dopes—and, needless to say, mostly women. Mary Hartman's mental equipment, informed by mass media, could not possibly help her cope with the world as she encountered it. Yet her predicament as a housewife was not essentially different from her predicament as a TV-addict, for the two conditions create and reinforce one another. The housewife, like her sisters who work for wages, looks to TV to make sense of herself and her labors. And television not only defines woman and work but at its most nihilistic, as with Mary Hartman, tells her just how crazy she is to turn on TV for meaning.

NOTES

1. Since families have different numbers of children, it makes sense to give the statistics this way rather than in terms of the numbers of working mothers who have children under specific ages. The figures are from the *1975 Handbook on Women Workers* (Washington, D.C.: U.S. Department of Labor Employment Standards Administration, Women's Bureau, Bulletin 297, 1975). The same figures are more accessibly arranged in a number of other Women's Bureau publications, including *Background Facts on Women Workers Today*. Most accessible of all are the somewhat older figures employed in the charts and tables in Lise Vogel, *Women Workers: Some Basic Statistics* (Boston: New England Free Press, 1971).

2. See, for instance, Melvin L. DeFleur, "Occupational Roles As Portrayed on Television," *Public Opinion Quarterly*, 28 (1964). For a later set of statistics, see Whitney M. Adams, Media Committee, National Capital Area National Organization for Women, Comment before the Federal Communications Commission in the matter of Notice of Proposed Rule Making, August 1971.

3. Not all these names were stored in my memory, which I refreshed by reference to the historical plot summaries in Robert LaGuardia, *The Wonderful World of TV Soap Operas*, (New York: Ballantine-Random House, 1974).

Index

343

individualism, 226, 301
Iverson, Lucille, "The Abortion" (poem), 286–287; "Outrage" (poem), 290–291

James, Henry, 101–102, 119, 128, 208
Jessup, Josephine Lurie, *The Faith of Our Feminists*, 13–14
"Job in a Laundry" (story), 246
Jones, Jennie, "American Standard" (poem), 296–297
Jong, Erica, *Fear of Flying*, 130n
Joyce, James, 120; *Ulysses*, 15–16, 130–131
Jung, Carl Gustav, 11

Kampf, Louis, xv, 22, 25, 55–57
Kerman, Judith, "Driving for Yellow Cab" (poem), 297; "Exmatriate" (poem), 273; "That Dream, At Last" (poem), 279
Kerr, Walter, 57–58, 60
Konek, Carol, *I Hear My Sisters Saying*, 226–227

Labé, Louise, 202
labor force (U.S.), women in, 313–315
lady knights, 152–153, 156, 158, 159, 162–163, 167–170
LaGuardia, Robert, 333
Lamb, Lady Caroline, *Glenarvon*, 210
landed gentry, 179–188, 190–199, 214–216
Lawrence, D. H., 49, 51
leisure, 77, 86, 157, 192–193, 198, 216; "colonized," 313; dialectical nature of, 90–91; and television, 310, 312, 313, 340–341
Lenin, Nikolai, 107, 108–109
lesbianism, 228, 301–302, 331
Les Liaisons dangereuses, 120
Lessing, Doris, 117–118, 129–130; *The Golden Notebook*, 122–123
Levertov, Denise, 253n; "About Marriage" (poem), 288–289; "The Mutes" (poem), 265–266

Levey, Michael, 25, 31–32, 33
Levine, George, 69
literature, 31–37, 200, 257; and historical situation, 53–67; redefinition of, 224–225, 230–232, 251–253; and social reality, 151–176, 179, 192, 214–222, 252–253, 299–301; sociology of women's, 204–207, 221–222, 224–225
Lorde, Audre, "Black Mother Woman" (poem), 271; "To My Daughter the Junkie on a Train" (poem), 288; "Who Said It Was Simple" (poem), 304–305
Lukacs, Georg, 48

McCarthy, Mary, 117, 130; "The Fact in Fiction" (essay), 127
Mailer, Norman, xvii
Mandiargues, André Pieyre de, 132
Mao Tse-tung, 15
Marcus, Steven 147n
Marcuse, Herbert, 93n, 112–113
marriage: for love, 153–154, 155, 156, 157–159, 162, 170–171, 174–176, 199; in poetry, 288–293; and property, 179, 181–188, 190, 198–199, 215; and social rôle, 188–191, 195–199
Marx, Karl, 20; on the bourgeoisie, 38; on the class nature of ideas, 5, 163; on commodity fetishism, xxvi–xxvii, 62–64; on consciousness, 8–9, 58–59
Marxist criticism. *See* criticism.
mass culture, 50–51, 67, 77, 81–92, 313
mass experience, 228–230, 233
Mayhall, Jane, "Tracing Back" (poem), 289–290, 292
Millay, Edna St. Vincent, 259
Millett, Kate, xvi; *Sexual Politics*, 15, 48, 51
Mitchell, Juliet, *Psychoanalysis and Feminism*, xv–xvi
Mitchell, Margaret, *Gone With the Wind*, 204
modernism, 22–26, 37, 44–45, 62
Monet, Claude, 37–39
monogamy, 100–101, 108, 146